The Professional Personal Chef
The Business of Doing Business as a Personal Chef

The Professional Personal Chef
The Business of Doing Business as a Personal Chef

CANDY WALLACE

GREG FORTE

AMERICAN PERSONAL & PRIVATE CHEF ASSOCIATION
★ PARTNERS IN ★
LIFESTYLE SOLUTIONS

WILEY

John Wiley & Sons, Inc.

Published by John Wiley & Sons, Inc., Hoboken, New Jersey
Published simultaneously in Canada

For general information on our other products and services or for technical support, please contact our Customer Care Department within the United States at (800) 762-2974, outside the United States at (317) 572-3993 or fax (317) 572-4002.

Wiley also publishes its books in a variety of electronic formats. Some content that appears in print may not be available in electronic books. For more information about Wiley products, visit our web site at www.wiley.com.

Library of Congress Cataloging-in-Publication Data:
Wallace, Candy, 1947–
    The Professional personal chef : the business of doing business as a personal chef / By Candy Wallace & Greg Forte.
       p.   cm.
    Includes index.
    ISBN-13: 978-0-471-75219-6 (cloth)
    ISBN-10: 0-471-75219-3 (cloth)
1. Food service management. 2. Cooks. 3. Entrepreneurship. I. Forte, Greg, 1952– II. Title.
    TX911.3.M27W352   2006
    647.95068--dc22
                                                                    2006013370

Printed in the United States of America

10 9 8 7 6 5 4 3 2 1

CONTENTS

A Note from Candy Wallace

In his book *Trendspotting* (The Berkly Publishing Group, 2002), Richard Laermer says, "Once something, anything, is put into practice by three people and a celebrity, it's a trend. The common trait shared by all trends is their ability to make a few smart people very, very wealthy." That's sardonic, but Laermer further distinguishes a trend from a fad in that a trend is something just emerging, whereas a fad is a flash in the pan. In his editorial about the personal chef industry in *Chef* magazine (September 2002), Brent T. Frei says that a trend is enjoyed by a few now, experienced by many tomorrow, and touches virtually everyone by next week.

These days in foodservice we hear a lot of talk about the future, because the foodservice industry is constantly changing. The personal chef career path may have started out as a fad in the early 1990s, but with the hard work of a small group of committed individuals it has grown to a trend and is now a legitimate culinary career acknowledged as such by the American Culinary Federation (ACF), which certifies personal chefs in partnership with the American Personal & Private Chef Association (APPCA).

Speaking of APPCA, I am the founder and executive director of the San Diego–based association and a working personal chef. The distinction between a trend and a fad hits home for me because many of my colleagues went on record about my decision to develop the personal chef career with the opinion that personal chefs were just a fad and would never last as a legitimate culinary career choice. I believe some even went so far as to say that personal chefs were not *real* chefs. The APPCA was founded over ten years ago but got off to a slow start because few in the industry considered working as a personal chef to families and individuals a viable career path. However, today, successful personal chefs are making comfortable, satisfying livings and their career path continues to become more mainstream each year. The staying power of this career choice is further evidenced by the APPCA offering professional personal chef certification through the American Culinary Federation. The future of the personal chef career is no longer up for debate. Personal chefs are here to stay, and this career choice will continue to flourish as more and more students choose to become personal chefs upon graduation from culinary school.

Newly emerging career choices in the culinary arts have required that culinary schools that have traditionally provided training almost exclusively for future line cooks now provide training for future personal and private chefs, food writers, food stylists and photographers, research chefs, and educators. Students entering culinary schools are no longer predominantly recent high school graduates. They may also be former or "recovering" engineers, lawyers, physicians, architects, software designers, administrators, or teachers who have elected to pursue a second career in foodservice but have no intention of cooking in a commercial situation on a line. Owning your own business in foodservice is no longer limited to owning a restaurant.

My work over the last twelve years has helped advance and legitimize the role of the personal chef and facilitated the successful startup of this new industry. I believed from the beginning that external validation of the personal chef was required to achieve stature among our culinary peers. That recognition occurred at the ACF 2002 National Conference in Las Vegas, where a certification agreement between APPCA and ACF led to the announcement of certification designations on two levels for personal chefs and the public validation of the personal chef career path as a legitimate culinary career by then ACF president, Ed Leonard.

As of June 2005, according to an industrywide survey commissioned by APPCA, approximately 8,000 personal chefs were operating in the United States. The number of clients served by those 8,000 personal chefs was estimated to be 72,000. This combination generates over $300 million in revenue annually.

The industry predicts that at the present rate of growth, within the next five years the United States will have nearly 20,000 operating personal chefs serving nearly 300,000 clients and contributing nearly $1.2 billion to the national economy.

Personal chef clients typically include dual-income couples with or without children; single, career-focused individuals; professional athletes and other high-profile clients; individuals with specific medical challenges; seniors who wish to remain in their own homes and live independently; single parents; and clients who enjoy fine dining.

Entrepreneur magazine ("Top 6 Homebased Businesses for 2004," by Paul & Sarah Edwards) designated the personal chef industry "one of the four fastest-growing businesses in the country." Who are these personal chefs? Where do they come from? Some personal chefs are female chefs who are raising families, while others are "dad" chefs who want to participate in their children's lives but feel they cannot if they are cooking in restaurants or hotels on nights, weekends, and holidays. Still other personal chefs are chefs "of a certain age," like me, who choose to cook for a living, but on our own terms. Yet others are younger chefs who do not feel compelled to pay dues for the next decade before owning a business of their own. Cooking for a living no longer means cooking on a line.

Personal chefs wear two distinct hats, one as a culinary professional and one as a small business owner. A personal chef business should reflect both the level of expertise and the personal requirements of the owner/chef. The way my personal chef business operates has nothing to do with anyone else's. Specificity is the key to success as a personal chef. What do you want to accomplish as a personal chef? Do you want more quality time with your family? money? freedom? It's all there. You have to make a plan and go get it.

What kind of special training does a personal chef need? Good question, and one that is often asked. Competency in the kitchen does not guarantee success as a business owner and operator. You may be an ace in the back of the house, but what do you know about running a successful business? Ask yourself the following questions:

- What form do you want your business to take?

- What licensing and regulations will you be subject to in your municipality?

- How do you construct a personal chef specific business plan?

- What specific level of service do you intend to offer, and to whom?

- How will you find clients?

- Once you find potential clients, what do you say to them?

- Customer service has never been a prerequisite in the back of the house, so how will you acquire the information necessary to customize a program for each client?

- What forms and paperwork are necessary to support each client and your business?

- How do you get media exposure for your business? Should you advertise—and, if so, where? Who can you talk to if you need advice or assistance?

These are just a few of the areas a personal chef training program can address by providing the information and expertise necessary to operate a legitimate, successful business. Knowing how to cook is only part of the challenge. You need to learn the business of doing business as a personal chef.

This text, *The Professional Personal Chef: The Business of Doing Business as a Personal Chef* is adapted from the American Personal Chef Institute training materials I first wrote more than ten years ago. I continually update this material and have been teaching it to students in different cities each month since then. To date, I have trained more than 5,000 working personal chefs across the United States and Canada, but my goal has always been to have culinary schools teach this program as an adjunct to the culinary skill and technique classes so necessary to culinary success. This book, which Chef Greg Forte, CEC, CCE, AAC, and I have written, is the culmination of my dream and my contribution toward fulfilling the lives and dreams of working personal chefs across the world by helping them launch successful personal chef services.

These past ten plus years have been deeply satisfying for me because my efforts and dedication have helped create a new culinary career path for culinary students. This path will continue to evolve, as no two personal chef businesses and no two clients will ever be the same. My effort has also been deeply satisfying from a commitment standpoint. "Paying it forward" to future personal chefs and my commitment to the culinary industry and the individuals who work in it each day is who I am. It is how we, as chefs and cooks, make our mark in the world. I cannot think of any other career that could make my heart sing.

I would also like to take this opportunity to thank my wonderful husband, and APPCA Webmaster, Dennis Wallace, without whose support, vision and contributions this industry would not have been able to grow and flourish as it has. Dennis, you have forwarded the action for personal chefs everywhere.

Make it personal.

Candy Wallace

San Diego, California

HOW THE STUDENT AND ENTREPRENEUR CAN USE THIS BOOK

This book is a primer on how to develop and operate your own personal chef business. It deals not only with broad concepts but also small details that can save you time and money as you develop your enterprise.

Each chapter features:

- **Learning Outcomes**: a list of key concepts that will be covered within the chapter

- **Key Words**: a list of key terms that will be presented and defined within the chapter

- **Discussion Questions and Activities**: open-ended questions and activities designed to stimulate thought and ideas relating to the key topics and concepts presented in the chapter

- **Key Words with Definitions**: a list of the key words, with definitions, presented within the chapter

- **Questions for Review**: true/false and multiple choice review questions that help reinforce understanding of the key concepts

- **"From the Field" Accounts with Discussion Questions**: true stories from the personal chef industry that demonstrate the application of a particular concept, together with thought-provoking questions

STUDENT RESOURCES

Companion Website: Includes samples of items and concepts mentioned in the chapters and in the appendix of the text, associated links, and additional resources to help students explore in greater detail concepts presented in the text.

RESOURCES FOR INSTRUCTORS

Companion Website: Includes teaching tips for key concepts, supporting PowerPoint slides for each chapter, additional resources relating to key concepts, and additional testing materials.

A Note of Acknowledgment from Greg Forte

It takes many talented professionals to make a book more than ink on a page. To all the personal chefs who were interviewed for this text: Thank you; your stories help in bringing the profession to life. We also owe a debt of gratitude to the instructors who took the time to read through our manuscript as we continued to develop it based on their continuous thoughtful feedback: Chef Heinz Lauer, from Creative Culinary Concepts, Las Vegas; Rob Hudson of Pikes Peak Community College; and Linda K. Rosner of Lexington College. To the gang at Rochester Institute of Technology, where this part of the journey started: I think of all of you often; thank you for being there.

A very special thank you to Cindy Rhoads, developmental editor for Wiley; I am sure I supplied you with some good laughs and tears as you patiently brought focus and direction to this text. I told you I don't know how you do it, and I still don't.

To all my past, current, and future students, my gratitude for everything you have and will teach me. Learning is interactive, and you have taught me so much.

A special thanks to Mary Petersen, a true believer in what culinary education is all about. Finally, without the support of my wife and family, this would have never been possible. Thank you for your patience, understanding, and love.

Remember: Quality is all.

Greg Forte

Sandy, Utah

THE EVOLUTION OF THE PERSONAL CHEF

Cooking is at once one of the simplest and most gratifying of the arts, but to cook well one must love and respect food.

—Chef Craig Claiborne (1920-2000), author and *New York Times* food critic

Culinary history has not officially recorded when the first personal chef opened his doors for business. Was it hundreds of years ago, when a talented chef cooked for several affluent families, traveling from one estate to another? Or was the first personal chef someone who cooked for a friend's family that had fallen on hard times and needed help with the day-to-day chores of the household? History provides us with clues, but determining when the personal chef profession emerged is open to discussion.

The Business of Being a Personal Chef

This text is about the business of being a personal chef. A personal chef is a chef for hire who provides a range of services and products to customers. Some personal chefs cook in four or five homes per week, leaving behind multiple customized meals that meet the taste and nutritional profiles of their clients. Others specialize in preparing menu items for dinner parties, catering events, or even teaching culinary classes. No matter which avenue they choose, personal chefs constantly strive to customize the food they prepare to meet the needs of their clients. The business of being a personal chef is based on providing the utmost in quality of service and cuisine.

Personal chefs operate with all the advantages and responsibilities that small business owners have. They plan, market, promote, pay bills, produce food, and do what they can to develop their business. Personal chefs come from all backgrounds. Some begin their career in this business with limited formal culinary training, while others have years of industry cooking experience. Still others are second-career culinary school graduates and cooks. Many professional personal chefs are certified by the American Culinary Federation.

As we interviewed successful personal chefs around the country so we could include their stories from the field, it became abundantly clear that they all share three common traits:

<table>
<tr><td>

Exhibit 1.1
Certification Levels for the Personal Chef as Recognized by the American Culinary Federation

</td><td>

Personal Certified Chef

For a chef with a minimum of two full years employed as a personal chef who is engaged in the preparation, cooking, serving, and sorting of foods on a cook-for-hire basis; responsible for menu planning and development, marketing, financial management, and operational decisions of private business; provides cooking services to a variety of clients; possesses a thorough knowledge of food safety and sanitation and culinary nutrition.

http://www.acfchefs.org/certify/pcc.html

Personal Certified Executive Chef

For a chef with advanced culinary skills and a minimum of seven years of professional cooking experience with a minimum of two years as a personal chef; provides cooking services on a cook-for-hire basis to a variety of clients; responsible for menu planning and development, marketing, financial management, and operational decisions; provides nutritious, safe, eye-appealing, and properly flavored foods.

http://www.acfchefs.org/certify/pcec.html

</td></tr>
</table>

- *The love of cooking and serving great food.* Personal chefs understand what good food can mean to their clients on a personal level—it's more than just taste.

- *The desire to service their clients' needs, even if a client isn't entirely sure what his needs are.* Personal chefs help their clients determine what their needs are as they develop partnerships with those clients. This might be called the *hospitality spirit of service.*

- *The enjoyment and satisfaction that come from being one's own boss.* However, as you will learn for yourself as you go into the business world, self-employment is not for everyone!

While there are many similarities between personal chefs and private chefs, it's important that we distinguish between these two culinary professions. A private chef is one who is employed by a specific person or organization exclusively. She earns a paycheck and is responsible for providing her culinary services to one person or group. She works scheduled hours, cooks menus to satisfy the needs of her employer, whether a family or an organization. As pointed out previously, a personal chef is a chef for hire who works for herself as a small business operator. There is no exclusivity agreement involved, and she can choose the number of clients with whom she will associate and for whom she will prepare customized menus.

As the profession began to gain popularity among culinarians and the attention of the media, many critics called personal chefs a fad profession that would be around only as long as it was fashionable. However, over time, this supposed fad became a trend and gave chefs and cooks around the world the opportunity to work with food on their own terms. The personal chef trend has become a legitimate career path in the culinary industry and a viable alternative career for culinarians looking to leave traditional cooking situations.

In the May 2004 issue of *Entrepreneur* magazine, Paul and Sarah Edwards named the personal chef business as one of the top four hottest home-based businesses to start in the United States. Along with growth has come recognition and validation by industry professionals and governmental entities. In 2003, the American Culinary Federation in partnership with the American Personal & Private Chef Association adopted specific certification requirements for Personal Certified Chef (PCC) and Personal Certified Executive Chef (PCEC). This marked a turning point in the recognition of personal chefs by their culinary peers around the world.

Using This Text

This text is about the business of being a personal chef. As a culinarian, whether you are enrolled at a culinary school, a serious cooking hobbyist, or an industry professional looking for a career change, your skill and expertise will become the foundations of your personal chef business. This book is not intended to be a resource for recipes and cooking methods, except when they are used as examples. Rather, the goal is to provide you with a roadmap of the tasks that must be completed as you launch and develop your personal chef business. Each chapter in this text includes the following features:

- Learning outcomes
- Bolded key terms with definitions
- Review questions
  - True/False
  - Multiple choice
  - Discussion/Activities
- "From the Field" interviews and stories from working professional personal chefs that highlight how working personal chefs have approached specific aspects of their businesses. These interviews include discussion questions to help drive thoughtful group discussion in the classroom.

Organization of the Text

Chapters 2 through 6 focus primarily on what must be done to ensure your personal chef business is well organized and that you've investigated everything required to legally run your own business. Chapters 7 through 10 discuss the market research, marketing tools, and strategy needed to seed your target market so potential clients are aware that your personal chef business exists and clear about the quality of service and level of customization you offer. Finally, the last two chapters cover a day in the life of a professional personal chef and opportunities that have the potential to help you grow your business once you have launched it successfully and have a set of loyal clients.

EACH CHAPTER IN A NUTSHELL

- Chapter 1 provides a brief history of the business of being a personal chef and discusses the future of this career path for culinarians.

- Chapter 2 covers the forms of business ownership and the tax liabilities associated with each.

- Chapter 3 is about operating your personal chef service legally.

- Chapter 4 discusses the importance of developing a sound business plan and defines its components.

- Chapter 5 covers the vision statement and mission statement and their importance as the foundation of everything your business does. It also highlights the elevator speech and how it helps you and your business make a good first impression on potential clients.

- Chapter 6 deals with financial planning for your personal chef business.

- Chapter 7 is about the forms of business marketing a personal chef might use.

- Chapter 8 provides a detailed account of the services the professional personal chef can offer clients and the sales methods he can use to promote them.

- Chapter 9 focuses on the optimal forms of advertising available to professional personal chefs.

- Chapter 10 covers customer service and its critical importance to the success of a personal chef business.

- Chapter 11 describes a day in the life of a personal chef.

- Chapter 12 presents opportunities that have the potential to expand a personal chef's business.

This text provides you with the information you need to start a business that will allow you to cook on your own terms while supporting your passion for serving wonderful, delicious foods in an effort to make a positive change in people's lives.

From the Field

Chef Candy Wallace, *The Serving Spoon*

ONE CHEF'S EVOLUTION

As personal chefs, we are paid to shop, cook, and nurture.
—Candy Wallace, Founder and Executive Director,
American Personal & Private Chef Institute and Association

"My grandmother was a chef. She taught me the way you show your family and the world you love them is through food," says Candy Wallace, founder of the American Personal & Private Chef Institute and Association (APPCA). Candy started cooking in a family-owned restaurant as a teenager but promised her grandmother she would go to college "because cooking is a hard way for a woman to make a living," as her grandmother said. Good to her promise, Candy graduated from the University of Maryland with a degree in political science.

She lived in Washington, D.C., and worked for a congressman during the day. On the weekends, she returned to her roots by planning and cooking dinner parties for government officials. "Washington is the dinner party capital of world," she says. "Dinner is the way people entertain and network, which provides for an exciting mix of international cuisines." A few years later she moved to Chicago and opened a lobbying office for a food manufacturer. Again, Candy found herself doing dinner parties on the weekends for clients, many of whom worked at the radio station where her husband was general sales manager.

Eventually, Candy moved to the West Coast and began an entirely new career working as a national media buyer for a photo chain—but she continued to plan and cook for weekend dinner parties. In addition, she decided to cook part time at a local restaurant to satisfy her passion for cooking for others.

One evening at her corporate job, she had an epiphany and decided to leave corporate America to follow her passion for food and service. Knowing she wanted to continue to cook professionally, but on her own terms, she resigned and entered the new world–the world of a personal chef.

"I wanted to find a way to blend my culinary skills with my business skills in an effort to serve multiple clients as an independent business owner, one client at a time. I was going to make it personal and cook the freshly prepared foods the clients wanted to enjoy, but I would cook for them in *their* homes." Recalling her grandmother's advice to "keep it simple and be true to the harvest," she opened a personal chef business called Candy Wallace, Personal Chef, later The Serving Spoon.

This business was a success, due mainly to Candy maintaining her goal of "taking care of my clients the way I take care of my friends and family. I took the time to learn what they liked to eat and how they liked to eat. I also found out whether or not they had allergies, sensitivities, or whether or not there were certain tastes and textures they simply did not enjoy." Knowing that cooking is more than food, she specialized in customizing her clients' foods by "getting to really know them." One of her first clients needed to lose weight, so Candy researched healthy recipes containing foods that not only fit the profile for weight loss, but that he would also enjoy. He lost over 75 pounds!

Candy's business is as much about service as it is about food. "No one cared what anyone wanted anymore," she states. "Service was becoming a thing of the past, so I made certain that providing scrupulous personal service was as much a part of my business as the delicious meals I prepared for my clients. Clients would literally fall into my arms, they were so pleased. When Mom and Dad are both working, the family is forced to catch meals on the fly. What I wanted to do was to bring families back to the table to enjoy one another along with the freshly prepared foods they wanted, and I knew what they wanted because I asked them." She felt "they had every right to ask for what they wanted because they were paying me, and it was my job to provide it."

As she continued to develop her new career, Candy learned how much the service she provided could affect a family or an individual. The concept of bringing the family back to the dinner table, where they could enjoy healthy and delicious meals cooked in their own home, was powerful. "People get tired of eating out all the time. Sometimes they want to have good food in their jammies while curled up on the sofa, and the personal chef business provides a service that allows clients to do just that." The service she designed would supply Monday through Friday meal support for busy, hungry professionals who appreciate palate-specific meals prepared from fresh ingredients.

A Change of Direction

Candy received a fair amount of press coverage as a personal chef, which drew the attention of the business editor of the *San Diego Tribune*. He arranged to tag along with her and wrote a feature article about her and the business of being a personal chef. Within a week of the article's publication, she received over 300 phone calls from people either wanting service or looking for more information about becoming a professional personal chef. "Almost half the calls were from professionals who wanted to change their careers," she recalls. "I had no idea so many people were unhappy in their jobs and would rather be cooking. Some wanted to become my assistant to learn about the industry, while others wanted to tag along," she says. This abundance of interest led her to start a personal chef organization in San Diego, which she founded to provide education and networking resources for people who wanted to become professional personal chefs. At the time, her husband, Dennis, told her to stop talking about the profession and all the resources available and "write it down." She took his advice and wrote her first training manual intended for the professional personal chef.

Candy held classes for prospective chefs once a month at the San Diego personal chef chapter, and students did "tag-alongs" as part of their education. Membership grew exponentially and Candy became an invaluable advocate for personal

From the Field...continued

chefs, matching chefs with clients as the calls came in. This group of personal chefs became close and supportive of one another, something Candy discovered when Dennis had a heart attack. The group contacted all of Candy's clients to arrange for continuation of their service while Candy took time off to help with her husband's recovery. It was during this time she realized she wanted to take her program national to promote the personal chef career path. The result is the American Personal & Private Chef Institute and Association (APPCA).

During the past twelve years, Candy has trained more than 5,000 chefs who have entered the culinary field as professional personal chefs. She has worked hard to validate this nontraditional culinary career path and, in the summer of 2002, signed a charter representing official national recognition of this career path by the American Culinary Federation (ACF). "I always wanted a third-party accredited certification. Although the APCA could certify personal chefs, it would mean more coming from an outside professional organization such as the ACF," she says. The ACF offers two levels of personal chef certification: the Personal Certified Chef and a Personal Certified Executive Chef. More information on these certifications is on the ACF website at www.acfchefs.org.

During the last few years, the personal chef business has enjoyed enormous growth. Print and electronic media have covered stories about personal chefs around the country. Throughout the United States, culinary schools have invited Candy to present a program on career options in the culinary industry and how to do business as a personal chef, and the international culinary community is taking an interest in her work as well. APPCA presents regional seminars and workshops to chefs who wish to enter the personal chef industry.

Candy's contribution to the growth of the personal chef industry was recognized with the prestigious Award of Excellence as International Entrepreneur of the Year in 2003 by the International Association of Culinary Professionals (IACP). She is currently on the board of directors for the San Diego chapter of Les Dames d'Escoffier and is a mentor and national speaker for the IACP, Women Chefs and Restaurateurs, and the ACF.

People may argue about when the first personal chefs began working but culinarians' desire to cook on their own terms initiated a legitimate alternative career path that is constantly evolving.

Many of the personal chefs interviewed for this book report they no longer have to explain what a personal chef is and how they differ from caterers and private chefs to local health departments and other governmental licensing agencies. Whether recognition leads to greater demand or vice versa makes no difference. This culinary career path serves the needs of many chefs and gives them great satisfaction as they provide customized service and foods to their clients. The personal chef business is growing at an astounding rate, becoming more mainstream, and will continue to grow into the foreseeable future.

In an interview we had with Irena Chalmers, internationally known author and food lecturer, she talks about the growth and attraction of the personal chef industry to culinary students. Her insights on the personal chef profession are very interesting.

Irena Chalmers, award-winning cookbook author and food writer, instructor at the Culinary Institute of America, states that students are drawn toward the idea of becoming a personal chef because they like the idea of freedom and independence associated with being your own boss. "The personal chef industry is an extremely good option for a man or woman because they have flexibility with their time" she states. "People are excited about being their own boss, this gives them the ability to use their knowledge and passion and be flexible with their time."

When asked about the perceived value of using a personal chef she stated, "Think about the money you spend each week at the supermarket and how much of the food is thrown away or wasted. Economically it might make sense to have prepared food waiting for you in the refrigerator when you get home from work which can be very lovely and wonderful." Over the past years, industry has made it easier to cook, but so many people don't want to cook, its does not matter how easy it is, it is something that is not captivating, especially if someone else will do it for you. Some people think of cooking for themselves as a waste of time."

FORMS OF OWNERSHIP

The hardest thing in the world to understand is the income tax.
—Albert Einstein, 1879-1955

Introduction

When starting your own business, you must decide which type of ownership you'd like. The most common forms of business ownership are *sole proprietorship, partnership,* and *corporation.* Each form of ownership offers advantages and disadvantages along with different tax implications. The way you structure your personal chef business ownership will affect your tax liability and management options. The form of ownership you choose will have long-term financial consequences.

This chapter explores common forms of ownership and their associated tax advantages and disadvantages.

Learning Outcomes

After reading this chapter, you will be able to

✎ Identify the tax advantages and disadvantages of
    a. Sole proprietorships
    b. Partnerships
    c. Corporations
    d. Subchapter S corporations
    e. Limited liability companies (LLC)

✎ Discuss the differences in management responsibilities between each form of ownership.

✎ Describe a general partnership, limited partnership, joint venture, and limited liability company.

✎ Identify the liability advantages of incorporation.

✎ Discuss the personal liabilities for a sole proprietorship.

✎ Describe the four taxes your personal chef business may be responsible for.

Key Terms

Sole Proprietorship
Limited Partnership
Subchapter S
   Corporation
Incorporation
Income
Loss
Liability
Shareholder
Gross Income
Income Tax
Excise Tax
Sales Tax
State Unemployment
   Tax
Gross Receipts
Profit
Partnership

Joint Venture
Limited Liability
   Corporation (LLC)
Assets
Deductions
Capital
Partnership
   Agreement
Capital Stock
Net Income
Self-employment Tax
Self-employment
   Income
Federal Insurance
   Contributions Act
   (FICA)
Office Expenses
Inventory
General Partnership

Corporation
Dividends
Gains
Operating Agreement
Personal Liability
Domestic Corporation
Expenses
Employment Tax
Tax Obligation
Federal
   Unemployment Tax
   Act (FUTA)
Revenue
Cash Basis
Sales Tax License
Payroll
   Unemployment
   Taxes

Types of Ownership for Your Business

A sole proprietorship is an unincorporated business owned by one individual. It is the simplest form of business organization to start and maintain. The business has no existence apart from you, the owner. Its **liabilities**, or financial obligations; a responsibility or debt, are your **personal liabilities**. As a result, you undertake the risk of the business for all **assets** owned, whether or not they are used in the business. Assets are defined as the value of items owned by a business or an individual. You include the **income**, which is money received during a period in exchange for a product or service and the **expenses** or money spent by the business on your own tax return. Most personal chefs choose to operate as sole proprietorships.

The major benefits of a sole proprietorship include:

- You, the owner, have complete control. When you look in the mirror, you are looking at the person in charge of your company!

- A sole proprietorship is the easiest and least expensive business type to start.

- You, the owner, receive all the income from your personal chef business.

- It is easy to dissolve.

The major disadvantages of a sole proprietorship are:

- You, the owner, assume total responsibility for all debts. This liability may put your personal assets at risk.

- It may be more difficult to raise **capital**, meaning money or other assets owned by a company or an individual that can be converted to money as a sole proprietorship than under the other forms of business.

- Benefits such as health and dental insurance may not be fully tax deductible.

Most personal chefs choose to this form of ownership. Some maintain sole owner-ship for the life of their business, while others choose to take on an alternate form of ownership as the nature of their businesses evolves.

Sole Proprietorship

Advantages	*Disadvantages*
Easier to Start	Harder to Raise Money
Easier to Raise Money	Less Tax Deductions
You Get All of the Income	You Are Liable
You Have Complete Control	

Exhibit 2.1
Advantages and Disadvantages of Sole Proprietorship

A **partnership** is the legal relationship between two or more persons who join to carry on a trade or business. Each person contributes money, property, labor, or skills and expects to share in the **profits** and **losses** of the business. A partnership must file an annual information return to report the income, **deductions** or the amount that may be deducted from a tax return, gains, and losses of its operations, but it does not pay in-come tax. Instead, it passes through any profits or losses to the partners. Each partner includes his or her share of the partnership's income, etc., on his or her tax return.

A partnership is based on a legal agreement that clearly states how the profits, or monies left within a business after all operating expenses are met, or losses which occur when the business' expenses exceed its income, will be shared, how deci-sions will be made, how new partners will be admitted, and how the partnership will be dissolved, if necessary. This agreement should also include how much capital (and in what form) each partner will contribute to the partnership. There are three forms of partnership to consider.

A **general partnership**, the simplest form, assumes all partners are equal within the business unless a written agreement states otherwise. A **limited partner-ship** offers some protection to the partners by limiting liability to the extent of each partner's investment. A **joint venture partnership** is similar to a general partnership except that it exists for a limited period and dissolves at the com-pletion of a project.

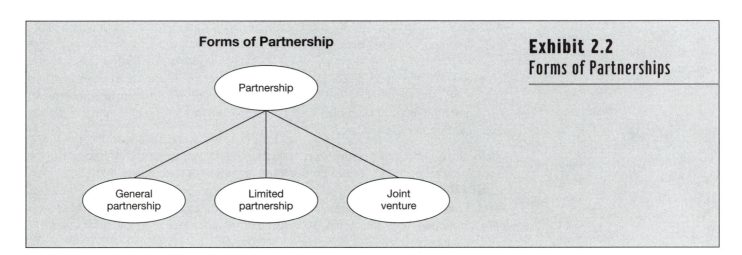

Forms of Partnership

Exhibit 2.2
Forms of Partnerships

These are the advantages of a partnership:

- It is easy to form, although it does require legal agreements.

- The larger the partnership, the better its ability to raise capital.

- Partners can pool their individual skills to create competitive advantages for the business.

- Tax reporting is relatively easy.

These are the disadvantages of a partnership:

- Profits and decisions are shared, which may result in disagreements.

- Each partner may be liable for the actions of the other.

- Should a key partner leave the partnership, the business may be forced to dissolve.

Clearly, if two or more chefs open a personal chef business together, forming a partnership is the optimal form of business ownership for them. It is easy to establish, and the amount of paperwork involved is manageable. Like a sole proprietorship, this form of ownership may last for the life of the business, but it may also change as the nature of their business warrants.

A **corporation** involves selling stock to shareholders in order to raise capital. A corporation generally takes the same tax deductions as a sole proprietorship to calculate its taxable income, but it may also take special deductions. The profit of a corporation is taxed when earned and then is taxed to the shareholders when distributed as **dividends** or the share of the profits received by the stockholder from a company. However, shareholders cannot deduct any loss of the corporation.

Forming a **Subchapter S Corporation** may offer additional tax advantages beyond those of a corporation, for your business. A **domestic corporation** can avoid double taxation (once to the corporations and again to the shareholders) by electing to be treated as an S corporation. An S corporation generally is exempt from federal income tax, other than tax on certain capital gains and passive income. Its shareholders include on their tax return their share of the corporation's separately stated items of income, deductions, loss, and credit as well as their share of non–separately stated income or loss on their tax returns.

A **limited liability company (LLC)** is another form of ownership, but it is not permitted in all states. If it is allowed in your state, forming an LLC may offer benefits that other forms of ownership do not. An LLC is an unincorporated business entity, meaning it is a cross between a corporation and a partnership. Like a corporation, an LLC protects its members from personal liability for the debts and obligations of the company. Like a partnership, an LLC is typically formed by filing a certificate of formation with the appropriate state office, such as the Secretary of State. As in a partnership, the members of an LLC typically enter into an **operating agreement**. This agreement not only establishes clear guidelines on how the LLC is managed but also how the members relate.

Where the number of **shareholders** who must be U.S. residents is limited under the S corporation form, LLCs have no such restrictions. For this reason, the LLC is particularly attractive to non–U.S. citizens who own a small business in the United States. An LLC can have more flexibility in management because it is controlled by the members' agreement and not by the Business Corporations Act in a particular state.

Unless the LLC elects to be taxed as a corporation, it is taxed as a partnership—that is, both the income and deductions of the LLC are passed through to members for inclusion with their personal income tax returns. LLCs have a limited life cycle that is agreed upon by the owners at start-up. This life cycle can be extended with an agreement of all the owners. LLCs cannot have more than two of the four characteristics that define corporations:

- Centralization of management

- Free transfer of ownership interests

- Limited liability to the extent of assets which means the total amount of liability cannot exceed the corporation's assets.

- Continuity of life

Characteristics of LLCs

Central management

Free transfer of ownership

Continuity of life

Limited liability

Exhibit 2.3
Characteristics of LLCs

The formation of an LLC is more complex than that of a general partnership, but it may prove a more worthwhile form of business, especially when one or more of the owners are non–U.S. residents or if you have a nontraditional management structure and need more flexibility than the standard officers-and-directors arrangement for corporations governed by the state's Business Corporation Act. If tax considerations are a driving factor, you can achieve the same pass-through taxation of a corporation by electing to be an S corporation.

Incorporation

All the forms of ownership mentioned so far in this chapter have advantages and disadvantages. A more sophisticated form of ownership is the **incorporation**. To incorporate your personal chef business, you issue and sell stock to investors. Corporations are chartered by the state in which they reside and are considered by the law to be a unique entity—that is, separate and apart from those who own it, the shareholders.

Forming a corporation requires more time and money than the other forms of ownership. Corporations are regulated by federal and state agencies and generally result in more paperwork than either sole proprietorships or partnerships. The advantage of incorporating your business is that it may offer protection in the form of reducing or eliminating personal liability. When a corporation enters into a transaction, it is the corporation and not the shareholders that is held responsible. When you are starting up a new business or a corporate entity, your bank may require a personal guarantee because your company does not have a credit history. As a rule, however, a shareholder's liability is limited to the amount he or she invested in the company. Under normal circumstances, creditors cannot reach beyond the assets of the company. The same is true with a lawsuit. It is the corporation, not you, who will be sued, assuming there are no unusual circumstances, such as fraudulent undercapitalization. Not only do corporations and LLCs offer some protection against personal liability, they also offer important tax considerations, which are discussed later in this chapter.

Taxes

Businesses as well as individuals pay local, state, and federal taxes. The form of business you choose to operate determines what taxes you must pay, how you pay them, and what form you use to report them. You can refer to the Internal Revenue Service (IRS) website at http://www.irs.gov for more information.

It is highly recommended that you consult an attorney, certified public accountant, or your local branch of the Small Business Association (SBA) for assistance in choosing the correct form of ownership for your business.

Personal chefs most often choose sole proprietorships. A sole proprietorship has no existence apart from you, the owner. Its liabilities are your personal liabilities, and you undertake the risks of the business for all assets owned, whether or not used in the business. You include the income and expenses of the business on your own tax return. For more information on sole proprietorships, see IRS Publication 334, "Tax Guide for Small Business."

A partnership must file an annual information return to report the income, deductions, **gains** meaning the increased value of your business or investment, and losses, of its operations, but it does not pay income tax. Instead, it passes through any profits or losses to its partners. Each partner includes his or her share of the partnership's income, etc., on his or her tax return. For more information on partnerships, see IRS Publication 541, "Partnerships."

In forming a corporation, prospective shareholders transfer money, property, or both for the corporation's **capital stock** which is the amount of stock authorized for issue by the corporation. A corporation generally takes the same deductions as a sole proprietorship to figure its taxable income. A corporation can also take special deductions. For more information on corporations, see IRS Publication 542, "Corporations."

No matter what form of business you choose to create, you must pay four general kinds of business taxes:

- *Income tax.* This tax is paid by most people who have taxable income, or business or personal income. It is the most common form of tax in the United States. It is paid to the federal government as well as many state governments.

- *Self-employment tax.* This is a Social Security and Medicare tax primarily for individuals who work for themselves. It is similar to the Social Security and Medicare taxes withheld from the pay of most wage earners.

- *Employment taxes.* If you have employees, you must file employment taxes. These taxes include Social Security and Medicare taxes, federal income tax withholding, and federal unemployment taxes.

- *Excise taxes.* These are taxes imposed on the manufacture or sale of certain products; the operation of certain kinds of businesses; the use of various kinds of equipment, facilities, and products; and payments received for certain types of services.

Each state and county has its own tax regulations, so it is important for you to research the required taxes in your local area in addition to the federal tax regulations relevant to your type of ownership. That being said, there are some generally accepted guidelines related to handling your business **tax obligations**, or monies owed by a person or organization to a government entity. It is strongly suggested that you consult a tax consultant for help in determining which taxes are applicable to your small business based on the federal and state requirements and regulations in your area.

Self-employment Taxes, Federal

Self-employment income is that income you earn when someone else does not employ you. For example, if you receive a paycheck and taxes are withheld, then you are employed by a company. If you are paid for services rendered when you issue an invoice for the work you or your employees perform and taxes are not withheld, you are self-employed and must remit your taxes four times a year using IRS Form 1040ES.

When reporting your self-employment income to the IRS, use IRS Form 1040 Schedule C. There is also a short form of 1040 that you may be able to use. After you complete the profit and loss part of Schedule C, the income is carried to page 1 for inclusion in your taxable income. The same amount is carried over to IRS Form 1040SE, where your portion of Social Security is calculated and carried to pages 1 and 2 of IRS Form 1040. More information on self-employment taxes can be found in IRS Publication 533, "Self-employment Tax."

Self-employment Taxes, State and Local

Virtually every state applies taxes to small businesses. The way you structure your business may affect your tax obligation, as discussed earlier in this chapter. Some cities and counties tax personal property used in a business, while others have an income tax on all businesses operating within their jurisdiction. Contact your state and local government taxing authorities to determine which, if any, taxes your personal chef business must pay.

Sales Tax

A **sales tax** is a dollar amount added to the cost of a product or service. Sales tax is paid by the customer at the completion of a transaction. Many state and local municipalities have a general sales/service tax. As a business owner, you are responsible for collecting these taxes and then transferring them to the appropriate government agency. Although you are producing meals for your client, the food is a pass-through cost and no sales taxes are charged for it. As a personal chef, you provide a service, and your service fee is taxable in many locations. If you live in an area that charges sales tax, you must obtain a **sales tax license** which establishes an account for reporting and paying sales taxes to a governmental entity, from the state in which your business was established.

Other Taxes

If you have employees, you are responsible for withholding income taxes and deducting **Federal Insurance Contributions Act (FICA)** taxes from their paychecks. Employers not only must withhold taxes from their employees' paychecks but also must match a certain amount of some taxes for each employee.

You may also have to pay **Federal Unemployment Tax Act (FUTA)** taxes and **state unemployment tax**. The IRS has established guidelines, which can be found in IRS Publication 15 1/2005 Circular E, to help you to determine whether your business must pay FUTA tax. Contact your local state taxing agency to determine if your business needs to pay state unemployment taxes. In order to keep your payroll taxes in order, you may choose to use a payroll service company. For a fee, these companies determine each employee's tax obligations and the business's tax obligations and then print the paycheck and provide you with all needed reports. Remember, these companies charge a fee for this service. Some business owners choose to save money by calculating these tax obligations themselves, but time spent calculating **payroll unemployment taxes** for federal, state, and local taxing agencies is time spent away from promoting and selling your services.

Important Considerations

Many owners of home-based businesses deduct office expenses, such as money spent on common office items such as paper, copy costs, and supplies, for their home office. The IRS has established tests to determine if this sort of deduction is acceptable. Generally, a home office can be deducted when the home area is the principal place of business or professional activity. For example, you are a doctor and see most of your patients at an office within your home. In this case, a deduction for the home office is acceptable. A tax dispute may arise when you have a principal place of business elsewhere but use a part of your home for occasional work or administrative paperwork. Occasional use is not sufficient for a home office deduction. If your deduction is questioned, you must prove that the area is used regularly and exclusively to meet with customers, clients, or patients. Based on the Supreme Court's tests in the *Solomon* case, you may not deduct the cost of a home office if you use the office only to do administrative paperwork. Further information can be found in IRS Publication 587.

Another tax consideration is whether or not the business is really a business or simply a hobby. The question of whether an activity, such as dog breeding or collecting and selling coins or stamps, is a hobby or sideline business typically arises when losses are incurred. As long as you show a profit, you may deduct the expenses of this sort of activity. But when expenses exceed revenue and your tax return is examined, an agent may allow expenses only up to the amount of your revenue and disallow the remaining expenses that make up your losses. At this point, you must prove that you are engaged in this activity to make a profit. IRS Publication 535 provides additional information about the differences between a business and a hobby.

Conclusion

The form of ownership you choose for your personal chef business affects many facets of its operation. Whether you operate your business by yourself or have active partners or invested partners, planning appropriately and having a complete understanding of the ramifications of each type of ownership are essential. Because each state has different laws regarding these types of ownership, and because these laws continuously change, it is strongly recommended that you consult a business lawyer, accountant, or a business support agency such as the Small Business Administration or Service Corps of Retired Executives (SCORE) to determine the best form of ownership for your needs.

Determining the type of ownership for your personal chef business is the first step in forming your business plan. Decisions made now affect not only how the business is run but also the tax responsibilities for everyone involved.

For more in-depth discussion on forms of ownerships, we recommend to the following books:

Home-based Business for Dummies, 2nd Edition, Paul Edwards, Sarah Edwards, and Peter Economy (John Wiley and Sons).

Small Business Owners Manual, Joe Kennedy (Career Press, June 2005).

Key Terms

Sole Proprietorship
A simple form of ownership where one individual has complete ownership of the business.

Liability
Financial obligations; a responsibility or debt.

Personal Liability
Responsibility for debts or actions against the business.

Assets
The value of items owned by a business or an individual.

Income
Money received during a period in exchange for a product or service.

Gross Income
Total income before deductions.

Net Income
Sometimes referred to as the *bottom line*; a company's total profit.

Expenses
Money spent by a business.

Capital
Money or other assets owned by a company or a individual that can be converted to money.

Partnership
A form of ownership where two or more individuals own a business

Profit
Monies left within a business after all operating expenses are met.

Loss
When expenses exceed income.

Deductions
As a tax term, the amount that may be deducted from a tax return.

General Partnership
A form of ownership where two or more individuals own a business and are equals in the eyes of the business.

Limited Partnership
A form of ownership where two or more individuals own a

business, but each is liable only to the extent of his or her investment.

Joint Venture Partnership

Similar to a general partnership except that it exists for a limited period and dissolves at the completion of the project.

Partnership Agreement

A contract between two or more persons that obligate money, labor, and or skills that each offers the business. Also determines the sharing of profits and losses between signing members.

Corporation

A form of ownership where stockholders share in the ownership. Stock is sold to shareholders in order to raise capital.

Domestic Corporation

A U.S. corporation doing business in the state in which it is incorporated.

Shareholder

A person who holds shares of stock in a company.

Dividends

The share of profits received by a stockholder from a company.

Subchapter S Corporation

A form of ownership that enjoys tax advantages beyond those of a corporation.

Operating Agreement

An agreement among business partners that defines responsibilities and management relationships.

Limited Liability Corporation (LLC)

A form of ownership that limits the liability of the business. It is not permitted in all states.

Incorporation

Becoming a corporation.

Gains

The increased value of business or investment.

Revenue

Total sales during a given period.

Gross Receipts

The total of all receipts. See Revenue.

Inventory

The goods and materials in stock; may be referred to as a dollar amount.

Cash Basis

An accounting method whereby receipts are recorded during the period they are received and the expenses in the period in which they are actually paid.

Capital Stock

The amount of stock authorized for issue by a corporation.

Income Tax

Taxes on personal or business income.

Employment Taxes

Taxes paid on behalf of a company's employees.

Excise Taxes

Taxes imposed on the manufacture or sale of certain products.

Tax Obligation

Monies owed by a person or organization to a governmental entity.

Self-employment Income

Money or its equivalent received over a period by a self-employed person.

Self-employment Tax

Social Security and Medicare taxes paid by individuals who work for themselves.

Sales Tax

A tax levied on retail sales or services that is collected by the provider or retailer.

Sales tax license

A license which establishes an account for reporting and paying sales taxes to a governmental agency.

Federal Insurance Contributions Act (FICA)

A tax levied in equal amounts on both employees and employers.

Federal Unemployment Tax Act (FUTA)

A federal tax that funds state workforce agencies. Paid by an employer.

State Unemployment Tax

A state tax, usually paid by employers, to fund state workforce agencies.

Payroll Unemployment Taxes

A percentage of gross payrolls paid to a governmental entity by the employer.

Office Expenses

Monies spent to cover common office items such as paper, copy costs, and supplies.

Review Questions
True/False

1. Each form of ownership has different tax obligations.

2. A sole proprietorship is similar to a corporation, except for the number of shareholders.

3. A sole proprietorship is the easiest form of business to start.

4. A partnership is a relationship between two or more persons.

5. A subchapter S corporation is just a smaller version of a large corporation.

6. A joint venture is a form of a partnership.

7. In a sole proprietorship, the assets and liabilities of the business are yours.

8. Gross income is monies left after all expenses are deducted.

9. FICA is a federal agency that inspects small businesses for tax fraud.

10. As a small business owner, you are responsible for reporting your self-employment income and tax.

Multiple Choice

1. Which is not a form of ownership?

   a. Partnerships
   b. LLC
   c. Dual proprietorships
   d. Subchapter S corporations

2. Which statement is not true concerning a sole proprietorship?

   a. It is the easiest form of business to start.
   b. A single person is in complete control.
   c. It is easy to dissolve.
   d. It always contains only one employee, the owner.

3. A partnership should be

   a. Based on a legal agreement that clearly defines each person's roles, risks, and rewards.
   b. Formed only after a business has been in business for at least one year.
   c. Confined to only two partners.
   d. Based on a broad understanding of each person's role, risk, and reward.

4. A joint venture is a form of

   a. Corporation
   b. Sub S corporation
   c. Partnership
   d. Sole proprietorship

5. LLCs share many traits of a

   a. Corporation
   b. Sub S corporation
   c. Partnership
   d. Sole proprietorship

6. A form of ownership that offers protection against personal liability is a

   a. Corporation
   b. Sub S corporation
   c. Partnership
   d. Sole proprietorship

7. A shareholder is

   a. A working partner in a company.
   b. A consultant to the company.
   c. A person who bought stock in a company.
   d. A person who owns an entire company.

8. Self-employment taxes are

    a. Paid to cover Medicare and Social Security.
    b. Taxes that sole proprietors and partnerships do not need to pay.
    c. Paid by employees of a company.
    d. A pass-through tax.

9. Sales tax is a good example of a tax that is

    a. Paid to cover Medicare and Social Security.
    b. Paid by a sole proprietorship.
    c. Paid by employees of a company.
    d. Is a pass-through tax.

10. The IRS considers ____ when determining if a business is a business or a hobby.

    a. The total losses of the business.
    b. The type of ownership of the business.
    c. Proof that the business is engaged in activity to make a profit.
    d. The size of the business.

Discussion Questions & Activities

1. Divide a group of students into three equal groups. One group is the sole proprietorship, another partnership, and the third a corporation. Have each group report on their ownership style advantages and disadvantages as related to

    a. Tax ramifications
    b. Ease of ownership
    c. Support of ownership
    d. Growth potential

2. Decide which form of ownership would be the best form for your personal chef business and discuss why.

3. Interview businesspeople who run their own small business. Determine why they picked the form of ownership of their business. Would they change their form of ownership, should they have the opportunity? Why or why not?

4. Divide into groups of three or four students. Go online and pick a large foodservice corporation such as McDonald's, Brinker International, or Darden Restaurants. Go to the website and scan their annual reports to shareholders. Report to the other groups about the information found in the shareholders' report. Relate this style of information reporting to what is needed in a sole proprietorship or partnership.

From the Field

Roundtable discussion with

Chef Jim Davis, *The Really Good Food Culinary Services*
Chef Alison Sturm, *Wish Upon a Chef*
Chef Jackie Alejo, *Cooking for You*

FORMS OF OWNERSHIP

Most personal chefs choose a sole proprietorship as their initial form of ownership. Chef Jim Davis of The Really Good Food Culinary Services says, "I can tell you from my experience that we operated as a sole proprietorship for the first four years. We incorporated only after we moved into a commercial kitchen operation. In most cases, personal chefs elect to start out as sole proprietorships. It is the least expensive and the least intrusive form of ownership and requires the least amount of reporting. There are exceptions, of course, but in general, sole proprietorships serve the purpose for most personal chefs starting up their businesses."

Chef Alison, owner of Wish Upon a Chef, located in Hot Springs, Arkansas, states, "I operated as a sole proprietorship when I started as a personal chef, and even now that I'm in a commercial kitchen doing catering and running a second revenue stream of gourmet-to-go meals and specialty foods markets, I still operate as a sole proprietorship."

Chef Jackie Alego of Cooking For You! says, "With proper insurance coverage, you should really not have to be overly worried about protecting your personal assets. That being said, some folks find they feel better with proper insurance and forming an LLC."

As discussed in this chapter, a sole proprietorship is an unincorporated business owned by one individual. The business has no existence apart from you, the owner. Its liabilities are your personal liabilities, and you assume the risk of running a business that turns out to be unsuccessful and risk all the assets you own in the process. A limited liability company is an unincorporated form of business ownership that offers protection to its members from personal liability for the debts and obligations of the company. Recall that this form of ownership is not permitted in all states. If the purpose of establishing an LLC is to protect your personal assets, Chef Jim Davis states, "Even if you form an LLC or a corporation, you are its only employee and asset. If you make somebody sick, no matter what form of ownership you have established, they will pierce the corporate veil and get at your personal assets. That's why you have liability insurance. With this insurance, you relieve yourself of that liability and pay somebody else, the insurance company, to assume it for you."

As your business grows and expands, you might consider different forms of ownership, such as Chef Davis did when The Really Good Food Company moved into a commercial kitchen. Others choose to stay with their original form of ownership. They all agree that it is best to talk to an attorney, tax attorney, or local business advisory association that understands the laws that apply to your state.

Discussion Questions

1. Chef Jim Davis started his personal chef business as a sole proprietorship; then, after expanding into a commercial kitchen, he switched the business to that of a corporation. What are the advantages associated with his decision to change the form of ownership of his business?

2. Chef Alison also expanded her business into a commercial kitchen, yet she chose to remain a sole proprietorship. Speculate on why she did so. What are the advantages and disadvantages of changing from sole proprietorship to another form of ownership?

OPERATING LEGALLY

> Haste in every business brings failures.
> —Herodotus, 484-430 B.C.

Introduction

Every business has to deal with local, state, and, possibly, federal regulations. Being a small business owner sometimes requires great patience and perhaps even a sense of humor when filling out all the forms needed to start your personal chef business. This chapter introduces you to the generally accepted requirements most small businesses must meet before officially opening their doors. Remember, every location has different requirements, and you may even have to deal with different state, county, or local offices in order to determine the requirements for your business location.

Learning Outcomes

After reading this chapter, you will be able to

✍ Explain the steps needed to operate a small business legally.

✍ Discuss the importance of a food handler's certification.

✍ Describe the term *DBA* and its advantages for the personal chef.

✍ Explain the requirements for a Employee Identification Number.

✍ Discuss the importance of obtaining general liability insurance.

✍ Describe bonding.

Key Terms

Safe Food Handler's Certification

ServSafe

Limited Liability Corporation (LLC)

Chapter C Corporation

DBA

Bonding

Corporation

Sole Proprietorship

Subchapter S Corporation

Employee Identification Number

Local Business License

General Liability Insurance

Partnership

Personal Service Business

National Restaurant Association Educational Foundation (NRAEF)

National Restaurant Association (NRA)

American Culinary Foundation (ACF)

American Personal Chef Association (APCA)

Legitimize the Business

You would be surprised at how many small businesses operate without securing the proper licensing. Business owners who take this approach are usually trying to cut corners, save a few dollars, and open their business faster. They feel the licenses are not worth the few bucks required to obtain them. However, if you do not obtain the proper licenses or insurance for your business, you may face fines, forfeiture of the business, legal action, and even imprisonment. It is simply not worth risking all of this, especially as most business licensing is easy to obtain.

STARTING OFF ON THE RIGHT FOOT

In order to legitimately operate your personal chef service, in your city, you should secure and maintain the following five items:

1. **Safe Food Handler's Certification** (also called *food sanitation card*) which proves you have taken and passed a locally or nationally recognized foodservice sanitation course. Information on locally or nationally recognized programs can be obtained through the local department of health or environmental protection.

2. Registration of a **DBA**, or "Doing Business As," which is a fictitious name statement for the name of your business. This protects your use of the name (in your city/county *only*) for five years. You must then renew the DBA.

3. **Employee Identification Number or Tax ID Number** which is an identification number assigned to your business by the IRS.

4. **Local business license** issued by a governmental agency as proof of official or legal permission to operate a business (if required). Remember to register your business as a **personal service**, not a cooking company. Because you are a personal service and not a catering business, you do not need to have a commercial kitchen.

Personal Chef Versus Caterer

Remember, as a personal chef you are a service provider, cooking only in your client's home. You are not a caterer, which would require a commercial kitchen.

---

5. **General liability insurance**, health insurance, and bonding. Insurance coverage protects the business against specified kinds of loss. Bonding is a form of insurance.

Once you have completed these requirements, you are in full compliance with your municipal regulations and can operate your personal chef business with confidence.

Safe Food Handler's Certification

It is important to obtain a **safe food handler's certification** before opening your business. In some locations obtaining a food sanitation card through the local department of health suffices. Most, if not all, academic culinary programs require students to pass a foodservice sanitation exam during the course of the program. Local health departments usually accept documentation of the successful completion of a culinary sanitation course and waive their own test. However, most sanitation certifications must be renewed periodically, so you should always make sure your certification is up to date.

If you need to take a sanitation course, the educational branch of the **National Restaurant Association Educational Foundation (NRAEF)** offers a nationally recognized and Conference for Food Protection-approved food safety programs, called ServSafe, which can be taken online at www.nraef.org. Your local community college, local chapter of the **National Restaurant Association** a trade organization offering services to the foodservice industry, or local chapter of the **American Culinary Federation**, the largest chef's organization in America, offering professional levels of nationally recognized certifications, may also offer brick-and-mortar classes in sanitation for those who enjoy the traditional classroom setting.

DBA

Name recognition and branding are crucial to business success. You must own a **corporation** or **LLC** in order to open a bank account or other related accounts using a business name rather than your personal legal name. If you own a **sole proprietorship**, such as a personal chef service, you are required by law to file a **DBA** to receive money or hold a bank account under a business name. A DBA (Doing Business As), also known as a *fictitious name statement* or an *assumed name,* helps establish a brand for the business. A DBA is typically filed in person or by your legal representative in your county recorder's office. Once filed, the DBA officially states you are conducting business using a name that is different from your legal name. It gives your personal chef business legitimacy and makes it easier to keep your personal and business accounts separate.

Imagine your real name was Ned Overdone or Susan Poortaste. A personal chef business with a name like these would be doomed for failure simply because of the negative response the public would have to the owner's last name. Filing a DBA enables you to call your business Ned's Personal Chef or Meals in Your Home by Susan. These names would definitely be more appealing to the public.

On the other hand, if you are lucky enough to have a name that might enhance your personal chef business, by all means use it. For example, if your legal last name is

Jones, you might name your business Jones Personal Chef Services. In this case, you would not need to file a DBA.

In most states, DBAs protect the use of your registered name for five years. However, some states do not require a DBA to be unique, which means you may share your business name with another business. With this in mind, a little research can ensure you create an original name for your business. Many states supply a list of DBAs within a city or county on the state's business website.

Requirements for obtaining a DBA vary from state to state. Check with your local Small Business Administration office or online at your state or county business website.

Employer Identification Number

An **Employee Identification Number (EIN)**, which may also be called a *federal tax ID number*, is an identification number assigned to your business by the IRS. These numbers are used by many forms of business and are easy to obtain. You are required to have an EIN for your business if you:

- Pay wages to an employee(s).

- Form a **chapter C** or **subchapter S corporation** or **partnership**.

- File pensions which are monies paid into an account, either by a business or employee, that is used for retirement or excise tax returns.

If you are a sole proprietor with no employees or pension plans and collect no excise taxes, you do not need an EIN. As a sole proprietor, you can use your Social Security number for tax purposes. The IRS has free publications to provide further information about EIN. To obtain an EIN, you need to complete IRS Form SS-4. It is wise to obtain an EIN before opening your business. Most financial institutions require an EIN to open accounts for either a corporation or a partnership.

Business License

You must have a local **business license** in order to conduct business. This license may be issued by a local government, such as a town or city, or by the county in which the business is based. When applying for your business license, remember these four key points:

1. You are a home-based small business.
2. You have no employees other than yourself (if this is true).
3. Because your clients pay you in advance to purchase their groceries, you may be considered a shopping service.
4. You do not require a commercial kitchen license or special zoning permits, as you will be cooking *only* in your clients' kitchens.

Keep in mind that yours is a personal service business rather than a food preparation/cooking business.

Personal Service Business

A business that creates revenue by providing a service, not a product.

You do not sell food you prepare in your home but rather provide a service within your client's home. In some localities, this concept may be misunderstood. It is important that health departments and licensing agencies understand you will be cooking all the food in the client's home and not elsewhere. As a personal chef you plan menus, shop for the necessary ingredients, and prepare all the food items in the client's kitchen. A personal chef is unlike a caterer in that caterers require the use of a commercial kitchen.

Insurance

As a small business owner, it is critical that you recognize the risks associated with operating your business. As an independent business owner, you are quite vulnerable, and you need all the protection you can garner.

We live in a litigious society where more and more people file lawsuits, whether they are justified or not. During the last several years, general liability insurance coverage geared specifically to the personal chef industry has been made available. Organizations such as the American Personal & Private Chef Association (APPCA) can assist you in obtaining this insurance. Annual premiums are reasonable—$400–$600 per year in 2006—and you and your business are protected from any sort of liability.

Exhibit 3.1
American Personal & Private Chef Association Logo

General liability insurance provides coverage for damages that you, as a business owner, are legally obligated to pay if bodily injury or property damage is the result of an occurrence within your operation or arises due to your negligence in maintaining your premises or operations. It also provides, unless excluded, coverage for bodily injury or property damage caused by your products after you have relinquished possession to others or from your operations after they are completed. Such coverage includes:

- $1,000,000 in liability and medical expenses

- $1,000,000 in personal and advertising injury

- $300,000 in fire damage legal liability

- $10,000 in medical expenses for any one person

- $2,000,000 aggregate

When shopping for insurance, work with organizations that understand the needs and risk associated with the personal chef business. Look for a policy with a low deductible and one that can be tailored to meet the needs of your business. The policy should be underwritten by a nationally recognized and rated insurance company. Research several companies for the most competitive premiums, and find companies that offer renewal discounts.

Bonding

Bonding is not usually required of an independent business owner, as you are also covered by general liability insurance. However, you should consider bonding if you have employees, as clients occasionally ask whether or not your employees are bonded. The purpose of a bond, whether it is referred to as a fidelity bond, theft bond, or surety bond, is to bond an employee to an employer and pay the claim for any theft damages filed by a client. Damages will be paid to a client only if your employee is convicted of an actual theft, and a conviction may be difficult to get.

Bonds are not terribly expensive. If you have employees and you find it gives your clients peace of mind to know they are bonded, you might want to consider spending the extra $100–$200 per year for this coverage.

Conclusion

Many small home-based business operate without obtain the necessary permits and licenses. The owners think they are saving money, but they are opening the door to possible legal action against the business. Obtaining the proper licenses and permits allows the business to grow and expand without the fear of fines or possible imprisonment.

Insurance can be reasonably inexpensive and offer the business protection against loss. With all the forms of insurance offered today to the small business owner, dealing with a trusted agent can ensure proper protections for a fair price.

Key Terms

Safe Food Handler's Certification
Proof of taking and passing a locally or nationally recognized foodservice sanitation course.

DBA
"Doing business as;" a fictitious name under which a business operates.

Employee Identification Number or Tax ID Number
Identification number assigned to your business by the IRS.

Local Business License
A document issued by a governmental agency as proof of official or legal permission to operate a business, issued by states, counties, municipalities, or other such governmental agencies depending on state laws.

General Liability Insurance
Insurance that covers the business for bodily injury or property damage the business may incur.

Bonding
A form of insurance that protects customers against theft or other actions of a business's employees.

Personal Service Business
The nature of a business that provides service to a customer.

National Restaurant Association Educational Foundation (NRAEF)
The educational branch of the National Restaurant Association.

National Restaurant Association (NRA)
Trade organization offering services to the foodservice industry.

ServSafe
A national recognized training program for foodservice sanitation and food safety practices.

American Culinary Federation (ACF)
The largest chefs' organization in America offering professional levels of nationally recognized certifications.

Corporation
A form of ownership where stockholders share in the ownership.

Limited Liability Corporation (LLC)
A form of ownership that limits the liability of the business.

Sole Proprietorship
A simple form of ownership where one individual has complete ownership of the business.

American Personal & Private Chef Association (APPCA)
The largest organization representing the personal chef industry.

Bond, Fidelity, Theft, or Surety
See Bonding.

Chapter C Corporation
A form of ownership that enjoys tax advantages beyond those of a simple corporation.

Subchapter S Corporation
A form of ownership that enjoys tax advantages beyond those of a simple corporation.

Partnership
A form of ownership where two or more individuals own a business.

Review Questions

True/False

1. Small businesses must obtain proper licensing, or the owner may face fines and imprisonment.
2. The term *DBA* means a business is operating under the name of the owner, such as Candy's Personal Chef Service.
3. Because the personal chef business is a service business, the owner need not obtain a safe food handler's certification.
4. In most states, a DBA protects the user's registered name for eight years.
5. All forms of business are required to have an Employee Identification Number.
6. A personal chef business is considered a catering business.
7. General liability insurance protects you against losses associated with weather or theft.
8. A small business does not need liability insurance.
9. Bonding is another form of insurance.
10. A personal chef business is considered a home-based small business.

Multiple Choice

1. In a legitimate small business, the owner has

   a. Secured proper licensing.
   b. Gotten permission from a financial institution to operate.
   c. Been licensed by a professional organization.
   d. Both b and c are correct.

2. A possible consequence of not legitimizing your business may be

   a. Loss of the business.
   b. Fines.
   c. Imprisonment.
   d. All of the above.

3. To avoid confusion about whether your business is a catering business or a personal chef service, your personal chef business should be licensed as a

   a. Catering business.
   b. Take-out restaurant.
   c. Personal service business.
   d. Delivery service.

4. A business "doing business as"

   a. Is operating under a fictitious name.
   b. Can only be a corporation.
   c. Is allowed to operate in multiple states.
   d. Must use the last name of the owner within the name of the business.

5. General liability insurance covers the business against losses resulting from

   a. Weather.
   b. Acts of negligence.
   c. Robbery.
   d. Lack of sales.

6. Which form of business does not need an EIN?

   a. Chapter C corporation.
   b. A partnership.
   c. A sole proprietorship.
   d. A business that pays excise taxes.

7. In most states, business licenses are issued by

   a. Banks.
   b. State government.
   c. Local or county government.
   d. Federal government.

8. In obtaining a business license, a personal chef business should be listed as a

   a. Personal service business.
   b. Catering business.
   c. Food production business.
   d. Restaurant.

9. Bonding is a form of

   a. Licensing.
   b. Advertisement.
   c. Glue.
   d. Insurance.

10. Sanitation certifications
    a. Should be posted for all to see.
    b. Must be renewed periodically.
    c. Should be paid for in advance.
    d. Are not needed in most locations.

Discussion Questions & Activities

1. Name your personal chef business using a DBA. Compare this name with those of other students and examine the differences. Find the shortest name that clearly states what the business is.

2. Contact your local government and report on what types of permit and license are required in your area.

3. Review sanitation guidelines and find the Critical Control Point (CCP) for a personal chef. Include CCP for the following:
    a. Purchasing food and transportation from the grocery store to the client's home.
    b. Storage of food items being used in the client's home.
    c. Effective sanitation techniques used in the client's home while doing mise en place.
    d. Proper cooling and storage of food items.
    e. Reheating instructions for the client.

4. Interview an insurance agent or broker on the forms and types of insurance offered for the small business owner. Report to the class on your findings.

From the Field

DBAS AND LICENSING

As you recall from studying this chapter, a business that is "doing business as" is called a DBA. A DBA allows you to call your personal chef business almost anything within reason. Some states are easy to work with when filing a DBA, while others have a more detailed process with more specific requirements in place. In New York State, Chef Carol Ricket had to file her DBA with the county clerk for each county in which she was going to cook. Chef Meredith Erickson of Whisk for Hire says, "In Maryland, you do not need a business license to operate as a personal chef. However, I do recommend that you register your business name." She adds, "For starters, so no one else can use it. You also get a piece of paper from the state of Maryland that serves as proof that you are a legitimate business. This comes in handy when buying from wholesalers, getting into trade shows, or getting a business discount."

Chef Renee of Queenie's Kitchen Personal Chef Service says, "Here in Colorado, the DBA cost $8.00 when I filed for it, and I had to have the registration paperwork in order to open my business bank account. My business license is actually a county sales tax registration that didn't cost anything."

Problems *can* occur with a DBA. Chef Kendri Burkett of Savor the Moment, located in Kansas, recalls, "I got a letter from a law firm informing me that my use of Savor the Moment is a trademark infringement. In Kansas, they don't have such a thing as a DBA, and I had decided not to go to the hassle and expense of trademarking the name when I started my business a year and a half ago. The law firm representing the trademark holder contends that she has a nationwide business and is concerned that my use of the mark Savor the Moment is likely to cause confusion among consumers." After careful consideration, Chef Burkett changed the name of her business to A Touch in Thyme.

A trademark is a word, phrase, symbol, or design, or a combination of these elements, that identifies and distinguishes the source of the goods or services of one party from those of others. Trademarks, when federally registered, can trump DBAs when the trademark holder can show harm or dilution of the value of the trademark by the DBA. Additional information about trademarks, including how to register, can be found at www.uspto.gov.

From the Field...continued

In some states you do not need a business license to operate as a personsal chef; in others, you do. It is your responsibility to check with local government authorities. Some chefs have to jump through hoops to become a legal business entity. Chef Judy Erlandson of Sound Cuisine Personal Chef Service says, "Here in Jefferson County, Washington State, I have had the privilege of paying $235 for my zoning home business application, plus $80 to a title company for a list of neighboring property owners. I even had to post two public notice signs in my front yard, just in case passersby might want to know what I'm up to. My state business license was another $20. I suspect that a lot of low-impact home businesses just don't bother getting the home business permit, but I wanted to be official and not worry about getting caught later. The price we pay to do business. . . . "

Paying the price for not being a licensed business operator can be devastating. You could lose your business, pay fines, and even spend time in jail. As Chef Erlandson puts it, "It's the price we pay."

Discussion Questions

1. Chef Burkett of Savor the Moment had to change the name of her business because of tradmark infringement. This name change could affect business due to the loss of name recognition, and there are added expenses for changing all business materials that included the original name. What would be the best way of going about changing your business name? Could you make it so both your current and potential clients perceive this name change as a positive event? If so, how?

2. Each state and sometimes each governmental agency has different requirements for obtaining a business license. Investigate the area where you live and determine the steps you must take to obtain your license. If you are lucky, you live in one of the states where you have nothing to do because a business license is not required to operate a business?

THE BUSINESS PLAN

Eat and drink with your relatives; do business with strangers.
—Greek proverb

Introduction

It is important for you to have a framework or a written blueprint for your business because it will enable you to anticipate problems, recognize opportunities, outline your marketing program, and attain your financial goals. You should use the research you gather relating to the personal chef industry as a foundation for your business venture blueprint. The information you collect and analyze as you conduct your investigation of the industry will enable you to set realistic financial goals for your business and to lay the foundation for your road to success.

Preparing a **business plan** is critical to your success as a business owner. This document defines the scope of your business and identifies your goals and objectives. A good business plan not only helps you address unforeseen problems the business encounters but also enables you to pinpoint organizational strengths and weaknesses. It provides the guidance you need to make intelligent and informed decisions that affect the future of your business. A good business plan need not be long, but it should explain in detail certain components of your business.

You may need to present a business plan when seeking financing from a bank or **investors** who commit capital for either interest costs or financial gains to help you open and operate your business until it starts to earn a profit and becomes self-sufficient. Banks and other lenders often require a start-up business to include a business plan as part of the loan application.

The process of writing this plan can be long and tedious, but you should not rush through it. Many excellent texts focus entirely on how to write and research an effective business plan. In this text, we introduce the basics of preparing such a well-written business plan, which is a mix of research, planning, and professional aspirations. Spend as much time as you need to make your business plan as specific as possible. The time you spend now will save you money and headaches later.

Learning Outcomes

After reading this chapter, you will be able to

✎ Identify the purpose of a business plan.

✎ Discuss sources for the research required to write a business plan.

✎ Identify the parts of a business plan.

✎ Describe the key features of a management business plan.

✎ Explain the importance of a financial business plan.

✎ Explain the importance of an assessment of strengths and weakness when formulating a business plan.

Key Terms

Business Plan
Small Business Administration (SBA)
Management Business Plan
Financial Business Plan

Mission Statement
Chamber of Commerce
Competitive Advantage
Vision Statement
Investor

Capital
Profit
Overhead Cost
Strength/Weakness Assessment

Writing the Business Plan

Writing your first **business plan** may seem a daunting task, as it requires research, honest self-reflection, and realistic planning. Most first-timers will rewrite their business plan numerous times, with each draft becoming a more useful tool. Personal chef Meredith Erickson owner of Whisk for Hire says, "The business plan is a living document and comes off the shelf twice a year to get adjusted. It's a plan, but it can be thrown in the fireplace and you can start a new one without large capital investment. We can reinvent ourselves as many times as we want."

A Business Plan

A business plan for a business is much like mise en place for a chef.

Keeping the following questions in mind as you write your business plan will save you time and help focus your effort:

- What is your best method of research?

  - If you are computer and Internet savvy, much of your research can be done using the search engine of your choice.

- What resources are available in your community?
  - A local library may have all the information you need.
  - The local office of the **Small Business Administration (SBA)**, a federal agency that provides support to small businesses, can be a wonderful resource.
  - The **chamber of commerce** in many communities can be an excellent source of information, since it is an association of business persons that promotes the business interest in the community.
- How familiar are you with your sales area?
  - Have you lived there for years and know the area well, or are you new in town? Being new to an area might require you to do additional research.
- What services will your business provide?
  - What is the scope of your business? Will you be providing high-end restaurant-style foods or home-style comfort foods?
  - Do you have the resources to prepare medically modified diets?
- Who will be your customers?
  - Why will they choose you to provide those services?
  - How will your customers find your business?
- Do you have the financial resources needed to start your personal chef business?
  - If not, where will those resources come from?
- What strengths do you bring to your business? Are you a great cook, an outstanding planner, or a great salesperson?
- What weaknesses do you bring to your business? Do you feel uncomfortable selling your services or closing a deal?
  - How will you overcome these weaknesses?

Honest reflection is important when considering the strengths and weaknesses you bring to your business. We all excel at certain things, and making the best use of your skills will give you a **competitive advantage** when you open your business. We also all have weaknesses, and recognizing those weaknesses and formulating a plan to address them will strengthen your business. Chef Erickson explains, "You have to be honest with yourself. If you are the type of person who only cooks a certain way, you need to accept that and make it the backbone of your business plan." Many of the chefs interviewed for this text agree with Chef Erickson's statement. By being honest about what you love doing—and, just as important, about what you dislike doing—you can focus your business plan around your passion.

Parts of the Plan

A business plan can be broken into distinct parts. The first consists of a description of your business, including both a **mission statement** which defines your business' measurable objectives and a **vision statement** defining the values of the business. The second section addresses the organization of your business. (If you will be the sole employee of your business, this section may be rather short.) The third section outlines the methods you will use to market your new business. The fourth section refers to the finances necessary to open and operate the business as well as your realistic financial projections. You will learn more about mission statements and vision statements in the next chapter.

Writing your business plan is an evolving process. It is not unusual to go through several iterations before you are satisfied with it and consider it workable. It is important for you to take time to think about what you are trying to communicate through the business plan and put your ideas on paper so you can refer to them as needed.

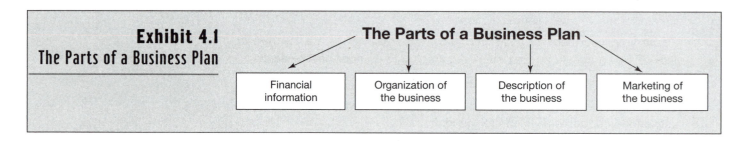

Exhibit 4.1
The Parts of a Business Plan

The Parts of a Business Plan

| Financial information | Organization of the business | Description of the business | Marketing of the business |

Two Types of Business Plan

> **Define your business goals clearly so that others can see them as you do.**
>
> —George F. Burns (1896-1996), comedian

There are two types of business plans, one used to manage your business and the other used to obtain financial resources. While both plans share much information, it is important to remember who will be reading each plan and what you want the reader of each to do with the information it contains. If you are writing a business plan for a start-up company, be sure to provide a clearly written description of your business strategy. What makes your personal chef business different and better than its competitors? This can be articulated in a short summary—no more than three points—within the business plan.

Your **management business plan** should describe your services and products and how they set you apart from the competition. Focus on your most competitive advantage and fully explain how you will use that advantage in your business. You should also describe other core factors in detail. These important areas might include your ability to market your services or your ability to cook certain styles of food. You should focus on what sets you apart from other companies in your field. Do you have experience in cooking tasty food for people on medically restricted diets? If so, you have a strategic advantage over your competition. Being honest with yourself is critical when determining these strategic advantages. For example, just because you enjoy cooking Northern Italian cuisine does not mean it is an advantage you can leverage against your competition.

The **financial business plan** should be used when obtaining **capital** from a financial institution or **investors**. Although much of the information within a management business plan is included in the financial business plan, the latter should focus on the potential **profits** of the business providing realistic financial projections. Of course, it is also important to acknowledge the financial risks associated with opening a personal chef business. Financial institutions are more likely to supply capital to a business that has presented an honest account of both the potential for success as well as the risks involved in starting a business from scratch.

Note that the capital start-up costs for a personal chef business are rather modest. Most of the personal chefs interviewed for this book agreed that taking out a loan to start your business may put you at a disadvantage. Some chefs work as employees as they start their independent business, thus earning income and avoiding debt. Others have the support of family members to offset the modest cost. Chapter 6 details financing the start-up costs associated with your personal chef business.

Issues to Consider as You Prepare Your Business Plan

As you collect information for your business plan, possibly the most important part is information about yourself. This **strength/weakness assessment**, if done honestly, allows you to focus on the advantages you bring to your business while identifying areas in which you need improvement.

Things I know I do well	Things I could improve on
Things my friends think I can improve on	Things my friends think I do well

Exhibit 4.2
Strength/Weakness Assessment

Try this window approach to help you to identify both your strengths and areas where you need improvement.

Draw this box on a larger piece of paper and fill in the upper box. Fold the paper in half so the upper half is not showing and then have friends and family fill out the lower half.

If done honestly and openly, this can become a powerful tool in identifying and leveraging your strengths. By knowing your weaknesses, you will be able to formulate a plan to improve yourself in those areas. Remember, be honest and deal only with traits that may affect the success of your business.

Some people have trouble completing this simple exercise; some don't like self-criticism, while others are unrealistic about their strengths. This approach to self-assessment may help identify those strengths and weaknesses. The following questions and suggestions will help focus your ideas as you start to write your business plan. Use these answers along with input from others to help write this vital framework for your business's success.

Preparing the Idea

1. Define the idea for your business on paper in no more than 25 words.
   a. Who will want my service?
   b. Where am I going to find these clients?
   c. What shall I name my business?

Personal Inventory

2. Write a short self-description.

   a. What skills do you bring to your business? What are your competitive advantages based on your skill set?

   b. Are you committed to making the business a success?

   c. What weaknesses do you have that need improvement?

   d. Do you really want to be your own boss?

      i. What will you like about being your own boss?

      ii. What will you dislike about being your own boss?

   e. Do you need the help of others?

   f. What motivates you in forming this business?

   g. How much time are you willing to spend on the business?

   h. Do you enjoy selling?

   i. Are you comfortable with closing the deal?

Your Service

3. Why are your services better than those of other personal chefs?

   a. What are the specific services you are offering?

   b. Who are your customers?

   c. What are you going to charge for your services?

   d. What technical skills do you have that can be leveraged as an advantage?

Finances

4. Remember: A business is not a hobby.

   a. Do you have the start-up money you need?

      i. Does your family have another income to live on while you start your business?

      ii. What changes in your or your family's lifestyle will you have to make when you first start your business?

      iii. Can you work another job while starting your new business?

   b. What is the realistic amount of financing you need to start your business, if any?

   c. Where can you borrow money, if needed?

   d. What is your daily **overhead cost** or the cost associated with fixed expenses such as rent, debt service, and administration?

   e. What insurance does the business need?

   f. What accounting procedures do you plan to follow? Are you disciplined enough to follow them?

   g. What sort of profit do you plan on making?

The Operation

5. The day-to-day life of the business

   a. Can you run your business from your home?

   b. What type of transportation do you need?

    c. What type of equipment will you need?

        i. Food-related equipment, such as coolers space or storage space

        ii. Business-related equipment, such as a fax machine, business phone lines, a copy machine, and a personal computer

    d. From what governmental sources must you obtain licenses?

    e. Are there professional associations or networking groups you can join?

Sales

6. Selling the service

    a. How will you develop collateral material? That is, will you do it yourself or use a graphic professional?

    b. Where will you advertise the business?

    c. How will you handle customer relationships?

    d. What sort of publicity events will the business do?

    e. What sort of charity events will the business do?

Controlling the Business

7. Procedures and paperwork

    a. Will you need an accountant?

    b. Will you use a computer to help with the paperwork and accounting?

    c. How will you choose your banker?

    d. What system will your business use to track sales, expenses, profits, and losses?

    e. How will you manage your time?

These are important questions to consider thoughtfully as you plan your business. Some can be answered with a simple yes or no, while others require detailed responses. Use your answers to these questions as the foundation of your business plan.

Conclusion

The business plan defines your business in a clear and precise way. It tells the reader who you are and what products and services you provide. It clearly identifies the strengths and weaknesses of the business. It need not be long, but it should clearly describe your personal chef business and its professional goals. There are two types of business plan: the management plan, which is used to control and manage the business, and the financial plan, which delineates clear objectives for the financial health of the business. For the purposes of the personal chef business, these plans can be combined into one document.

Start by putting words on paper to describe what you want to accomplish with your business—what you want your business to do. Then, evaluate what you wrote and reduce the wording, but keep the key elements. A good business plan takes time and research to write. A well-written plan is the foundation of the business.

You can learn more about writing and researching a business plan by studying *Business Plans Kit for Dummies,* 2nd Edition, Steven D. Peterson, Peter E. Jaret, and Barbara Findlay Schenck (John Wiley and Sons, 2005).

Key Terms

Business Plan

A document that defines the scope of your business and identifies your goals and objectives.

Investor

A person or financial institution that commits capital for either interest cost or financial gains.

Small Business Administration (SBA)

A federal agency that provides support to small businesses.

Chamber of Commerce

An association of businesspersons that promotes the business interest in a community.

Competitive Advantage

Strengths that give a business advantage over similar businesses.

Mission Statement

A clear statement of your business that defines its measurable objectives.

Vision Statement

A short, clear statement that defines the values of a business.

Management Business Plan

A clear statement that describes an organization's services and products.

Financial Business Plan

A clear statement of realistic financial projections for a business.

Strength/Weakness Assessment

A self-assessment which helps you to focus on the advantages you bring to your business while identifying areas in which you need improvement.

Profit

Monies left within a business after all operating expenses are met.

Capital

Money or other assets that a company or a individual owns that can be converted to money.

Overhead Cost

Cost associated with fixed expenses such as rent, debt service, and administration.

Review Questions

True/False

1. A good business plan helps address unforeseen problems.
2. A good business plan points out the business's strengths and weaknesses.
3. A good business plan can be written in little time with little research.
4. A business plan, once written, should never be changed.
5. Being familiar with your sales area gives you an advantage when writing your business plan.
6. Weaknesses need not be addressed in a business plan.
7. A business plan should include a mission statement, a vision statement, and a vision outcome.
8. The financial business plan is based on financial projections and budgets.
9. Being able to cook delicious, healthy foods might be considered a competitive advantage.
10. The management business plan states your hours of operation.

Multiple Choice

1. A business plan should include all but the following:
   a. A mission statement.
   b. A short self-description.
   c. Your family history.
   d. A vision statement.

2. A business plan should be:
   a. Rewritten or adjusted as needed.
   b. Once finalized, never changed.
   c. Rewritten only if the business is changing direction.
   d. Both a and c.

3. The type of business plan presented for a loan is a:
   a. Management business plan.
   b. Profit projection business plan.
   c. Financial business plan.
   d. Mission and vision statement.

4. In writing a business plan, it is important to:
   a. Be honest with yourself when evaluating your skills, abilities, and weaknesses.
   b. Define your business goals.
   c. Do meaningful research.
   d. All of the above.

5. A competitive advantage:
   a. Is what you do well and enjoy doing.
   b. Is what you do well and do not enjoy doing.
   c. Involves your ability to raise large sums of money for your business.
   d. Is what you do well and enjoy doing that might be an advantage over the competition.

6. A business plan contains:
   a. Mission statement, vision statement, and personal statements.
   b. Vision statements, mission statements, organizational outline, and financial information.
   c. Organizational outline, marketing plan, and personal statements.
   d. Personal statements, visions statements, and financial information.

7. A personal inventory includes:
   a. How much cookware you own.
   b. An evaluation of your skills and weaknesses.
   c. Your commitment to making the business a success.
   d. Both b and c.

8. In defining your product and service, you need to:
   a. Define who your customers are.
   b. Define how you cook all your food items.
   c. Define your staffing.
   d. None of the above.

9. Overhead is:
   a. A fixed cost, such as rent.
   b. A cost that changes as sales change.
   c. Another word for profit.
   d. A cost that is paid one time.

10. The Small Business Administration and your community's chamber of commerce are:
    a. Government agencies that provide advertisements for local business.
    b. Federal tax collection agencies.
    c. State-run promoters of business.
    d. Organizations that support business development.

Discussion Questions & Activities

1. The business plans of many organizations can be found online. Pick a well-known company and research its business plan. Most publicly traded corporations post copies of their business plan online.

2. Compare the business plan of a charity organization to that of a for-profit organization.

3. Form groups with two or three other students. Each group is starting a personal chef business. List the competitive advantages within each group by focusing on the talents and strengths of each group member.

4. Invite a small business owner to class to discuss his or her original business plan and how the plan has changed over time.

5. Answer the framework questions. Compare your answers with those of your fellow students and instructors. Ask for honest feedback. Does the feedback support your answers? Why or why not?

From the Field

Meredith Erickson, Personal Chef, *Whisk for Hire*

Formulating Your Personal Chef Business

Meredith Erickson has a degree in marketing and considerable experience in the retail food industry. She began her career as a manager for a retail kitchen store, and eventually moved into educational planning for the grocery business. Always around food, she enjoyed cooking and serving good food to friends and family. However, after being in the retail food business for several years, she found the demanding schedule, which required her to work long hours, weekends, and holidays, was no longer appealing. She investigated many options when she decided to make a career change and chose to start a personal chef business in 1999 in the suburb of Washington, D.C., where she was a long-time resident.

She found the personal chef business appealing because she would be her own boss, and the challenge of running her own business excited her. She would also enjoy a more flexible work schedule than her current arrangement, and she would be around food again—something she missed as she continued to move up the corporate ladder of retail food business.

As she began to plan her new business, she projected budgets based on scenarios by asking, "Can I afford to make this business work? What impact will this new business have on my family and lifestyle?" She did some number-crunching and calculated three budgets:

1. Bare-bones budget based on the absolute minimum of sales and profits.

2. A more optimistic budget that assumed meeting business tax liabilities, saving money for vacations, and earning enough profits for the business to grow.

3. The golden budget, which exceeded all financial expectations.

To analyze the feasibility of each of these budgets, she calculated the number of clients she expected to contract and multiplied that total by the cooking dates. Once she determined which of the budgets was most realistic, she used it to formulate her business structure and calculate the price she needed to charge each client for her services in order to meet or exceed her financial goals.

Because she knew the area well, she did not need to include as much demographic information as most formal business plans require. Also, little relevant statistical information was available at the time. She analyzed the demographics of her geographic area and targeted potential customers by identifying people who were clearly pressed for time and who were comfortable assigning tasks to strangers such as nannies, dog walkers, and groundskeepers. It became abundantly clear that this group of potential clients was accustomed to paying others in order to get personal time back. Later, as she began to enjoy the success of her business, she realized that a lack of personal time was characteristic of all her customers.

Meredith was able to use her writing skills to create a competitive advantage over the competition. She concentrated on writing her menu in a way that made her entrées and services sound fun. "When I walk down a street in a strange town and I decide where to eat, I am going to go where the menu sounds like it is fun." Some formally trained chefs write menus with only the simplest of descriptions, but the vivid descriptions on Meredith's menu left customers with little doubt that they would enjoy eating her creations.

Aside from her creative menu, she realized she needed to develop a marketing plan in which synergy played an important role. "Don't put all of your hopes into one thing. [Success] is a combination of everything working together. You never know what is going to work for you and when. Brochures, business cards, websites all work together to create the synergy needed in a marketing plan."

Meredith developed an elevator speech to help market her business to the public. She sparked curiosity by working the phrase "since I started my own business" into every conversation. She found people were intrigued and asked for more information about her business, which gave her the opportunity to describe her personal chef service and how it benefited her clients.

Her business plan was nontraditional, but she was able to parlay her financial and writing skills into a competitive advantage, which helped her to create a successful business. I asked Meredith if she had any advice for an individual starting a personal chef business. In response, she provided the following to-do list:

1. Do not neglect the business part.
2. Set up your books.
3. Learn basic bookkeeping.
4. Know how to track costs.
5. Be honest with yourself.
6. Know what your goals are.
7. The business plan is a living document; revisit yours at least twice a year.

Although this list has nothing to do with the cooking or customer service aspects of a personal chef business, completing these tasks will ensure the greatest chance of success for those starting out in this industry.

Discussion Questions

1. Chef Erickson did considerable self-reflection before starting her personal chef business. Make a list of personal commitments you would have to make or change to make a personal chef business work.

2. Chef Erickson formed three budgets as she was planning her business. Do the same by writing a just-making-it budget, a moderate budget, and a golden budget. Aside from the profit, what makes each budget different? Describe how each budget could be realized by a personal chef business. For this exercise, do not dwell on the numbers; consider instead the act of doing to get things done.

3. Without much valid statistical information available in a database, what other factors would you consider when defining who your customers might be?

4. Describe your competitive advantages and how you can apply them in your business.

THE BIG THREE

chapter 5

If you don't know where you're going, any road will get you there.
—Lewis Carroll (1832-1898), author

Introduction

A well-written business plan defines the organization and its set of goals. The plan is guided by the vision statement and the mission statement. Both of these are short, to-the-point sentences that define your business. This chapter addresses the sometimes difficult job of writing these essential sentences. It also discusses your elevator speech—another tool that, if properly used, helps ensure your success.

Learning Outcomes

After reading this chapter, you will be able to

✎ Define a vision statement and mission statement.

✎ Identify your own values for your vision statement.

✎ Differentiate between a vision statement and a product statement.

✎ Relate a vision statement to a mission statement.

✎ Compare the effectiveness of the vision and mission statements of different organizations.

✎ Write an effective vision statement.

✎ Write an effective mission statement.

✎ Judge the effectiveness of a elevator speech.

✎ Identify types (purposes) of the elevator speech.

✎ Write an effective elevator speech.

Key Terms

Business Plan	Vision Statement	Mission Statement
Product Statement	Values	Executive Summary
Elevator Speech	Universal Statement	

Vision Statements

A vision statement guides you in your work. It provides direction, gives meaning to your activities, and helps you determine how to allocate your resources to achieve the goals or mission of your business.

Your vision statement provides a set of fundamental reasons for your company's existence—you haven't created your business just to make money. As with your company's values or the principles, standards and qualities that are core to the business, the key to a compelling vision statement is authenticity, not uniqueness. When properly conceived, vision is broad, fundamental, and enduring. If Walt Disney's vision statement had said, "We exist to make cartoons for kids," the company, most likely, would not exist today. "We exist to make cartoons for kids" is based on the business formula of "We exist to make *x* products for *y* customers." This is not a global statement, fundamental and enduring. It is a **product statement** that clearly defines the advantages of a particular product, not a vision statement.

Indeed, a visionary company continually pursues but never fully achieves its vision. For instance, Disney captured the enduring quality of a vision when he said, "Disneyland will never be completed as long as there is imagination in the world." His company will never outgrow its core value of "bringing happiness to millions."

The vision for your business emerges from your **values**. Values and vision keep the individual, community, and company on track. The time taken to identify your values and develop a vision statement for your business will pay off by decreasing the time you spend trying to decide policy, make decisions, and resolve disputes.

A vision statement should be short, not more than two or three sentences. You want it to state what your business does and what you are striving to achieve. This statement is not only for today but for tomorrow as well—it should be forward thinking. As you develop your vision statement, consider these questions:

1. What service or products do you produce or are planning to provide?
2. Who is your market? What is its demographic profile? Do you have more than one market?
3. What characteristics, values, and qualities do you want to be known for providing?
4. What are your broad financial goals?
5. What do your see your business looking like in five years?
6. What is it going to take to get there?

Begin writing your vision statement by writing what comes to mind as you respond to each of these questions. You may want to do a first draft, sleep on it, and then review it and rewrite it as needed. You may need to write numerous drafts to find that perfect combination of words, but it will come to you. Remember, vision statements are constantly evolving as you and your business evolve. A vision statement is not meant to be set in stone!

Mission Statements

With a good vision statement written, the mission statement becomes more self-evident, but it still requires honest self-reflection and thought. A **mission statement** consists of a set of values your business upholds to achieve its goals and objectives during its day-to-day activities.

Your Mission Statement

A mission statement contains a set of values.

This particular statement says a lot about your business. You should think of it as an **executive summary** that articulates your business's story and ideals. There are many thoughts on what a good mission statement should include, but most experts agree on these points:

- A mission statement clearly defines your business:
  - Who you serve
  - Your purpose
  - How you will achieve your purpose.
- A mission statement is no longer than a few sentences.
- The objective(s) set out in a mission statement should be measurable.

Your mission statement should reflect your personality and that of your company. Larry Kahaner, author of *Say It and Live It: The 50 Corporate Mission Statements That Hit the Mark* (Doubleday, 1995), states, "People tend to pooh-pooh mission statements as something that makes us feel good. But they can be true management tools if they're used all the time."

Mission statements are not static documents; they are evolving and should be reviewed and changed as needed as changes occur within your business. As your business grows and expands, it may outgrow the mission statement you initially articulated. It is a good practice to plan a yearly review of your mission statement to ensure it is still consistent with your business model. You might be surprised at how much your business has changed!

The ideal mission and vision statements should say everything about your business in a simple way. Consider this statement: "We are ladies and gentlemen serving ladies and gentlemen." This motto of the Ritz Carlton Hotel Company says in eleven simple words what the organization considers to be its core values and goals.

The goal of the Traveling Culinary Artist is to provide services that will support and benefit individuals and families by creating tasty mealtime solutions for today's busy households with all the savory flavors of home. Furthermore, these services are aimed at reducing time-related stress while promoting delectable healthy eating habits.

—Mission statement for the *Traveling Culinary Artist*, Chef Jim Huff

Using Your Vision and Mission Statements

Both of these statements give your organization rules by which to operate by highlighting what is important to you and your business. Sharing these statements with clients and prospective customers lets them know you are a directed and striving business. When your clients are informed about you and your business, they are better equipped to spread the word by providing referrals.

Be ready to live your vision within your business and the business model you create. Creating, articulating, and writing these statements often leads to increased growth and movement. Remember, they tell others what you sell, who you are, and what you value.

The Elevator Speech

An **elevator speech** is a short oral introduction to who you are and what you do. It is an ad about your product and services you share with people you meet, when you are networking, and whenever the opportunity arises.

It's called an elevator speech because you want to be able to share it in the space of the time you'd spend talking to someone while riding in an elevator—between 20 and 45 seconds. The key to an effective elevator speech is sharing enough information so people can understand what you offer or what you do and at the same time making them curious enough to ask you for more information.

To be effective, an elevator speech should be:

- Benefit driven
    - The most important thing people want to know about your product and services is "What's in it for me?" Benefits are the things that will appeal to people about your product or service, whether they are prospective purchasers or networking connections. Make sure your elevator speech outlines the way your product and services ease your customers' pain or needs, or gives them pleasure.

- Customer-centric
    - Your elevator speech must speak to the people who will be buying your product or services.

- Concise
    - Keep it simple and to the point. Potential customers must understand right off the bat what you do, and they must be able to explain it to others. Keep it in laymen's terms.

- Interesting
    - Include what is most compelling about your product or service. Don't be afraid to use colorful, emotional language. Research shows that people buy with their emotions and then use logic to justify their buying decision afterwards. For example:
        - Dine out—in your own home.
        - Personal chefs bring families back to the table.
        - I perform culinary miracles in your own kitchen.

- Conversational
  - Be natural with your speech. Write it out so it sounds like you are speaking with friends or colleagues. Deliver it so your warmth and genuine enthusiasm shine through. A person who truly enjoys what he does is irresistible, and customers will want to share in the enthusiasm.
- Smooth
  - Practice, practice, practice so you can say it naturally without hesitating or fumbling over your words. Practice in front of a mirror, or make a video of your practicing. Practice in front of your loved ones and friends so delivering the speech is second nature when anyone asks what you do.
- Focused but flexible
  - You'll need several versions of your speech for different networking opportunities. These versions should vary in length depending on how much time you have to deliver them. They should include specific information to address the specific needs of the different groups you interact with. For example:
    - Your elevator speech to a group of hungry, time-pressed lawyers may contain a little different information than the version you use for a group of individuals with specific medical challenges.
- Positive
  - Always put your product or service in an optimistic, positive light. Don't be vague or wobbly or uncertain about what you do and the value it brings your clients.
- Believable
  - Be genuine and humble about what you do. Try not to abuse the truth or oversing your own praises. Most people find genuineness and humility attractive and enticing.

ELEVATOR SPEECH WORKSHEET

Your elevator speech must be benefit driven, not feature driven. Answer the following questions to start formulating your elevator speech.

1. What does your product do for people?
2. What need does it fill?
3. What benefit does it provide?
4. What problem does it solve?
5. What makes your product or service unique and attractive?
6. What makes it stand out from your competitors?

Remember to think in terms of what your customers say or what you like them to say about your product—special service, price, location, selection, service, quality, testimonials, etc.

A SAMPLE ELEVATOR SPEECH

This sample of an elevator speech tells potential clients what Jane Does does and how her services can benefit them in less than 30 seconds.

"My name is Jane Doe, and I am a professional personal chef. That means I develop customized meal programs for my hungry, time-pressed clients and provide delicious meals for them prepared from all fresh ingredients in the safety of their own kitchens. I even package and store their meals with specific handling instructions so they can be enjoyed at their convenience. When my clients come home from a long day, they don't have to worry about what's for dinner anymore! They can enjoy delicious, healthy meals in the comfort of their own home."

Your elevator speech, or **universal statement**, is often the first impression you make on potential customers, and because you get to make a first impression only once, you should spend some time developing an elevator speech that memorably represents who you are and what you do. It's an enormously important part of your success.

Chef Meredith Erickson invites people to hear her elevator speech by incorporating in a conversation the words "since I started my own business." This, of course, sparks curiosity from the listener, who opens the door for Chef Erickson to deliver her speech. Chef Jim Huff has mentally filed different speeches to fit different situations; these rehearsed speeches allow him to respond to questions with concise information about his business. Chef Shari Aupke's elevator speech is very direct, leaving the listener with no doubt about the services her business provides.

Whatever form your elevator speech takes, a well-rehearsed, smooth speech can be a valuable tool in creating new business.

Conclusion

"If you don't know where you're going, any road will get you there." This statement defines the importance of the vision and mission statements. Both statements define your business, how it operates, what it values, and how the business will honor those values. Vision or mission statements are not statements on making money, but rather statements that help create the conditions in which your business will succeed.

The elevator speech is your brief, conversational business advertisement, presented to friends, colleagues, and potential clients. The speech promotes you and your business. An effective elevator speech opens the door for the recruitment of new clients.

Key Terms

Business Plan
A set of goals and responsibilities that precisely defines your business.

Vision Statement
A clear statement that provides a set of fundamental reasons for your company's existence.

Mission Statement
A clear statement of your business that defines measurable objectives the business strives to achieve.

Product Statement
A statement that clearly defines the advantages of a particular product.

Values
Principles, standards, and qualities that are core to the business.

Executive Summary
A short, focused presentation or paper that deals with the main points of a business. It should articulate your business' story and ideals.

Elevator Speech
A short oral introduction to your business that is presented as an impromptu speech.

Universal statement
See Elevator Speech.

Review Questions

True/False

1. A business plan should include a vision statement and mission statement.

2. The vision statement is a list of financial goals for a business.

3. A vision statement is broad in nature.

4. A product statement is a wide-ranging statement on the goals of a business.

5. Values are the worth of a service or product.

6. Mission statements are general statements that define the financial purpose of a business.

7. An executive summary is a short focus paper or presentation that articulates your business story.

8. Mission statements, once finished, should never be changed.

9. A elevator speech is a short speech you can use about your business as opportunities arise.

10. A good elevator speech is broad in nature.

Multiple Choice

1. A good vision statement is:

   a. A projection of financial goals of your business.
   b. A standalone statement that tells people who you are and what you do.
   c. Part of a business plan.
   d. Both b and c.

2. A product statement is:

   a. The same as a vision statement.
   b. The same as a value statement.
   c. The same as a mission statement.
   d. The same as an elevator speech.

3. Values for your business should be:

   a. Reflected in your mission and vision statement.
   b. Reflected only in your mission statement.
   c. Not posted, for they have little worth.
   d. Ambiguous in nature.

4. A mission statement is a:

   a. Set of statements that tells others about your daily activities.
   b. Set of statements that tells others about your goals and objectives.
   c. Set of statements that tells your employees what type of work to do.
   d. Set of statements that is filed with your tax returns.

5. A good mission statement includes:

   a. Who you serve and why.
   b. The hours of your business.
   c. How much money you plan on making.
   d. The reasons the client will save money when using your service.

6. A mission statement should list:

   a. Financial goals that are measurable.
   b. Objectives that are measurable.
   c. Hours of operation.
   d. Specific details on how the business operates.

7. Once written, a mission statement should be considered a:

   a. Living document.

   b. Nice idea, but not one that applies to the daily business.

   c. Document that will not change; the business must change to meet the mission statement.

   d. Document to be filed with the business tax returns.

8. Your vision and mission statements are:

   a. Rules your business operates under.

   b. Values your business has.

   c. Shared with others.

   d. All of the above.

9. A elevator speech is:

   a. A long talk about your business, presented in front of a group of people.

   b. A short, planned speech that tells people about your business.

   c. A made up as the situation requires.

   d. An extension of your business plan.

10. A good elevator speech is:

   a. Customer-centric, concise, and interesting.

   b. A method to tell customers your prices.

   c. A speech in which you use charts and other media.

   d. Not an effective way to advertise your business.

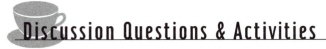

Discussion Questions & Activities

1. Using the Internet, research the vision statement and mission statements of an organization, nonprofit or for-profit. Many times the vision statement and mission statements are posted on a company's main website or within the stockholders report. Report to class on the statements and discuss how the company is meeting its goals—or failing to do so.

2. Create a fictitious organization and write a vision statement for it. Share the statement with your fellow students. Have your classmates report what type of organization you have created.

3. Write a vision statement for your personal chef business. Share this statement with others and note their feedback.

4. Using your vision statement from question # 3, write a mission statement. Again, share this statement with others for feedback.

5. Write an elevator speech. Practice presenting it. Present it to your class and ask for constructive feedback. Rework the speech and repeat the process.

6. Discuss the different types of elevator speeches you may need. Examples: one for a family of five who like basic comfort foods, and one for a couple who like to explore unfamiliar cuisines.

From the Field

Mission Statements

Jim Huff, Personal Chef, *Traveling Culinary Artist*

"The goal of the Traveling Culinary Artist is to provide services that will support and benefit individuals and families by creating tasty mealtime solutions for today's busy households with all the savory flavors of home. Furthermore, these services are aimed at reducing time-related stress while promoting delectable healthy eating habits." This is the mission statement of Jim Huff's personal chef business, Traveling Culinary Artist.

Jim's personal chef business opened two years ago, after he decided to leave a successful career in the retail toy business. Having learned to cook at the ripe old age of thirteen, when his mother rejoined the workforce, he found a passion in food. Later in life, he honed his cooking skills by serving seven-course meals for New Year's Eve dinner parties that he cooked with his wife and best friend. These dinner parties led the three of them to open a small catering business that specialized in dinner parties and backyard weddings. As time progressed, the catering business closed, and Jim started a career with a large national toy retailer. Fifteen years later, after leaving the retail toy business, he rediscovered the passion he had cooking healthy and tasty meals for others.

After reading an article about personal chefs in a local newspaper, he reflected on what his friends had said during his catering career. "Just make extra and put it in my freezer so when I get home I can heat it up." Now there was a business that would allow him to do exactly that—a business that would allow him to follow his passion for cooking and feeding people, and of course eating!

Jim's first clients were on special diets, which made him a bit anxious. These special diets required research and careful planning to ensure he was meeting their needs. With the help of members of the American Personal & Private Chef Association (ACPPA), he started creating meals that were not only satisfying but also met all the dietary guidelines his clients required.

Jim states on his website that he meets the needs of clients with special diets by researching recipes, shopping, preparing, and storing healthy, tasty cuisine. This turns out, for his clients, to be an incentive to follow the prescribed diet. This is true for seniors, heart patients, diabetics, and anyone else with diet restrictions. Having a personal chef can be a strong motivation for staying on the diet.

Jim measures his success by asking his clients for feedback. He includes a menu-specific feedback form with each item he prepares. His goal is to make food the client enjoys and not necessarily what he himiself enjoys cooking. His clients tell him they feel that he is looking out for their interest. Jim states, "If it was all about me and my food, I would have a five-star restaurant in Manhattan."

For Jim Huff and his personal chef business, Traveling Culinary Artist, it's all about his clients and preparing the healthy food they love.

Discussion Questions

1. Considering the information presented in the chapter, do you think Chef Huff's mission statement is an effective mission statement? If so, why? If not, how would you change the mission statement to be more effective?

2. Does the mission statement give the reader an idea of the values on which Chef Huff's business is based? If so, please describe those values. If not, what values are missing?

3. Does the feedback from Chef Huff's customers support the mission statement? If so, why? If not, what is missing?

chapter 6

FINANCES

Lack of money is no obstacle. Lack of an idea is an obstacle.
—Ken Hakuta, author and entrepreneur

Introduction

How do you know if you really are in business? If your bottom line is in the black, or your income exceeds your expenses, you are making a profit! The personal chef business can be profitable *only* if you control your expenses. As a small business owner, you are responsible for generating your income. Remember, no one is going to pay you for your vacation or sick time as they would if you were employed by a company.

Learning Outcomes

After reading this chapter, you will be able to:

✎ Determine start-up costs for launching a new business.

✎ Define fixed costs and identify those associated with the personal chef business.

✎ Define variable costs and identify those associated with the personal chef business.

✎ Assess lenders' qualifications.

✎ Describe the key elements of a loan proposal.

✎ Identify the significance of your credit rating.

✎ Evaluate loan requirements.

✎ Explain the importance of cash management when running your own business.

Cash flow
Cash
Cash flow projections
Sales/Revenue

✎ Assess a breakeven analysis.

✎ Define profit for a business.

✎ Identify the as-purchased (AP) price of a food item.

✎ List the factors to consider when determining the edible portion (EP) cost of a food item.

✎ Determine how the yield percentage of a food item is calculated.

Key Terms

Start-up Cost	Short-term Loan	Cash Flow Projections
Fixed Cost	Variable-rate Loan	Working Capital
Capital	FICO	Inventory
Default	Outflows	Gross Receipts
Fixed-rate Loan	Negative Cash Flow	Edible Portion Cost
Credit Report	Operating Cash Flow	Elasticity of Demand
Cash	Breakeven Analysis	Estimated Taxes
Positive Cash Flow	Session	Loan Proposal
Capital Strategy	Yield	Gross Profit Percentage
Income	As Purchased (AP)	Gross Income
Sales Revenue	Food Cost	Quarterly Tax Payments
Breakeven Point	Assets	Portion Control (PC)
Net Profit	Profit	Average Gross Profit Per Sale
EP	Debt Loan	Average Gross Profit Percentage
Sales Mix	Long-term Loan	Cash Management
Deductions	Hybrid Loan	
Expenses	Cash Flow	
Variable Costs	Inflows	
Equity		

Estimating Your Start-up Cost

In order to start your personal chef business without adding emotional or financial stress to your life, it is necessary for you to have a sound estimate of what starting up will take. This estimate must be as realistic as possible so you can calculate the financial support you need to get your business up and running. Many first-time entrepreneurs underestimate their **start-up cost**. Other common mistakes include not accounting for the **expenses** associated with items such as uniforms and web hosting services. If you are the sole income earner in your household, make certain you have sufficient funds to cover your family expenses for at least three to six months before you launch your new personal chef business.

It would be foolish for you not to take advantage of the resources already available to you when estimating your start-up cost. If you have office or culinary equipment at your disposal, use what you have rather than investing in new equipment. Invest in additional or new equipment or other assets when you are generating an income from your business.

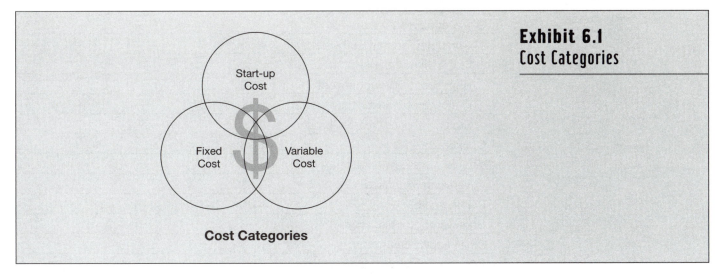

Cost Categories

Exhibit 6.1
Cost Categories

There are several categories of cost. Costs associated with your business consist of fixed costs, one-time start-up costs, and variable costs. **Fixed costs** are those expenses you pay on a regular basis, such as rent or transportation. These costs tend to stay the same month after month and do not change as business volume increases or decreases. **Variable costs** are those expenses directly related to a sale. Food is a good example of variable cost; the food you buy depends on the menu you plan for each client. One-time start-up costs are those expenses you incur once only, during the development phase of a new business, for the lifetime of the company. Some examples are the security deposit on the lease of a building or a set up fee to open a business checking account.

The best estimates for each of these costs come from doing your homework and educating yourself about your options. To estimate insurance costs, for example, contact two or three insurance agents. Professional trade associations, such as the American Personal & Private Chef Association (APPCA), can also help you estimate start-up costs. Other possible resources include the local Small Business Administration (SBA) office, a small business development center, and friends and family who currently operate small businesses.

The following chart is designed to assist you in identifying the costs you must be prepared to cover when starting your personal chef business. These items are traditionally considered start-up costs. However, you may incur other costs not identified here or for which you have not yet determined accurate estimated cost.

DBA publications	$
Business license	$
Bank fees for setting up accounts	$
Safe food handler's certification	$
General liability insurance	$
Professional service (start-up)	
Legal	$
Accounting	$
Graphic design	$
Telephone/Voice mail	$
Cell phone	$

Office equipment	
Computer, printer, software	$
Fax, scanner, copier	$
High-speed internet access	$
File cabinets, desk, chair, lights	$
Stock stationery, cards, brochures	$
Cookbooks	$
Vehicle	$
Advertising expenses	$
Printing cost	$
Cookware, utensils, knives	$
Small appliances	$
Carrying containers, thermal bags	$
Dry pantry stock	$
Storage containers	$
Uniforms, shoes	$
Linens	$
Cash reserves	$
Other	$
Other	$
Total	**$**

> **Finance is the art of passing money from hand to hand until it finally disappears.**
>
> —Robert W. Sarnoff (1918-1997), president of NBC, 1956, and RCA, 1965

Once you've made an educated projection of your start-up costs, determine the source for the money needed. If you have personal savings you can use to cover this cost, you may wish to use those funds, but there may be a better way. Compare the money your savings is earning in the bank or as an investment to the cost of borrowing the same amount of money from a financing agency. For example, if your money invested in stocks shows an 8 percent return and you can borrow the same amount for 7 percent, you might be better off borrowing the funds while maintaining your stock investments. It is critical to discuss financing options with a financial consultant before making a decision. A key reason many small businesses fail is they are not adequately financed at start-up. Remember, you will not be making a profit for a while when starting your business, so you must be prepared to cover these expenses some other way.

Finding Capital

Before shopping for capital, you must be prepared to answer the following questions;

- How much do you need to borrow?
  - Add start-up costs plus other anticipated expenses.
- How urgently do you need these funds?
  - You might be able to find better terms if you are not under pressure to find a loan quickly.

- What is the risk to the lender?
  - Lenders look differently at loans backed by equity, the value of items owned by a business, and loans considered debt loans. You may have **equity** in a house that you can borrow against at a much better rate than a **debt loan** which is repaid over a specified period of time. The lender does not gain an ownership interest in the business and the debt obligations are typically llimited to repaying the loan with interest. Loans of this type are often secured by some type of asset. Remember, when using equity for a loan, you are placing that equity in jeopardy should you be unable to meet the terms and default on the loan.

- What terms and interest rates are available?
  - Interest rates change based on the time frame of the loan. A short-term loan has a different rate than a long-term loan. A **short-term loan** requires a financial obligation of less than one year, while a **long-term loan** requires a financial obligation lasting more than one year. It might also be to your advantage to compare a **fixed-rate loan**, one with a fixed interest rate for the life of the loan, to a **variable-rate loan** where the interest rate can rise or fall over the life of the loan, to a **hybrid loan** which combines elements of both a fixed-rate and variable-rate loans.

Once you have answered these questions, you are ready to apply for a loan.

When you apply for a loan, you must prepare a **loan proposal**. This proposal is linked directly to your business plan. Within the loan proposal you should explain who you are, the business opportunity, and your background. Of course, when explaining your background, you should highlight your unique qualifications and why they make you right for this particular business opportunity. You must also explain how much you need to borrow, your terms, and how you intend to repay the loan. Because the personal chef business is new to the market in many areas, you should not assume the loan committee is familiar with this industry. Use specific details and statistics from the industry that will validate your business proposal. Your business plan should be attached to the loan proposal along with realistic financial projections for at least one year or until you envision the business will show a positive cash flow.

Before requesting a loan from a financial institution, make sure your credit rating is good and accurate. Here are a few simple steps to follow before approaching a bank for your loan:

Get a personal **credit report** which provides a historical account of a person or business' use of credit. The Fair Credit Reporting Act requires each of the nationwide consumer reporting companies (Equifax, Experian, and TransUnion) to provide you with a free copy of your credit report once every twelve months at your request. To order your free report, call 1-877-322-8228, go to www.annualcreditreport.com, or mail a completed Annual Credit Report Request Form to Annual Credit Report Request Service, P.O. Box 105281, Atlanta, GA 20348-5281. The request form is available only at www.ftc.gov/credit. Allow fifteen business days following your request to receive your report.

If you are in a hurry to receive your credit information, many online services will provide you with your credit report and **Fair Isaac & Company (FICO)** score within minutes—for a fee. Some sites offer "free credit reports," but a careful reading of the site requirements often shows that while the report itself is free, you must sign up for a fee-based service you may not want. Be careful when applying for something you can get free from the nationwide consumer reporting agencies.

Should you find a questionable item, write the reporting agency explaining why you are disputing an item. Make sure you include all relevant information. Credit reporting companies must investigate items in question within thirty days, unless they consider the dispute frivolous. When the investigation is finished, the company must provide you with the written result and a free copy of your report if the dispute results in a change to your overall credit report. The reporting company will also forward their findings to other credit reporting agencies to ensure your credit rating is accurate going forward based on the necessary change. For more information on credit reports, visit the Federal Trade Commission website at www.ftc.gov/bcp/conline/pubs/credit/freereports.htm.

Lenders consider other factors as well when you apply for a loan. With this in mind, you should be able to respond to the following questions both in your loan proposal and in person.

- **How do you plan to repay the loan?**   Lenders want to see sources of repayment, such as cash flow from your personal chef business or some form of collateral. Because your business is a start-up, you will not have a cash flow history, but you should have a realistic **cash flow projection** for the first year of the business.

- **How much of your personal money do you plan on investing in the company?**   Lenders want to see that you have your own money invested in your company because a significant personal investment in your own company will encourage you to ensure the success of the business.

- **What is the exact purpose for the loan?**   Using your start-up cost estimates, show the lender exactly how the loan will be allocated to enable your business to operate.

- **What type of person are you?**   When lenders are determining whether or not to approve a business loan for a start-up company, they want to know what type of character you have. Have you owned other successful small businesses? If so, it is important to make sure the lender is aware of them. Your educational background and experience in the business are also important. Being a personal chef and graduating from a culinary program often go hand in hand. A little bragging about your culinary background when you are making your loan proposal can go a long way.

- **Do you have references?**   A lender may require a list of both professional and personal references. Your references should be people who are willing to tell the lender what a wonderful and hardworking businessperson and chef you are.

Cash Management

The number-one reason many small businesses fail is poor control of all income and expenses within their organizations. Understanding basic concepts of this **cash management** will help you plan and deal with the unforeseen difficulties and pressures all businesses experience.

- **Cash** is real money stored in the business's bank accounts. It does not include other assets such as inventory, equipment, or property. Assets such as these can be converted to cash, but they are not considered cash until they become real money.

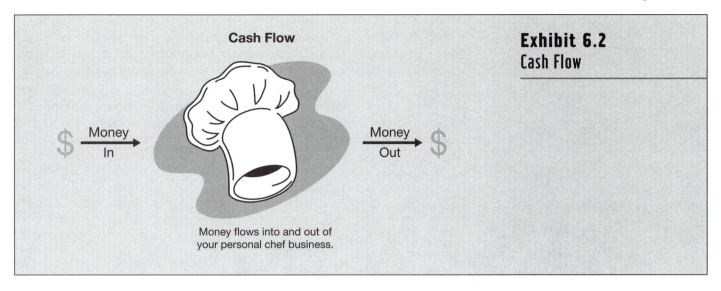

Cash Flow

Money In → 🍳 → Money Out

Money flows into and out of
your personal chef business.

Exhibit 6.2
Cash Flow

- Cash flow is simply money moving in or out of your business. **Outflows** include checks for employees, creditors, or suppliers. **Inflows** include cash you receive from your customers. A **positive cash flow** is a good sign of financial health. This indicates more money is flowing into the company than is flowing out. A **negative cash flow** is the opposite; more money is flowing out of the company than is flowing in. Negative cash flow may indicate financial problems and should be investigated and corrected as soon as possible. *During the start-up phase of the business, it is common to have a negative cash flow, but this must be temporary and planned for.* Eventually, as the business becomes established, it will earn a profit and have a positive cash flow.

- **Cash flow projections** are simply reports that predict your business cash flow for both the short and the long term. They are used to help manage cash and to strategize about ways to grow and expand the business. Short-term projections—those under one year—are used to manage daily cash and to assist in management direction and positive growth. Long-term projections, or those from three to five years, are used for planning capital strategy to meet the future business needs.

- **Operating cash flow**, also can be called **working capital**, is capital that comes from the sales (**income**) of your business minus all operating expenses. As your operating cash flow increases, your business ability to take advantage of growth circumstances increases.

- **Sales revenue** is the total cash you bring into the business over a given period.

- **Average gross profit per sale** is the monies left after you have subtracted the direct cost from the sale.

- **Average gross profit percentage** is your average gross profit converted into a percentage. Simply divide the average gross profit by the average selling price. For example, if your client paid you $200 for services rendered, and your gross profit is $100 for that sale, your gross profit percentage is 50 percent—that is, $100 (average gross profit) divided by $200 (average selling price).

- **Breakeven analysis** is a calculation that helps you determine when your business will be able to cover all expenses and begin to make a profit. First-time business owners often make the mistake of thinking that the first $1,000 in sales

> Money was never a big
> motivation for me,
> except as a way to keep
> score. The real
> excitement is playing
> the game.
>
> **—Donald Trump, founder and CEO of Trump Organization**

will cover $1,000 of the start-up cost. This is simply not the case because you must deduct the cost of **inventory**, or goods and materials in stock used to generate that $1,000 in sales. To calculate your **breakeven point**, or the point at which income from the sale of a product or service equals the invested costs and expenses, resulting in neither profit nor loss, calculate your fixed and variable costs. Fixed costs are those that do not change based on the amount of sales. Fixed costs may include, for example, the lease payment on the vehicle used for the business. They remain constant during a business cycle no matter what the production level is. Variable costs change with sales volume. These costs may include food purchased for a client.

Exhibit 6.3
Formula Used to Calculate Breakeven Point

$$\frac{\text{Fixed Cost}}{\text{Gross Profit Percentage}} = \text{Breakeven Point}$$

To calculate your breakeven dollar amount, divide your estimated total fixed cost by your gross profit percentage. This calculation determines the amount of sales revenue you need in order to break even. For example, if your fixed cost for a month is $1,000 and you have a gross profit percentage of 50 percent, your breakeven amount per month is $2,000, or $1,000 (fixed cost) divided by 0.50 (gross profit percentage). Remember, this number does not include profit or any salary for yourself!

It is important to note that good cash management involves knowing how much money is flowing out of your business compared to how much money is flowing into your business. You must be able to control your cash and to determine when, where, and how your cash needs occur. Being able to financially meet your cash needs helps ensure business success.

Figuring It All Out—Just How Much Money Am I Going to Make Anyway?

Of course, we must not forget that you are running your business to make money. All the sweat, late nights, and hard work should be rewarded, and part of that reward is your ability to make money. Before we look at how to estimate how much you are going to make, let's clarify these simple terms:

- **Sessions**: For a personal chef business, a session involves you going to a client's home and preparing meals. A session may be one where you prepare five different complete meals for a family of five, or it may be one where you prepare three different lunches for a single client.

- **Gross receipts**: The number of sessions per month multiplied by the price for each session. For example, you do 40 sessions per month at a rate of $350 per session. Your gross receipts are $14,000, or 40 sessions × $350 (rate charged per session).

- **Total variable cost**: Variable cost per session multiplied by total monthly sessions. For example, your variable cost per session is $175 and your total monthly sessions is 40 sessions which results in a monthly total variable cost of $7,000, $175 × 40.

- **Total fixed cost per month**: Remember, this cost tends to be the same every month—hence the term *fixed*. We use a monthly fixed cost of $2,000 for the example.

The following example uses amounts from the terms listed above.

- Number of sessions per month = 40

- Income per session = $350

- Total gross receipts = 14,000 (40 × $350)

- Variable + fixed monthly cost = $9,000

- Net profit = $5,000 ($14,000–$9,000)

This net profit of $5,000 is also considered your bottom line or the company's total profit. Your pay, all associated payroll taxes, other taxes, and monies set aside for the business are deducted from this net profit or income. If your net profit is not enough to cover all these expenses, you must employ strategies to increase it.

Calculating Net Profit		
Number of sessions	40 per month	
Income per session	$350	Multiply
Total Gross Receipts	$14,000	
Variable + Fixed Cost	$9,000	Total Expenses
Net Profit	$5,000	

**Exhibit 6.4
Formula Used to Calculate Net Profit**

The first and most logical strategy is to cut costs without cutting quality or service to your clientele. Perhaps you are using USDA Choice meats for most of your cooking. If your client wants beef stew, you can use a lower grade of meat due to the long, slow cooking method used to prepare stew. This represents a simple way to reduce your cost. Other ways may include shopping at a membership warehouse such as Costco or Sam's Club. Although you might be buying in larger quantities, you should be paying less per unit than at a regular food market. As long as you can use all items purchased, you will be saving money.

Parts of many foods purchased are unusable. **Yield** is the difference between what you bought and what you can actually use. Consider a head of lettuce. You purchase a 1-pound head of lettuce. After removing the outer leaves and the core, you have only 12 ounces of the lettuce available for service. The 4 ounces of trim cannot be used. If you are planning to serve 8 salads, 2 ounces each, the pound of lettuce you bought will not be enough.

Yield is also affected by cooking food items that lose moisture and shrink in the process. If you want, prepare eight 4-ounce servings of pot roast, a 2-pound roast will not be enough; shrinkage, depending on cooking method, can be as much as

30 percent. The goal of wise shopping is to put the lowest **edible portion (EP) cost**, which is the cost of a portion of food after trimming or processing, on the plate.

Some foods do not have yields. If you buy 90-count baking potatoes and, after baking, each potato serves one, there is no yield. Many chefs refer to these items as **portion control**, or **PC**. An example of a PC is a New York strip steak. If your clients decide to have a 10-ounce New York strip steak and you buy pre-cut 10-ounce New York strip steaks from your butcher, each steak is a portion for one.

Many factors go into calculating EP cost, but the most critical to the personal chef may be personal skills, storage space, available equipment, and time. Let's look at the price for a 6-ounce portion of fresh salmon. Consider that both portions of fish are of the same quality for this example. At your fishmonger, a whole salmon (gutted, head on) costs $3.50 per pound, with an average size of 8 pounds. This price is the **"as purchased" (AP)** because it is based on the entire product before trimming or processing. Your fishmonger also sells salmon fillets, skin off, pinbones removed, for $6.49 per pound; again, this is the AP price. Which salmon do you buy to get the lowest EP cost to the plate? In this case, the EP price may depend on your skills at filleting an 8-pound salmon in your client's home. If you are good at filleting, you might get 4 pounds EP after breaking down the 8-pound salmon. Your yield for the entire fish is 50 percent. Yield is calculated by dividing the EP by the AP (4 lbs / 8 lbs = 50%). Using this 50 percent yield, you can determine the EP cost of salmon bought whole, which is $7.00 per pound. The EP cost is calculated by dividing the AP cost by the yield ($3.50 / 0.50 = $7.00). In this example, you would save 20 cents per portion if you purchased the salmon fillet from the fishmonger.

Of course, if you are a superstar at filleting salmon and could get a 60 percent yield, or if you could use the salmon body for stock and make salmon croquettes out of some of the body meat, you might be better off buying the whole fish. Remember, you must also take your time into consideration. Do you have space to break down a whole fish and the skills and equipment to do so? If your time or space is limited, you might be better off buying the fillets from your fishmonger rather than the whole fish. Your goal of getting the lowest EP cost to the plate must be weighed against these other factors.

Another way to change your net profit is to raise your prices. Economists use the **elasticity of demand** curve to determine the effects of price increases or decreases. This simply means there is a point where you will lose customers as you raise prices. A price increase of 5 percent may not affect any customer, while an increase of 10 percent may result in the loss of 5 percent of your clients. Prices on food change daily, sometimes hourly, and some clients understand this. Be cautious when raising your prices, be aware of how much your clients will be willing to pay for your service, and stay within that range.

Net profit is also affected when you change your sales mix. The **sales mix** is the combination of the total amount of items you sell, listed by profit. If you offer a New York steak at a profit of 20 percent, try to persuade the customer to choose the higher-priced and higher-quality fillet of beef so you make a 30 percent profit. You can also package your meals with added value. If you sell your New York steak entrée for $10.00 and it is popular, but you sell a single dessert for $3.00 and it has poor sales, try packaging the steak with the dessert and offering the two together for $12.00. Even though your cost percentage is higher when selling the package, so will gross income, which will decrease the variable cost percentage.

Increasing the number of sessions or amount of business done during a month also has a positive effect on your profit. Of course, as an independent businessperson, there is only so much time you can spend working during a given day. If you are already maxed out, consider hiring an employee to help expand your business. If you have time to add more sessions to your month, of course, that would affect your profit in a positive way. In order to determine how extra sessions will affect your profit, determine how much you make per session.

- First, determine your fixed cost per session, which is your monthly fixed cost divided by the number of sessions per month. For example, 40 sessions per month with a fixed cost of $1,000 per month equals $25 per session ($1,000 / 40).

- Now, determine your variable cost per session, which is your monthly variable cost divided by the number of sessions per month. For example, 40 sessions per month with a variable cost of $4,000 per month equals $100 per session ($4,000 / 40).

- Then, determine the profit per session, which is the price per session minus the fixed cost per session combined with the variable cost per session. In this example, you charge $200 per session; that minus $25 (fixed cost) and $100 (variable cost) equals a profit of $75 per session ($200–$25 − $100 = $75).

This simply states that your profit will increase by $75 for every new session you do per month. The profit per session can help you determine how many new sessions you will need in order to reach your financial goals for your personal chef business.

Major Expenses

The two major expenses you incur as a personal chef are food and labor. You are the labor, and the food you provide is your service. Within the foodservice industry, **food cost** is often used as a benchmark against which you can measure other performance indicators. Within the business, food cost is usually indicated as a percentage. The percentage is the total cost of food divided by your income. For example, if you spend $40 for a session and you charge $160 to the client for the session, your food cost is 25 percent ($40 / $160 = 0.25%). This 25 percent food cost states that every dollar of income costs you 25 cents in food. Remember, when determining food cost, the cost of food and the income must be incurred during the same period.

The labor cost for most personal chefs is the fee for preparing the meals in the client's kitchen. There is a hidden side to labor costs, which includes the cost in time of running your business. Time-intensive activities such as grocery shopping, bookkeeping, marketing, and a host of other activities must be included in your labor cost. In most personal chef businesses, the owner is the sole employee and burdened with all the responsibilities of the business. A service charge of $25 per hour may at first sound fair, but when you calculate the true labor cost, that $25 might be reduced by half! Your time is worth money. Be fair when charging for your time, but be fair to both yourself and your clients.

Those new to the industry tend to neglect the business part. Set up your books, learn basic bookkeeping. Learn to track things, to set up and run accounts.

—Meredith Erickson, personal chef, Whisk for Hire Personal Chef Service

TIPS FROM PERSONAL CHEFS

It is recommended that you track and analyze your income and expenses weekly. It is a good idea to set aside a day and time once a week to do your tracking. Chef Candy Wallace prefers to do her tracking on Friday mornings. Of course, you may choose to hire a bookkeeper or use a bookkeeping program such as Quicken. Whatever system you choose to use, be sure your business's expenses and income are tracked regularly. An early sign of poor cash management is not tracking and analyzing your income and expenses in a timely manner.

The advantage of weekly tracking is that every week you will see if your business is profitable or not. Regular tracking helps you pinpoint potential problems sooner rather than later so you can correct them before revenue is lost due to breakdowns within the day-to-day business operation. You will be able to answer questions like these: Am I charging enough? Do I need to do more sessions? You will be able to recognize bad spending patterns and be able to correct them before they become major problems. You will not have to file quarterly tax payments, or estimated tax payments made for each financial quarter of a given year, the first year you are in business, but it is recommended that you have your finances reconciled quarterly so you will not face any big surprises come April 15, Tax Day. A good ballpark figure is to estimate taxes at 10 percent of your gross profit. After the first year of business, you will be required to make quarterly **estimated tax** payments based on the amount of taxes you expect to be responsible for during a business cycle of 3 months, if you made a profit during your first year. Many businesses are not profitable for the first few years, but the personal chef industry tends to be an exception.

It is important for you to determine what method of keeping track of your expenses works well for you and to use that method. Replacing lost receipts takes time and causes frustration. The use of a business credit card helps simplify recordkeeping. Every month you receive a statement of all expenses incurred on the business credit card. If your accounting period works the same as your credit card statements, recordkeeping is even easier.

Food receipts for ingredients used when recipe testing (your family or friends might enjoy being the guinea pigs) are allowable **deductions** which decrease taxable income. Occasional receipts for restaurant meals are also deductible if you were conducting research on a new food trend or technique you intend to offer to your clients. Use your own discretion, but be careful not to abuse this deduction.

You should always carry an envelope or file with you to hold any and all receipts for business-related cash purchases. At the end of each week, write yourself a reimbursement check. You may be surprised at how much miscellaneous cash you spend.

If you are using a leased vehicle for your business, both a percentage of the lease and the auto insurance are deductible business expenses, along with vehicle maintenance. If not, and you are using your own vehicle, keep a daily log of mileage for business purposes. Keep this journal in your glove compartment and use it daily so you can receive the proper deduction.

Your records should also include the categories of income and expense. These categories can be specific or broad. If the categories are too specific, you may end up with so many they are difficult to manage. If, on the other hand, they are too broad, they become meaningless. The following is a list of suggested accounting journal categories.

Income

Personal Chef Service	$____	Other		____
Catering	____	**Total Income**		$____

Expenses

Personal Chef Service

Cash Reimbursement	$____	Uniforms / Shoes	____
Recipe Development	____	Linens / Laundry	____
Food	____	Equipment / Cookware	____
Utensils / smallwares	____	Rentals	____
Containers	____		

Office

Permits / Licenses	____	Internet Service	____
Stationery / Printing / Copy	____	Web Hosting	____
Advertising*	____	Domain Registration	____
Yellow Pages	____	Insurances**	____
Phone / Voice Mail	____	Memberships / Dues	____
Cell Phone	____	Books / Magazines	____
Postage	____	Vehicle or Mileage	____
Office Supplies	____	Gas / Oil / Maintenance	____
Computer and Supplies	____	Auto Insurance	____
Hardware / Software	____		

Professional Services

Accounting	____	Graphic Design	____
Legal	____	Bank Fees	____
Web Design	____	Taxes	____

Other

Owner Salary	____	Assets Purchased	____
Reserves (savings)	____	**Total Expenses**	$____
Container Deposit	____	**Net Profit / Loss**	$____

*Advertising includes marketing and promotion.
**Insurance includes all insurances.

Conclusion

Running a personal chef business is no different than running most other businesses. In order for any business to be successful, it is necessary to control costs, manage cash flow, and make the correct purchasing decisions. Managing your cash flow is more than knowing how much is going out or how much is coming into the business at any given time; it also involves controlling both fixed and variable costs. Determining profit and planning for profit are also part of the business process.

Recall that the number-one reason many small businesses fail is poor cash management. Good cash management involves controlling your cash flow, both the monies flowing into your business as income and the monies flowing out as expenses. Good cash management is simple. It involves:

- Anticipating when, where, and how your cash needs will occur.

- Knowing your best sources for additional cash.

- Being prepared to meet those needs when they occur.

All too often, small business owners feel their knowledge of their business is enough to ensure their success. They do what feels right to them and some are lucky—but many are not, and they become a sad statistic when their business fails. It is not enough to know how many clients you have this or next month. You must figure cash flow over many months by knowing;

- Your estimated income

- Your average gross profit per sale

- Your average gross profit percentage

- Your breakeven point

Cash flows in and out of the business constantly. Your control of that cash will keep your business in business for a long time.

Key Terms

Start-up Cost

A one-time cost that occurs during the development phase of a new business. Examples are licenses and professional fees.

Expenses

Money spent by a company.

Assets/Equity

The value of items owned by a business.

Fixed Costs

Costs that are constant and remain the same during a business cycle, no matter what the production level is.

Variable Costs

Expenses directly related to a sale. This cost that changes as the business volume increases or decreases.

Profit

Monies left within a business after all operating expenses are met.

Capital

Money or other assets that a company or a individual owns that can be converted to money.

Debt Loan

A loan that is repaid over a specified period. The lender does not gain an ownership interest in the business, and the debt obligations are typically limited to repaying the loan with interest. Loans of this type are often secured by some type of asset.

Default

The inability to meet the terms of a loan.

Short-term Loan

A financial obligation lasting less than one year.

Long-term Loan

A financial obligation lasting more than one year.

Fixed-rate Loan

A loan in which the interest rate remains the same for the entire term of the loan.

Variable-rate Loan

A loan in which the interest rate moves up or down based on the changes of an underlying interest rate index.

Hybrid Loan

A loan that shares components and characteristics of both fixed-rate and variable-rate loans.

Loan Proposal

Application for a loan that is linked directly to the business plan. You must explain how much you need to borrow and how you intend to repay the loan, and on what terms.

Credit Report

A historical account of a person or business's use of credit.

Fair Isaac & Company (FICO)

A standardized method of scoring the credit risk of an applicant.

Cash Flow

The movement of money in and out of a business.

Cash

Legal tender available to a business on short notice.

Outflows

The movement of money out of a business.

Inflows

The movement of money into a business.

Positive Cash Flow

An indication of a company's financial health. More money is flowing into the business than out of it.

Negative Cash Flow

An indication of a company's financial health. More money is flowing out of the business than into it.

Cash Flow Projections

Reports that predict the movement of monies through a business during a given business cycle.

Capital Strategy

Management decisions that determine the use of capital within a three- to five-year business cycle.

Operating Cash Flow

The movement of cash through a business at any given time.

Working Capital

See Operating Cash Flow.

Income

Money received during a specified period in exchange for a product or service.

Sales Revenue

Total sales during a given period.

Gross Profit Percentage

The dollar amount of a profit in terms of a percentage.

Average Gross Profit Per Sale

The monies left after you have subtracted the direct cost from the sale.

Average Gross Profit Percentage

Average gross profit converted into a percentage.

Breakeven Analysis

A calculation that helps you determine when your business will be able to cover all expenses and begin to make a profit.

Inventory

The amount of goods and materials in stock; may be given as a dollar amount.

Breakeven Point

The point at which income from the sale of a product or service equals the invested costs and expenses, resulting in neither profit nor loss.

Session

The act of cooking in a client's home kitchen; length of time does not matter.

Gross Receipts

See Sales Revenue.

Net Profit

Sometimes referred to as the *bottom line*. A company's total profit.

Yield

The amount of product remaining after trimming or processing. It is the difference between what you purchased and what you can actually use.

Edible Portion Cost

The cost of a portion of food after taking into consideration the yield of the food item after trimming or processing.

EP

Edible portion. Weight of product after trimming or processing.

Portion Control (PC)

Foods that are pre-portioned with a 100 percent yield.

As Purchased (AP)

The entire product before trimming or processing.

Elasticity of Demand

The measurement of demand for a service or good as its price increases or decreases.

Sales Mix

The combination of the total amount of items sold listed by profit for each item.

Gross Income

The selling price minus the cost of material.

Food Cost

The ratio of money spent on food to income created during a given period.

Estimated Taxes

The amount of taxes that a business expects to be responsible for during a business cycle.

Deductions

Allowable decreases in taxable income.

Gross Profit Percentage

The dollar amount of profit in terms of a percentage.

Gross Income

The selling price minus the cost of material.

Quarterly Tax Payments

Estimated tax payments made for each financial quarter.

Portion Control

Foods that are pre-portioned with a 100 percent yield. Example, an 8 oz New York Strip Steak that is a portion for one person.

Review Questions

True / False

1. Start-up costs for a business are generally one-time costs.

2. Good financial sense dictates that you have at least three months of cash reserves to cover household expenses while starting a small business.

3. Costs associated with your business include fixed cost, variable cost, start-up cost, and cash flow cost.

4. It is always a good idea to use personal savings for your starting capital.

5. A fixed-rate loan is one where the interest rate stays the same for the life of the loan.

6. A credit report is a recounting of your credit history.

7. When considering a loan request, financial institutions review such factors as how you plan to repay the loan, how much of your own money you are investing, and your marketing plan.

8. Cash management involves controlling both expenses and income.

9. Sales revenue is the total amount of cash your business brings in over a given period.

10. A breakeven analysis determines methods of payment for repairing capital equipment.

11. Variable costs tend not to change as business increases or decreases.

12. Net profit is your income.

13. Yield is the difference between AP and EP.

14. Typically, a portion control item has a yield of 80 percent.

15. To determine your fixed cost per session, divide your fixed cost for a period by the number of sessions for the same period.

Multiple Choice

1. The money spent to obtain your business licenses is a good example of a
   a. Fixed cost
   b. Start-up cost
   c. Variable cost
   d. Profit

2. Over time, start-up costs
   a. Increase.
   b. Decrease.
   c. Remain the same.
   d. Do not reoccur.

3. The cost of food used in a cooking session is a good example of
   a. Fixed cost
   b. Start-up cost
   c. Variable cost
   d. Profit

4. In an financial environment where interest rates are going up, it is better to have which type of loan?
   a. Fixed rate
   b. Variable rate
   c. Equity
   d. Long term

5. The number-one reason a small business fails is

    a. Poor location
    b. Poor business plan
    c. Hiring too many employees
    d. Poor cash management

6. Cash flow is

    a. The movement of money in and out of the business
    b. A measurement of profit
    c. The movement of capital into the business
    d. The ability of the business to make a profit

7. Sales revenue is

    a. The same as cash flow
    b. Total income minus total expenses
    c. Total income divided by total expenses
    d. Cash you bring into the business over a given period

8. A breakeven analysis determines

    a. The revenue needed to cover all expenses
    b. The revenue needed to cover fixed costs only
    c. The revenue needed to cover variable costs only
    d. The revenue needed to start the business

9. Total fixed cost per month is

    a. Fixed cost plus variable cost divided by 12
    b. Total yearly fixed cost divided by 12
    c. Fixed cost minus profit divided by 12
    d. Total yearly fixed cost multiplied by 12

10. EP refers to

    a. The total trim waste of a product
    b. The total yield of a product after trimming and cooking
    c. The amount of product that should be purchased for any given meal
    d. The AP of a product

11. To determine the yield of product,

    a. Divide the edible portion by the as-purchased size.
    b. Divide the as-purchased size by the edible portion.
    c. Divide the as-purchased size by the waste left after trimming.
    d. Multiply the edible portion by the waste left after trimming.

12. Which is not a factor that may influence the EP cost of a product?

    a. Season
    b. Skill of the chef
    c. Availability of equipment
    d. Transportation cost

13. Portion control refers to

    a. Ketchup and mustard
    b. An item whose EP is equal to its AP
    c. A item that must be peeled, washed, and cleaned
    d. A item that is packed in bulk

14. Packaging two items together, such as an entrée and a side dish, and offering them at a lower cost than both items sold separately can result in

    a. Higher cost
    b. Increased profit
    c. Lower cost
    d. A net loss in fixed cost

15. Within the foodservice industry, food cost is often referred to as a

    a. Dollar amount
    b. Percentage amount
    c. Fixed cost
    d. Start-up cost

Discussion Questions & Activities

1. In groups of three or four, identify start-up costs for a personal chef business, keeping in mind that you can use items (capital equipment) that you may already own initially. Identify each item as a fixed cost, variable cost, or one-time start-up cost. Use the list provided in this chapter on page 65, but expand on it as necessary.

2. Assign estimated costs to each item in your list. Research costs for business fees, legal services, accounting services, and design services. What costs could be trimmed if necessary? What would be the ramification of trimming these costs?

3. Break into groups of three or four. One group is the banker or lender, and the other groups are start-up businesses that need a loan. Each business group should write a loan proposal to be reviewed by the lender group. The lender group can award only one loan and must decide which group will receive it. In a class discussion, compare the loan proposals from both the requestors' viewpoint and the lender's viewpoint.

4. Order your free credit report and review it for any inaccurate information. Share your findings with your fellow students only if you are comfortable doing so. Remember to keep sensitive financial information private.

5. Do a yield test using a piece of beef that will be roasted. Start by weighing the meat before trimming or cooking; this is the AP weight. After trimming and cooking the meat, weigh it to determine the EP weight. Determine the yield and the yield cost of the meat. How would different methods of cooking affect the yield of the meat? If possible, cook one piece of meat in a hot oven and another in a low-temperature oven. Compare the difference in yield and in overall eating quality.

From the Field

FUNDING START-UP COSTS FOR YOUR NEW PERSONAL CHEF BUSINESS

"Start-up costs for a personal chef business will differ depending upon where your business is located. They will be a lot higher in a metropolitan area than in a more rural area," says Chef Jim Davis. Jim, who teaches seminars on the business of being a personal chef, adds, "I like to use the example that if you have transportation and if you have other means of support during the start-up period, then you can start this business on a medium-limit charge card."

This is what Chef Kristin Carlsen did when she started her business. "I got a credit card and used it solely for business expenses. I managed to land a client my first month, so I didn't even have to dip into personal funds to pay the minimum on the card. As the business has grown, I've been able to pay more than the minimum, and I now carry a zero balance on that credit card." She adds, "I got an airline credit card so I earn miles with all my purchases. I charge my clients' grocery purchases to the card and pay it off each month, letting my clients earn me miles. Turning a dream into reality takes some effort and planning, but it is worth every penny. People pay you to do what you love."

Chef Javier Fuertes of *The Dinner Maker* says, "Compared to other start-up businesses, this one is incredibly inexpensive. It can cost anywhere between $500 and $3,000. My start-up costs are somewhere in the middle of this range. I did put a big chunk of money onto a credit card. Now, I'm not saying go put all your expenses on a credit card, but at some point you need to decide whether you want to be patient and save up as much money as possible before going forward or just go for it and get a loan or put the money you need to pay expenses on a credit card."

A Different Perspective

Chef Meredith Erickson, owner of *Whisk for Hire*, says, "I would not recommend going into debt or taking out a loan to get this business going. There is no need. The start-up costs are low, and you can afford them by simply setting aside some money on a regular basis." She adds, "On average, it takes a personal chef six months to get what she considers a full schedule. Don't get me wrong—you may have several clients within weeks of opening your business. On the other hand, some chefs go six months or more without a regular client. How quickly you get going is dependent on many things such as your efforts, your demographic area, and even luck." Chef Erickson figures start-up costs to be about $1,200, which includes liability insurance, food safety certification, and marketing supplies. "You can go much higher with that figure if you aren't going to start out using cookware and other items you already own," she adds.

Chef Erickson also encourages personal chefs to "set aside a certain percentage or amount of money each month for a rainy day—strictly to help you through tight times. Our business can fluctuate; you can have a full schedule and be working gangbusters and suddenly lose three clients within the space of week."

How Much to Charge?

To create a successful business, you must control both income and expenses. As discussed earlier in this chapter, revenue must be profitable. It is easy for the first-time entrepreneur to fall into the trap of taking business just to take business. To repeat, revenue must be profitable. You decide the level of profit based on each cooking session you desire to schedule. Sometimes, potential clients will try to get you to lower your price per cooking session. This decision is yours—but remember, you have set your prices so they not only include profit but the cost of doing business as well.

Chef Jackie Alejo of *Cooking for You* says, "I have been told by potential clients that they have been quoted a low-ball price. From the beginning, I never low-balled or gave in to low-quality food and service in order to get some kind of money. A standard was set in stone!"

Chef Karen Gill of *Karen Cooks It*, LLC states, "Lately, I have been getting inquiries for different events, and it's amazing how the clients want to nickel and dime everything. 'Would you charge less if I grocery shop or made some of the dishes for the meal?' they ask. I have found that if that is the case, these people do not appreciate the value of the services I am offering: stress release, peace of mind, and a good meal."

Chef Jim Davis points out, "There will always be somebody that will do it cheaper. I have always been a proponent of establishing a general pricing scheme and then sticking to it. But I also recognize that sometimes, when you are getting started, you will go in cheaper because you have the time and need for cash. I can't argue with that approach, as long as that price doesn't become your regular price—and I would encourage personal chefs to make those fee adjustments very carefully."

Remember that the personal chef business is exactly that—a personal service supplied by you—when pricing your services. Your cost will depend on what the client wants and your own situation; take, for example, Chef Howard Lunt of *A Chef @ Home*. He says, "I take jobs for slightly less than my standard charge if I want to fill in a date."

For the personal chef who has a filled schedule or even a waiting list, it is not necessary to charge a price that is lower than his standard and accepted fee. For personal chefs just starting out, low-balling on price may set a precedent that makes it difficult to increase fees later. A common thought on pricing: "I wish I charged more when I opened my business."

Discussion Questions

1. Chef Erickson suggests a planning and saving approach to acquiring start-up capital. Assume this will be the method you use to fund your business. What are the advantages and disadvantages of this approach to funding start-up costs compared to charging expenses on a credit card or getting a loan to open your business? Consider the pressures of having to make payments, possible loss of income (by delaying your opening of the business to save), and potential lack of funding for your business. Which method would you choose to fund your start-up costs? Why?

2. When is it a good idea to charge less than normal for your personal chef services? Does charging less than expected create a pricing structure that might be hard to increase in time? If you have open slots and a potential customer asks you to reduce your price by 25 percent, would you do it? If so, why? If not, why not?

3. Speculate on how much price affects the clients who use a personal chef service. Is price the only issue they consider when enlisting a personal chef, or do they use the service to solve other problems in their lives?

IDENTIFYING YOUR MARKET

Identifying the level of service you intend to provide and to whom you will offer these services is an important part of designing a targeted marketing plan.

—Candy Wallace, Founder and Executive Director, *APPCA*

Introduction

It is important for a new business owner to understand what defines a marketing program and to realize its impact on the success of the venture. The challenge is developing a marketing program that will be effective. A good marketing program is based on the quality of the research you do as you develop the program. This research investigates three primary areas:

- Clients
- Client needs
- Competition

This chapter helps you understand the research required to create a good marketing plan.

Learning Outcomes

After reading this chapter, you will be able to:

✎ Define a marketing plan.

✎ Identify both primary and secondary methods of market research.

✎ Explain the difference between quantitative and qualitative data.

✎ Identify traits of potential clients.

✎ Discuss methods of marketing research data collection.

✎ Summarize the design of personal surveys.

✎ Discuss methods for increasing response rates for a survey.

✎ Distinguish among niche markets and identify the group of clients each represents.

Key Terms

Market Research	Marketing Plan	Survey
Primary Marketing Research	Market Research Plan	Formal Research
Qualitative Research	Statistical Analysis	Traits
Personal Survey	Geographical Representation	Niche Market
Secondary Research	Secondary Data	
Response Rate	Responses	
Competitive Advantage	Demographics	
	Quantitative Research	

Identify Potential Clients

Who are your clients going to be? The family of four next door with both parents working full time? The single doctor down the street? The senior couple a few blocks away? They all are potential clients. By identifying certain traits and characteristics of your potential clients, your **market research** or collection of information about people who buy from you or might buy from you, will educate you and help you develop a successful **marketing plan** to attract your targeted clients by putting strategies into action.

The first step is to identify who your clients might be. These potential clients will fit into broad categories that can be subdivided. These **demographic** categories include:

- **Age**. You may find a certain age group is more likely than others to use your services.

- **Income**. Obviously, the client must be able to afford your services.

- **Occupation**. Certain occupations require more time than others. People who tend to work long hours and bring work home may be in the market for great food prepared by someone else in their own home!

- **Family size**. New families and families with older children all want good food, but with more mouths to feed, there are more tastes to please.

- **Marital status**. Single clients are more likely to use your services since cooking for one can be a chore. A married couple who have different food preferences may also use your services as they still enjoy eating together.

- **Residence**. Apartment dwellers or luxury homeowners.

- **Interest and hobbies**. People who follow healthy trends in diet or enjoy dining out may be your next clients.

- **Education**. This may relate to client's occupation and income level. Traditionally, the client with a higher education may enjoy a greater income but may also have less time to enjoy some of the simpler rewards of life.

- **Ethnicity**. You can cook ethnic foods that appeal to particular ethnic groups.

- **Health**. Does the potential client's state of health require a special diet? Is the potential client a semi-athlete who requires a specific diet?

- **Lifestyles**. Potential clients may be used to assigning work and paying for others to provide personal services to them. Households that are used to paying for lawn service, cleaning services, or dog walking services may be especially interested in hiring a personal chef to cook their meals for them.

Primary Research

Original marketing data is called **primary market research**. The collection of primary or original data need not be complicated or expensive, but the process must be planned carefully.

Your **market research plan** must include the type of research to be conducted along with methods that will be used to analyze the data. The plan should include a budget and timelines marking the end of the research. Market researchers have two classifications of research, quantitative and qualitative. **Quantitative research** provides data that can be evaluated using **statistical analysis** or mathematical techniques to analyze market information. Such data are numerical values that, when analyzed, yield relevant information based on a small group of responses. The most common forms of quantitative research involve the use of **surveys** and other questionnaires.

Qualitative research is sometimes called the touchy-feely type of research. It requires an interpretation of the information gathered and does not require statistical accuracy. Collecting this kind of data can be time-consuming and expensive.

Surveys, if done properly, can provide you with valuable primary data about your potential clients. There are two types of surveys, each with advantages and drawbacks. A **personal survey** is one where you, as the market researcher, talk with people who you think should fit into a particular category of your potential clients. This type of survey is not time-efficient, and it can be tricky to decide who conducts it. For example, assume you decide to do this style of survey and you pick your local upscale supermarket as the location. First, you need permission from the store's management, who may or may not give it. If permission is granted, you must try to survey people as they exit the store, but they may feel you are hassling them as they go about their daily routine.

Another disadvantage of this type of survey is that you may unintentionally survey only a subgroup of your potential clients. Should you choose to conduct your interviews only on Tuesday afternoons, you are only dealing with those people who shop on Tuesday afternoon, which is not a good representation of your overall group of potential clients. You have not interviewed people who shop on Thursday evenings or Saturday mornings. Even though the **geographical representation** should remain somewhat constant, the demographic representation would change, and so your data would not include information about the larger group of the people with whom you want to do business.

Doing Market Research

Doing market research is much like doing homework for your business. Your market research need not be elaborate or expensive to be effective. Small, inexpensive efforts can help you find the required information. Knowledge gained from this research will help you make informed decisions about your business, such as where and to whom to market your business. Many times, new business owners underestimate the time required to complete good market research. When estimating your time requirements, it is best to be generous. Be prepared to rewrite your research tools a few times as your research becomes more targeted.

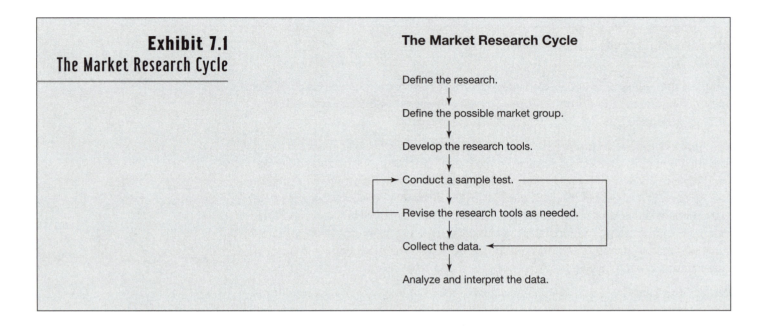

Exhibit 7.1
The Market Research Cycle

The Market Research Cycle

Define the research.

Define the possible market group.

Develop the research tools.

Conduct a sample test.

Revise the research tools as needed.

Collect the data.

Analyze and interpret the data.

The purpose of market research is to give you a better understanding of who your potential clients are. As you gather information, remember to blend all your data together and look at the big picture. Professional marketing researchers agree that market research should not be the only tool used when making marketing decisions.

Having knowledge about your local area is invaluable. Having a feel for the demographics of your area will help you assess the viability of your business. Targeted market research determines the average household income of your service area, traffic patterns, typical family size, work habits, and other such information, but you should also educate yourself about the local area.

You can do "marketing by driving around". Get in your car and drive around the area of interest. Look at the homes, the yards, the cars, the schools, and stop to check the menus posted in the area restaurants for types of entrées and prices. Know your area of service and your potential client's neighborhood.

Because the personal chef industry is a newly emerging business, only limited formal research data are available. **Formal research** is done by conducting the research yourself or by gathering primary raw data from other sources. **Secondary research** is the most common form of collecting data. This method involves reviewing data that has been interpreted by others. In many cases, this consists of third-party information in the form of published articles. Marketing research firms that specialize in particular areas may charge a fee for secondary data. **Secondary data** may also be obtained from sources such as a local chamber of commerce, your state or local business development center, or the Small Business Administration (SBA). Secondary data provided free of charge is often organized into broad categories and may not be specific enough to be meaningful to you. That is not to say this type of data is not useful; as long as it is combined with more specific data, it becomes useful in the broader sense.

Educational Attainment		
Population 25 years and over	509,453	100%
Less than 9th grade	18,214	3.6%
9th to 12th grade, no diploma	48,871	9.6%
High school graduate (includes equivalency)	122,409	24.0%
Some college, no degree	142,287	27.9%
Associate degree	38,041	7.5%
Bachelor's degree	93,213	18.3%
Graduate or professional degree	46,418	9.1%
Percent high school graduate or higher		86.8%
Percent bachelor's degree or higher		27.4%

Source: U.S. Census Bureau

**Exhibit 7.2
Profile of Selected
Social Characteristics
Salt Lake City, Utah, 2000**

As Exhibit 7.2 shows, examples of free secondary data include statistics on characteristics. Data to consider may include:

- Population counts
    - By age
    - By sex
    - By age
    - By race
- Household size
- Household ownership
- School enrollment
- Educational attainment
- Marital status
- Caregiver classification
    - Grandparents as caregivers
    - Employed caregivers
- Disability categorized by age and gender
- Household language
- Ancestry
- Employment status categorized by age and gender
- Average commute to work
- Occupations
    - Broad categories
- Household income
- Family income
- Average home value

- Mortgage status / payment average

- Rental occupancy and cost information

Obviously, not all these data may be useful to you as you do your market research, but some of it may be. Let's examine the income of households located in Salt Lake County, Utah, in 2000 based on the Profile of Selected Characteristics:

Income range	Numbers	Percentage
Less than $10,000	16,589	5.6%
$10,000 to $24,999	45,066	15.2%
$25,000 to $74,900	158,825	53.8%
$75,000 to $200,000+	74,810	25.5%

If one of the **traits** or characteristics, of a potential client is that the household income is above $75,000, the above table indicates that over one-quarter of the households in Salt Lake City, Utah, meet that qualification. When you combine your local knowledge and primary research, you are in a good position to make both management and marketing decisions.

Mailed Surveys

Mail surveys are a fairly cost-effective and time-efficient method of gathering the market data you need. Written questionnaires are easy to analyze, and many common computer software packages, when properly used, will help you analyze the data collected. Written surveys are also less intrusive than face-to-face surveys or phone surveys.

As with everything, there are disadvantages associated with written surveys, especially the possibility of low response rates. **Response rates** vary widely from one survey to another (3 to 90 percent), and if the rate for your survey is low, the value of the data that are collected is compromised. Another disadvantage of a written survey is the inability to probe **responses**. This can be overcome by providing space for comments or questions within the written survey.

Sometimes the quality of the responses may be questioned. It is natural to assume that the person filling out the survey is the person you addressed it to, but that may not always be the case. A questionnaire may be filled out by the wife, or husband, or even kids pulling a prank.

An effective survey is carefully planned and well written. As you plan a written survey, consider the following;

- What is the goal of the survey?

- How many questions will the survey have? (The fewer the better, in most cases.)

- How will you select the group to be surveyed?
  - Mailing lists can be purchased from research organizations, but for the new personal chef business, this may prove expensive and too large in scope.

- Neighborhoods can be surveyed in several ways. Leaving your mail survey attached to doors may work for some, but many times it ends up in the trash.

- Neighborhoods can also be surveyed by buying a ZIP code–specific mailing list. You do not have to send out 5,000 surveys to sample a neighborhood. One to two hundred well-written surveys with a response rate of 20 to 30 percent will supply you with the data you need to make informed marketing and management decisions.

- What will the cost of the survey be? Don't forget to include:
  - Paper and writing cost
  - Copying cost
  - Cost of envelopes and postage
  - Cost of return envelopes and postage
  - Incentives, if used

SURVEY DESIGN

We all have completed questionnaires we received in the mail, or maybe we have even completed them online. Some of these surveys are easy to complete and seem to focus on a specific issue or idea, while others seem to drift from one idea to another and include poorly worded questions. Meaningful surveys are well designed, with well-defined goals. As you develop your marketing survey, determine what your goal is in simple but specific terms before writing your first question. Decide how you intend to use the information gathered and focus the questions around that desired information.

As you write your survey, remember these important keys:

- Keep the survey short and to the point—the shorter the better. People are more likely to respond to shorter questionnaires than longer ones. Should you have too many questions, ask yourself how you are going to use the information collected from each.

- The first questions are the key; keep them interesting and focused. If the first few questions are boring, the survey stands a better chance of ending up in the trash than being mailed back to you.

- Use simple language, but don't be afraid of adding a touch of flair. For the personal chef, this flair might include using a few randomly placed high-end cooking terms within the questionnaire.

- Leave space for respondents to add their own comments.

A good question requires the respondent to be truthful and to provide concrete answers. Here is a poorly worded question: "Do you enjoy beef or chicken at dinner?" If the respondent answers yes, you, as the data collector, are not sure if she likes beef and dislikes chicken or likes chicken and dislikes beef.

Multiple choice questions are the most popular type of survey question because they are generally the easiest for the respondent to answer. As you design your questions and their associated responses, remember that each question should leave no ambiguity in the respondent's mind. The responses should be distinguishable from one another so there is only one correct choice for each respondent to answer the questions truthfully. Here is an example: "In desserts I prefer _____"

a. *Milk chocolate*

b. *Dark chocolate*

c. *White chocolate*

d. *No chocolate*

e. *All types of chocolate*

- Questions should flow seamlessly from one to the next. Transitions between questions should be smooth and logical. Many survey writers group similar questions in order to make the questionnaires easier for respondents to complete.

- The wording of a question is extremely important. Do not lead the respondent in her response, one way or another. A question such as "Wouldn't you like to enjoy delicious healthy food in your own home?" does not leave much room for any answer other than yes. Questions such as this do little to add to the quality of the information you are collecting.

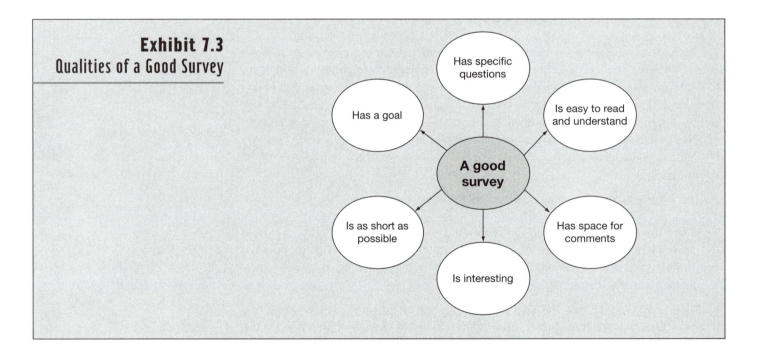

Exhibit 7.3
Qualities of a Good Survey

LAYOUT AND DELIVERY DESIGN

As you design your survey, remember, the goal is to gather meaningful information and to entice the respondent to fill out the survey and return it to you. Professional market researchers have found the following common characteristics tend to ensure the usefulness of a survey:

1. **Mail the survey** in a unique envelope. Eye appeal helps make an impression, and first impressions are important. Design an envelope that will make recipients curious about what is inside. Some research suggests that hand-addressed envelopes using commemorative postage stamps get a better response rate than those using machine-stamped mail permits or gummed labels.

2. **Provide a cover letter**. The letter should explain what a personal chef business is and persuade the respondent to complete the survey. Use the cover letter as a tool to inform the respondent about why the survey is important. Mention any incentive you may be offering, let the respondent know that a stamped, self-addressed return envelope is enclosed, and encourage a prompt response without issuing deadlines.

3. **Hand-sign your cover letter**.

4. **Give your questionnaire a short and meaningful title**.

5. **Print the return address on the questionnaire itself**; sometimes the questionnaire gets separated from the reply envelope.

6. **Provide a postage-paid, self-addressed return envelope**.

7. **Ensure the questionnaire is easy to read**. If you have decided to target a group of senior adults, you might consider using a size 14 font instead of a 12. Consider using color paper or color ink, but be careful of combinations, such as green ink on blue paper, that are hard to read.

8. **Use a high-quality method of publishing for your questionnaire**. The use of a good desktop publishing program and high-quality printing and paper will enhance the look and feel of your survey.

9. **Consider providing an incentive to respondents to motivate them to return the questionnaire**. This incentive could be as simple as a magnetic business card or something more elaborate, such as delivering a sample dessert to the respondent's household. The value of the incentive offered may directly influence the response rate. One market researcher reported that an incentive of 25 cents increased the response rate by an average of 16 percent, while an incentive of $1.00 increased the response by 31 percent. Even though an incentive adds to the cost of your survey, the money is well spent should an increase in responses result.

Niche Markets

The personal chef business allows you, the owner, to focus on the foods and style of cooking that interest you the most. Some chefs decide to be generalists, providing service to the widest range of clients, while others are more specific and specialize in preparing foods for senior adults with dietary restrictions or wealthy couples who enjoy high-end restaurant-quality foods in their home. As you design your tools to perform your market research, ask yourself the same questions you considered when developing your business plan and mission statement in chapter 4.

If there is a form of cooking you really enjoy and have knowledge about and expertise in, there may be a market for it. Good market research may confirm that a particular **niche market**, or smaller but profitable segment of a larger market, exists. A chef who specializes in preparing meals for diabetics or people with food allergies is catering to a niche market. Recall the concept of **competitive advantage** from chapter 4 and how you can leverage these advantages into your personal chef business. Of course, some niche markets require extra training, recipe research, and specialized marketing. While competitive advantages can help your personal chef business be profitable, they can also make it even more rewarding by allowing you to showcase your specialized knowledge or skills. Niche markets are smaller groups within the entire market group that share a particular trait. For example, a group of bodybuilders

> The man who does not work for the love of work but only for money is not likely to make money nor find much fun in life.
>
> —Charles M. Schwab (1862-1941), American industrialist

who want a high-protein, low-fat diet would be considered a niche. Exhibit 7.4 lists some target markets within the medical niche.

Exhibit 7.4 **Medical Niche Markets**	Postsurgical patients
	Presurgical patients
	Families with newborns
	Patients who require
	Low-sodium diets
	Low-fat diets
	Renal diets
	Low-protein/high-protein diets
	Soft or mechanical soft diets
	Low- or high-fiber diets
	Diets related to treatment for cancer
	Diets high in particular vitamins or minerals
	Diabetic diets

Remember, working in these niches may require you to consult with experts in relevant fields to ensure you are preparing meals appropriate for your client's dietary needs. For instance, when you cook for a client who is following a medically supervised diet, a consultation with a registered dietitian is appropriate. A word of caution: When researching specialized diets, approach a variety of creditable sources. As wonderful as the Internet can be, it also allows individuals with limited expertise to pose as experts in nutritional cooking. Use common sense and multiple sources as you investigate the requirements of specialized diets. The following list is a sampling of niche markets that a personal chef may explore:

- **Two-income families with children**: These families generally eat meals on the simple side, but the parents want to teach their children to make healthy choices so they can grow up to be healthy adults. They want meals prepared from fresh ingredients so their children can learn that food does not come in cardboard boxes and plastic trays that go into the microwave. They frequently want their personal chef to bring them back to the table as a family.

- **People with food allergies**: Approximately 11 million Americans suffer from true food allergies. Common food allergies include milk, eggs, nuts and peanuts, fish, shellfish, soy products, and wheat. Cooking for this group involves product identification and recipe modification.

- **Baby boomers becoming senior boomers**: With over 77 million baby boomers growing older, this niche market is huge. Seniors want to remain independent and vital as long as possible and wish to reside in their own homes rather than enter assisted living centers just to get meal service. Personal chef services can facilitate their desire to remain independent. As boomers age, their diets change as their taste changes. A personal chef in the right area might be able to take advantage of this market segment. Many of these clients prefer comfort foods that bring back memories of family dinner. This type of cooking might involve simple recipe modification to reduce fat or sodium while increasing vitamins and minerals. As people age, their senses of smell and taste tend to decrease. For this reason, a personal chef might use herbs and seasonings to spice up a meal. Also, as people age, their food consumption typically decreases as activity decreases. To ensure seniors are getting an adequate, nutritionally balanced diet, the personal chef may offer a dietary analysis of the meals being offered.

- **People on medically required diets**: Some people are on a diet supervised by a doctor. Enlisting this type of client can be both challenging and rewarding to you, emotionally as well as financially. Cooking for a client on a renal diet or on a modified soft diet requires special research, consulting, and possibly, extra equipment. Serving good-tasting food within such restrictions can be a rewarding challenge for any chef. A personal friend of these authors tells the story of how each week in his restaurant a particular customer would always order the same food, over-cooked by today's standards and sliced thin to allow her to eat it. One day, the chef approached the customer to find out why her food always had to be over-cooked and sliced into these bite-size pieces. The chef discovered the customer had problems chewing and difficulty cutting foods on a plate because of a medical condition. She still enjoyed good food, and her visit with her friends to his restaurant once a week was her treat to herself. On her next visit, the chef cooked a special meal for her, with all the foods sliced and cut but reassembled to simulate their original natural shape. Although this took place over twenty years ago, he still remembers the excitement and pleasure on her face as she enjoyed food that looked liked everyone else's. Sometimes, the simple reward of serving good food to good people is more rewarding than any financial gain. Meeting with the discharge counselors or diabetic and cardiac educators at the local medical center may be a good way to map out a plan to support medically specific needs of your clients who are patients under their care and supervision. You can then follow the primary caregiver's protocol as you create customized menus.

- **People who follow specific programs like Weight Watchers, the Zone, or South Beach**: You may find clients requesting personal chefs to follow these programs as they customize their menus. Many personal chefs are beginning to specialize in servicing clients with specific requests that help them stick to the requirements of various diet programs.

- **Wealthy couples (sometimes called DINKS, for Dual Income, No Kids)**: These fortunate folks may have entirely different tastes than other clients. In this case, you are cooking for two adults with adult tastes. Many times, these clients are interested in a wide range of tastes and flavors. One night, they enjoy the home-style comforts of a rich brown stew, while the next night they want an entrée with a Thai flair. These often young professionals, who do not have the time, desire, or knowledge to cook for themselves, may offer the personal chef the ability to expand her menu and cooking repertoire because they demand a wide variety of diverse foods and flavors.

- **Professional clients, married or single, who entertain business associates and clients in their homes for business dinners**: This situation presents an additional revenue stream for personal chefs who choose to supply this service.

- **Empty nesters**: These are couples with adult children who have left the house. Like well-off couples without children, these are older adults whose taste profile may consist of both family favorites as well as more adventurous meals, as they have traveled the world and eat adventurously. Now that their children are out of the house, they are once again becoming active, and while they enjoy good food, cooking is not something they choose to do.

- **Athletes of all ages who require special diets to help them reach nutritional goals**: High-protein, low-protein, or whatever food is in vogue may fit these clients' dietary needs.

- **Clients with temporary medical conditions**: A new mom may fit this category, or a person recovering from surgery or an injury. This type of client may require a special diet initially and then, as she recovers, she may revert to earlier tastes.

Conclusion

The goal of market research is to identify who your clients are, what they want, where they want it, and when they want it. The key to effective market research is neither the technique used nor the data gathered, but rather the compilation of useful information from a variety of sources. Local knowledge combined with basic market research should offer the personal chef enough information to formulate a marketing plan that is effective and will help him gain clients. Remember, clients' likes and dislikes are shifting constantly, so the information provided by market research must be timely.

A personal chef may be able to take advantage of niche markets. Doing so may require additional training or research but can pay off with a loyal list of clients.

Key Terms

Market Research
The act of collecting information about people who buy from you or who might buy from you.

Marketing Plan
An organized method that puts marketing strategies into action.

Demographics
A range of physical, social, and economic characteristics that exist within a given group.

Primary Marketing Research
Gathering information from firsthand sources.

Market Research Plan
An organized method of collecting and analyzing information from a target audience as part of market research.

Quantitative Research
A marketing research method that yields data expressed in numerical terms.

Qualitative Research
A marketing research method yielding data that do not require statistical accuracy.

Statistical Analysis
The use of mathematical techniques to analyze market information.

Survey
A method of obtaining primary data for a marketing research project, direct mail, or questionnaires.

Personal Survey
A method of obtaining primary data for a marketing research project using face to face interviews or questionnaires.

Geographical Representation
People who live in a physical area, such as a neighborhood, village, or town.

Formal Research
Formal research is done by conducting the research yourself or by gathering primary raw data from other sources.

Secondary Research
Collecting information using data previously published.

Secondary Data
Information obtained from published materials, such as books, magazines, or newspapers.

Traits
Characteristics of a group of potential customers.

Response Rate
The proportion of people who respond to a market research project.

Responses
Answers to a market research project.

Niche Market
A small but profitable segment of a larger market.

Competitive Advantage
Strengths that give the business an advantage over other similar businesses.

Review Questions

1. The purpose of market research is to identify traits and characteristics of potential clients.

2. It is best to identify the traits of a group and place them into subcategories before starting your market research.

3. A market research plan includes budget and timeline projections.

4. Quantitative research provides data that can be evaluated by statistical analysis.

5. A personal survey is the same as a mail survey.

6. Demographics refers to a large area where people live.

7. The type of research that involves collecting primary data is called secondary research.

8. An example of a trait is "All the people who live in the Denver area."

9. Mailed surveys offer a time-efficient and cost-effective method of gathering market data.

10. Most people respond to long surveys than to shorter ones.

11. A well-written survey leaves room for respondents to add their own comments.

12. A good survey question might be "Do you enjoy beef or pork?"

13. In a mailed survey, a cover letter allows you to explain the purpose of the survey.

14. For a mailed survey, you should always supply a postage-paid self-addressed return envelope.

15. A niche market is a large group of people who share a particular trait.

Multiple Choice

1. A market research project should
   a. Identify who your clients will be.
   b. Identify traits of potential clients.
   c. Identify categories for potential clients.
   d. Determine the age range of potential clients.

2. A market research plan
   a. Determines the type of research to be conducted along with the methods to be used.
   b. Determines if there is a market for a product or service.
   c. Helps define the results of a market research project.
   d. Is a statistical analysis of data.

3. Quantitative research is
   a. Information interpreted by the researcher.
   b. The touchy-feely type of research.
   c. Gathered by asking respondents open-ended questions.
   d. Provides data that can be evaluated using statistical analysis.

4. An example of demographic traits is
   a. Addresses where people live
   b. Income ranges broken into groups
   c. Last names
   d. Population counts

5. An example of secondary data is

 a. Information gathered by collecting raw data from other sources
 b. Information you gather yourself
 c. Information gathered from sources such as the chamber of commerce
 d. Information gathered from handing out surveys

6. Which is not a population category identified by a trait?

 a. A group of people who have incomes greater than $100,000 per year
 b. A group of people between 34 and 43 years of age
 c. The population count of a city or town
 d. A group of women with a income of over $100,000 per year

7. Response rate for mailed surveys refers to

 a. The percentage of completed surveys returned from a mailing
 b. The percentage of surveys not returned from a mailing
 c. The number of traits identified on a survey
 d. The number of written responses found on returned surveys

8. A well-written survey

 a. Has a specific goal.
 b. Is as short as possible.
 c. Uses simple language.
 d. All of the above.

9. Identify the good question for a mailed survey.

 a. Do you eat salmon or other cold-water fish more than three times a month?
 b. Which wine do you prefer with your meal, red or white?
 c. Do you enjoy beef at dinner?
 d. Are you on a low-fat, low-sodium, or low-protein diet?

10. A niche market is

 a. A smaller group of a larger market that has a particular traits
 b. A larger group of a smaller market that has a particular traits
 c. A group whose members change their eating style constantly
 d. A group of people who enjoy chicken or beef with dinner.

Discussion Questions & Activities

1. The Internet has many sites that offer surveys. Pick three of these sites and have a group analyze the quality of the questions posed within the surveys. Sort each question into one of three categories: (1) good questions with clear choices, (2) marginal questions with unclear choices, and (3) poor questions.

2. Rewrite the poor questions you identified.

3. Pick a food such as beef, chicken, fish, or root vegetables. Write a ten-question survey with the goal of determining your classmates' preferences with respect to the food how they like it served, and what foods they enjoy with it.

4. Write a cover letter for your food preference survey. Explain the purpose of the survey and how the information gathered will be used.

5. Visit government websites that provide demographic characteristics. Identify traits that may characterize a personal chef's potential clients.

From the Field

Chef Shari Aupke, *A Groovy Get Together*

MARKETING TO A NICHE OF THE TARGET AUDIENCE

For years, Chef Shari was a preschool teacher who also loved to cook and had a passion for food and people. Three years ago, she decided to change careers and become a personal chef. She chose to focus her efforts on a niche market within the personal chef business: dinner parties. She chose this niche because she enjoys cooking the meal and serving it but feels that interacting with her clients while they enjoy her food is just as important. "Being able to look out from someone else's kitchen to see clients having a good time and enjoying just being together" became the core of her personal chef business.

Some personal chefs specialize in cooking for clients and leaving the food in their cooler or freezer for later enjoyment. Others cook for clients weekly and add dinner parties as time permits. Chef Shari's personal chef business, A Groovy Get Together, only does dinner parties. "I was not interested in preparing meals weekly that would be frozen," she says. "I'm inspired to cook because I enjoy it. It's all about making people happy."

As she started her business, she quickly realized that for her there were two forms of payment; obviously, clients would pay for her service, but she also felt that the satisfaction she saw on their faces as they experienced the entrées she prepared specifically for them was another form of payment and equally important. "Eating and moaning is a good thing. I like to see people enjoying their food. When there is dead silence at the dinner table and all I am hearing is munching and moaning, I've done my job," she says proudly.

Each client receives a custom-designed menu that fits his flavor profile and the nature of the event he is hosting. She is proud of the time she spends getting to know her clients, not only their likes and dislikes but also their history and what makes them tick. Recently, she had a client who was planning a dinner party where he planned to propose to his future bride. He lived in another state and arranged everything with Chef Shari using phone, fax, and e-mail. She designed a custom menu for the dinner, arranged flowers for the table, and served the meal. The gentleman's girlfriend said yes to his proposal! "He proposed and she said yes, and I was part of that. What they had to eat that night will be forever ingrained in their heads." This is something that Chef Shari calls her emotional payment for her services.

To start her business, she decided to market her services to "people with enough cash flow who lived in big houses," she states. Business started out slow, but over time it grew to the point where she was exceeding her financial projections, as well as her emotional projections.

Her current methods for advertising include only two types. The first is the word-of-mouth advertising provided by her happy clients, and the second is a food column she writes regularly for two local newspapers, which includes her byline with the name of her personal chef business.

Chef Shari's personal chef business has become successful during the last three years. She loves what she does, and it is apparent that her clients share their love for food with her and value and appreciate the services she provides. She offers a little advice for new culinarians about to enter this field: "Just do it, just get out there and do it, but remember, there is a need to be human about it. Don't make it so much about the business as it is about human contact."

Discussion Questions

1. Chef Shari's business was slow to start. What forms of market research could she have used to increase her business in the first few months of operation?

2. As a dinner party personal chef, Chef Shari chose to cater to a niche market, and she enjoys the personal interaction with her clients. What other niche markets would also ensure direct interaction with clients?

MARKETING

Do you know what happens if you don't market? Nothing!
—Candy Wallace, founder and executive director of the American Personal & Private Chef Association (APPCA)

Introduction

One of the greatest needs for a new business owner is to develop a good marketing program and to recognize its impact on the success of his business. Long-term success depends on your ability to maintain a large pool of satisfied clients while adding new clients as your business warrants. Clients ebb and flow like the tide. Some will leave your services as they travel or move to different locations, while others may become periodically returning clients. A well-planned marketing program will keep your flow of clients steady. Your marketing program should focus on identifying, satisfying, and following up on your clients' needs. The personal chef rarely enjoys the wealth of resources other small business owners have at their disposal. Not only will you be responsible for the financial resources of a start up business, but you will be planning and creating your own marketing campaign as well.

Learning Outcomes

After reading this chapter, you will be able to

✎ Explain the similarities and differences between marketing and promotion.

✎ Identify a target market.

✎ Measure the performance of a marketing plan using various methods of assessment.

✎ Conduct marketing research.

✎ Describe the process of developing a marketing plan.

✎ Identify the marketing methods used by personal chefs.

Key Terms

Marketing
Marketing Plan
Geographical Area
Demographics
Promotion

Target Market
Profitable Sales
  Volume
Marketing Strategy
Advertising

Market Research
Maximizing Sales
  Volume
Marketing
  Expenditures

Marketing is a combination of promotion and advertising within the framework of a plan. All **marketing** programs should be aimed at convincing people to use or to continue to use your services. The development of the marketing plan takes research, focus, and the ability to execute its elements. A good **marketing plan** focuses on efforts to convince your potential customers that your services are the best. A marketing plan is a written document that details the actions needed to achieve specified marketing objectives. The style of advertising or promotion should enhance the image of the company and help draw new clients to your business. Advertising is any paid activity that calls attention to your product or service and promotion is anything done to highlight a business and its services to a target market. Promotion is usually less expensive than advertising.

An effective marketing plan has seven basic characteristics. It is:

1. Simple and easily understood by your potential customers
2. Truthful
3. Informative
4. Sincere
5. Customer-oriented
6. Specific
7. Cost effective

The Marketing Plan

To develop your marketing plan, you need a firm understanding of your own business. What services are you willing to provide? How far are you willing to travel? What type of services and food do you specialize in? The answers to these questions should have been covered in your business plan (see chapter 4).

As you develop the marketing plan for your personal chef business, you will conduct market research (see chapter 7), which will define your **target market** or one particular group to whom you are marketing your services, and help you develop a strategy for achieving your desired results. As you develop your plan, remember that achieving and maintaining **profitable sales volume** where you have a larger percentage of profit than the norm, is more important than **maximizing sales volume** or creating sales without regard to profit. Your marketing plan must be flexible so you can take advantage of seasonal changes, special events, and trends in dining.

The amount and type of market research you conduct will vary depending on the situation and the information you are trying to gather, but the purpose remains the same. As identified in chapter 7, the purpose of market research is to identify your potential customers. Gathering both information about the geographic areas and demographics will help you identify your target market. The collection and analysis of the data you gather from your market research will help identify your potential customers along with other important factors that must be considered in your marketing plan. For example, if the data shows that your potential customer is a family with two young children and both parents working, your marketing strategy should focus on this demographic. With this in mind, menus and meal plans that feature foods for both adults and children have a much greater chance of resulting in a sale than a plan that addresses adult tastes only. The purpose of the market strategy is to determine who your market is; based on the data you collect during the research phase.

Once your target market is identified, your marketing plan should be developed with these potential customers in mind. Your plan should include several forms of advertising and promotion as well as a working budget and an established method of evaluating the success of your marketing efforts. This evaluation will identify the style of marketing that returned the greatest sales and those that did not perform as expected. You use this information to choose future methods of advertising.

Because most personal chefs start their business with a modest budget, the amount spent on marketing may seem excessive. But funds spent to execute a well-thought-out marketing plan will be returned many times over in the future. Consumers may not realize their need for your service until educated by your marketing plan. The introduction of a new service to a community requires greater **marketing expenditures**, or funds spent on marketing expenses, than those of an established business type. Many existing businesses budget 2 to 5 percent of sales for advertising. New businesses, especially those introducing a new service to a community, may need to budget as much as 10 percent for the first year or two.

Advertising and Promotion

Good advertising gets favorable attention from the right people—those who need and will benefit from your service. The process of advertising can be summed up using the acronym AIDA.

Awareness: A good marketing plan creates awareness.

Interest: A good marketing plan creates interest in your services.

Desire: With interest comes desire for your services.

Action: The advertising recipient takes the action you want.

> Half the money I spend
> on advertising is wasted;
> the trouble is I don't
> know which half.
>
> —John Wanamaker, "the father of modern advertising" (1838-1922)

Promotion is defined as the actions taken to expose your services to particular target markets. Promotion can be inexpensive in that it may cost you your time only. For instance, writing a food article for a local publication, such as a newspaper or magazine, can initiate the process of exposing your business to potential customers. Promotion may also involve hard cost such as the food used to cater a charity event. Of course, the most valuable type of promotion is word of mouth. A happy client who refers your services to a potential customer can create a winning situation for all those involved.

Advertising helps further the growth and development of your services. Unlike promotional efforts, which can be of little or no cost, advertising can be expensive and is broader in scope than promotion. We are all familiar with television advertising, which can cost almost a million dollars a minute, depending on the airing time and date. Few, if any, personal chefs have a marketing budget that allows for the creation of prime-time television advertising. But there are excellent alternatives!

To understand the difference between promotion and advertising, consider the following. You have submitted a food-related article to a local newspaper in an effort to promote your personal chef business. The only cost incurred is the time you have spent writing the article and delivering it to the paper. The newspaper may use the article without delay or wait a few weeks before printing it. The article may also be edited to save space or reinterpreted to fit the needs of the paper. The services you highlighted in the article may not be identified by the reader due to the reworking. Finally, it's possible that your article was not written effectively to highlight your business's services, as some of the best chefs in the business find it extremely difficult to write articles for publication.

When advertising your business, you contact the newspaper to place an ad. In other words, you pay for a certain amount of space within the paper. The cost varies with placement and the day of publication. You determine the message and the timing of the advertisement. The paper may provide you with an advertising writer who will turn your ideas into text. Unlike that of a food-related article, the purpose of your advertisement is to inform and persuade potential customers to use your service. Advertising can be a powerful tool for creating an image and establishing name recognition for your business.

We all witness many forms of advertisement every day, and while some people may react negatively to a particular ad, others react positively; their interest is piqued by the business or service advertised. While the promotional food-based article does not focus on your business, the reading public may react more positively to the information presented in it.

Marketing has a cumulative effect. Responses may be slow at first but increase over time if the marketing plan is effective. Launching one-time-only marketing blitzes rarely achieves the desired results. The methods used in your marketing plan should be sustainable, measurable, and diversified for the greatest effect on the targeted market. Here are common methods of marketing for a new small business.

Business cards are an accepted essential for nearly every business. Business cards should, at a minimum, include your company name, your name, and contact information. You can also include a logo, if you have one, and a simple line describing what your business is all about. Your vision statement can serve you well on the business card.

Your business card may undergo a few transitions before you feel you have it just right, so you may not want to spend a substantial amount of money printing 1,000 or more right away. Many personal chefs start with laser cards and advance to professionally printed cards when they feel they have achieved the look they are after.

Remember, while you do not want to be sloppy in your business card creation, you also don't want to spend so much time on the design that you lose valuable time marketing your services.

Local newspaper / print media promotion and advertisement. Ads are run for a specific period. In daily or weekly publications, six-week flights work well. For monthly publications, arrange to run the ad six months straight. Most personal chefs interviewed for this text found newspaper advertising ineffective due to low response rates as compared to the cost of other forms of advertising such as direct mail or brochures which generated higher response rates. That is not to say that newspaper advertisement has no merit. However, use caution when considering running an ad in the local paper.

Contact: ENTRÉE NOUS

FOR IMMEDIATE RELEASE

BUSINESS NEWS/LOCAL

ENTRÉE NOUS, A PERSONAL CULINARY SERVICE NOW COOKING UP EXECUTIVE MEALS

Entrée Nous, a customized in-home personal chef service, is now available for busy executives and families in the North San Diego County area. Entrée Nous is owned and operated by Jessica Leibovich and offers "palate-specific" personal meals cooked from fresh ingredients in private homes.

Her clients appreciate the service. "It gives us precious time together at the end of a busy day. No shopping . . . no cooking . . . no cleaning up. For us, it's a luxury we can afford," says Sharon Esche, a small business owner and client of Jessica's. And her husband, Alexa, agrees. "When we add up the food and restaurant bills, we realize we aren't spending any more than we did before . . . but we're eating like kings."

Leibovich meets with clients to determine their specific dietary needs. Then menus are agreed upon and a cooking day is selected. "We shop for all the food, come into the client's home every other week for about four hours, and cook about ten meals. Then we freeze them and clean up the kitchen. We leave nothing behind but delicious smells and great food," says Leibovich. "And the cost is about the same that people are spending right now on food and restaurants."

Exhibit 8.1
Sample Press Release

Contact: ENTRÉE NOUS
Jessica Leibovich
000-000-0000

____@personalchef.com

FOR IMMEDIATE RELEASE

BUSINESS NEWS/LOCAL

ENTRÉE NOUS OWNER AND PERSONAL CHEF JESSICA LEIBOVICH AT NAWBO'S MONTHLY MEETING NOVEMBER 7

Jessica Leibovich, owner and head chef of Entrée Nous, a custom in-home personal chef service, will be the keynote speaker at the National Association of Women Business Owner's monthly meeting.

The meeting will be held at the Doubletree Hotel, 4500 Friars Road, in Hazard Center. Ms. Leibovich will speak on "Is It Time to Hire a Personal Chef?" and share insights on the personal chef industry and how to determine if a personal chef is right for you.

"For female executives looking for a healthier lifestyle, a personal chef may be just the answer, especially those with children. Take-out food, while convenient, is loaded with salt and chemicals," says Leibovich. "The time you save may not be worth the risk to your health and well-being."

Chef Jessica Leibovich is a member of the American Personal Chef Association (APCA) and can be contacted at 000-000-0000 or www.yourpersonalchef.com for more information. For meeting details and costs, call 000-000-0000.

Exhibit 8.2
Sample Press Release #2

Press Release and Publicity

Getting your name out there in print through interviews and/or articles is an effective alternative to PAID advertising, but can take some patience connecting with the right person. One thing to remember is this: Newspapers, radio, and TV stations are always looking for NEWS, and that's what you are!

You should call the local publications and broadcast stations and ask for the names of the Business Editor, Food Editor, Lifestyle Editor and segment producers for the broadcast stations since they are far more likely to read your material if it is actually addressed to them by name. Make sure you are submitting your press release to the appropriate person even if you are sending press release material by e-mail. These folks are busy, and if you have not done your homework and you send your information to someone who is no longer with the newspaper, the current editor is likely to throw your submission away. Do NOT be careless where your relationship with the press is concerned. You have ONE chance to make a first impression. Make certain it is a good one.

If you have a photo to send, and you are sending your press release electronically, you should submit your photo as a .JPG file. If you are submitting your information by regular mail you can send a color or black and white photo of you standing near food looking "personal cheflike".

You will want to follow up on your press release submissions by calling the person to whom you have submitted your information to confirm they have received it. This is a great way for them to be able to ask you questions or explore the possibility of setting up an interview, so the more genuine enthusiasm they sense from you, the better. Enthusiasm is contagious. One thing to remember when calling an editor—they are often working on deadline and you do not want to become a source of annoyance, so when calling, ask if they are busy or on a deadline. If so, make an appointment when the call might be more convenient. You want to be able to speak with that person to ask if there are any questions you can answer for them or further information you can provide them, so be cordial and develop a relatinship with that journalist so you may become the source they use for information on the personal chef industry.

Keep your press releases as brief as possible—one page is a great guideline for a basic release. Stick to the basic rules of journalism—answer the questions who?, what?, where?, and why? in your release, and stick to the main points.

Submit your press release in an acceptable form:

The top of your Press Release Page should raed like this:

- FOR IMMEDIATE RELEASE
- Contact Person: Include name, telephone/fax number, and e-mail address
- One or two line headline

The headline should be strong and tell the editor what the release is about.

> The *Yellow Pages* is a good method of advertising for established businesses, but it may not be a cost-effective choice for a start-up business. Many phone companies offer a combination of Yellow Pages advertisement and discount phone services that results in a cost-effective package.

Direct mail advertising can address narrow geographic and demographic areas. The advertisement letter itself should be personal, informal, or selectively directed. Postcards offer another method of direct mail.

The *sales letter* is a form of direct mail that is highly effective for some personal chefs. The letter is personal, informal, and selectively directed. Often, a handwritten envelope gains more attention than a typed one that has a mass mailing look. The letter itself can also be handwritten.

Postcards can be effective. They are less expensive to create and may be more cost-effective than brochures or letters. The message is delivered quickly and efficiently. The copy should be concise and similar to a newspaper ad, and you should use colorful card stock and graphics to grab the reader's attention. Postcards can be used effectively in three-month intervals. However, with a low or unsure bounce-back rate for most mailings, the nonresponse rate must be taken into consideration when comparing costs.

Brochures are a great tool for explaining what your business is about. A professionally produced brochure can convey information that other forms of print media cannot. A brochure can be more effective than a business card because it provides a detailed description of the service and its benefits. Many preprinted brochure paper designs are available for use with a laser printer or copy machine. This is less expensive than having 500 pieces printed, plus you retain the flexibility to make changes.

TIP: Choose a typeface no smaller than 10 point.

TIP: It should not take much more than a minute for anybody to scan your brochure, but those sixty seconds should be packed with memorable information.

The rule for time spent on creating business cards also applies to brochures. Do not spend so much time creating the material that you miss opportunities to distribute it.

Flyers are similar in concept to brochures and are effective whether they are mailed or personally handed to people. Flyers can also be in the form of bulletin board postings, which can be placed (with permission) in public places, including grocery stores and other retail food outlets. Another form of flyer is the door-hanger, although not all consumers appreciate having marketing materials left hanging on their doors.

Your vehicle. A growing number of personal chefs are using their vehicle as a traveling billboard by means of either removable magnetic signs or permanent vinyl lettering. Although significantly less targeted toward a specific audience, vehicle signage communicates to a high volume of viewers. Typically, the message is limited to a company name, telephone number, possibly a logo and a line or two about the service, making this a very large version of a business card.

The *Internet* can be a powerful marketing tool. While volumes can be written about this one topic, the same basic advertising guidelines pertain.

From a technical standpoint, you must choose:

*   To have your own domain (e.g., www.yourname.com)
*   To have your site as part of someone else's website (e.g., www.theirname.com/yourname.htm)
*   To purchase authoring software or use free tools available online
*   To pay for hosting directly or to use the services of a free host.

In a general sense, having your own domain, purchasing web creation software, and paying for hosting services ensures that your website to be truly yours. This one area can consume vast amounts of your time if you allow it to, so carefully consider whether you want a web page for your personal chef business at all, and if you do, whether you want to create it yourself or have a professional provide this service. The American Personal & Private Chef Association (APPCA) provides a web referral page for their members at no charge. They also provide web design and hosting to association members at a substantial discount.

Conclusion

Many personal chefs interviewed for this text stated that their website is their most productive form of advertising, especially for an already established business. New personal chef businesses should use multiple methods of both advertising and promotion to create a synergy within their marketing plan. What works for one personal chef business may not work for another. Some personal chefs enjoy designing flyers and brochures and sometimes lose sight of the purpose of marketing, which is to create new customers and to entice current customers to continue to use your services.

Key Terms

Promotion
Anything done to highlight a business and its services to a target market. Usually less expensive than advertising.

Advertising
A paid activity that calls attention to a product or service.

Marketing
A combination of promotion and advertising that results in either acquiring new customers or enticing current customers to continue using your business.

Marketing Plan
The written document that details the actions needed to achieve specified marketing objectives.

Target Market
A particular group to whom your services are marketed.

Market Research
The act of gathering geographic and demographic information concerning potential customers.

Profitable Sales Volume
Sales that create a larger percentage of profit compared to the norm.

Maximizing Sales Volume
The act of creating sales without regard to profit, which will generally be lower than the norm.

Geographical Area
A physical area, such as a neighborhood, village, or town.

Demographics
The range of physical, social, and economic characteristics of a given group.

Marketing Strategy
A combination of all the methods used within a marketing plan.

Marketing Expenditures
Funds spent on marketing expenses.

Review Questions
True / False

1. Marketing involves both promotion and advertising.
2. A good marketing plan is mainly concerned with how much money it will bring into the business.

3. You should see immediate results when launching a marketing plan.

4. The goal of a marketing plan is to persuade potential customers to use your service.

5. An example of a promotion is giving away small samples of food at a charity event.

6. All advertising is expensive, and most personal chefs can not afford it.

7. A newspaper ad is a form of advertising.

8. A business card is a form of promotion.

9. A brochure is more effective than a business card.

10. It is wise to spend a great deal of time on the design of a business card.

Multiple Choice

1. Marketing is
   a. Promoting a product or service.
   b. Paying for a product or service.
   c. Promoting and advertising a product or service.
   d. Advertising a product or service.

2. A good marketing plan
   a. Shows immediate results.
   b. Is costly.
   c. Tries to convince potential customers to use your service.
   d. Depends on print media.

3. In developing a marketing plan
   a. You should refer to your business plan to stay within its scope.
   b. You should plan to use natural food colors for your print media.
   c. You should not worry about a budget because of the sales the plan will generate.
   d. You should choose only one method of marketing your message.

4. It is not a good idea to
   a. Maximize sales volume at the loss of profit.
   b. Maximize profit at the loss of sales volume.
   c. Use different forms of promotion and advertising.
   d. Do market research before creating a marketing plan.

5. Generally, an established business spends
   a. More on marketing than a new business
   b. About the same on marketing as a new business
   c. Nothing on a marketing plan, because it is not needed
   d. Less on marketing than a new business

6. Which is not an example of advertising?
   a. Working a dinner party or charity event at no charge
   b. A newspaper ad
   c. A website
   d. A flyer or business card

7. A good business card
   a. Contains as much information as possible.
   b. Is printed on heavy black or dark blue card stock.
   c. Is easy to read and lists contact information.
   d. Contains both the vision and mission statement of a business.

8. Direct mail

   a. Should be used as a general mailing covering large areas.
   b. Is not a proper form of advertising for a personal chef business.
   c. Should be used as your only form of advertising.
   d. Should be used in a specific small area.

9. A website requires

   a. A hosting service or domain
   b. The services of a graphic artist
   c. A posting of all services and items you provide
   d. A link to websites that offer services other than those of a personal chef

10. A vehicle sign is much like

    a. A business card
    b. A flyer
    c. A website
    d. A direct mailing

Discussion Questions & Activities

1. Within a group, pick any common product from shoes to soda—anything that people use or any service people buy. Have each group member write a one-page marketing plan for the product. Consider who would buy the product or service and their age, gender, income, and other demographic issues. Compare the plans and present them to your fellow students.

2. Make a list of promotional ideas for a personal chef who is just starting his business. Estimate the cost of each idea and prioritize the list from potentially most effective to least effective.

3. Write a print copy ad for a new personal chef business. Refer to your business plan for background information as needed.

4. Using desktop software, design your first business card or flyer. Remember to use the suggestions as listed in this chapter.

From the Field

Chef Betsy Jaffe, *Home Cookin' Personal Chef Service*

MARKETING AND ADVERTISING YOUR PERSONAL CHEF BUSINESS

Chef Betsy Jaffe says, "Marketing can be time-consuming, but it isn't really complicated. Truth be told, hanging up flyers or passing out business cards isn't even marketing." Betsy started her personal chef business in a suburb of Washington, D.C. She wanted to stay in a narrow geographic area because D.C. traffic can be awful. "As a result, I had to be aggressive in my marketing while staying in a five-mile radius." This forced her to concentrate on a targeted market consisting of potential clients who lived within five miles of her home.

Before becoming a personal chef, Betsy had worked in marketing as a lobbyist and as a public relations director. She knew that in order to meet the goals she set for her personal chef business, her marketing efforts had to be targeted locally and affordable. She says the first thing she did was "get out there and get in front of people." She attended a few group meetings for networking professionals, as a guest, so she could try before she bought. "It is not enough to quietly pass out cards to other professionals. You must become interested in helping the members of the networking group succeed in their businesses, and in turn, they will help you to succeed in yours. The creed of all of these networking professional groups is 'Givers gain'."

She formed her own networking referral group with other professionals in her area. The group represented a variety of small businesses and referred potential clients to businesses within the group. Last year, this group generated over $120,000 in business referrals. Chef Betsy also developed a joint or hub website for the referral group where potential customers could visit and search for the services they desired. The website helped generate even more customers for all the businesses involved.

Chef Betsy also did cooking demonstrations during the summer at the local farmers' market in an effort to "get out there and get in front of people." She worked with the market organizers and cooked local produce as supplied by the farmers. She gave people who tasted the fresh-cooked produce recipes along with information on her personal chef service. Both the farmers and Chef Betsy benefited from this relationship. By providing cooking demonstrations at the farmers' market, she got free booth space where she cooked the local's farmer's produce. This is an excellent example of promoting her personal chef business while featuring locally produced fresh foods.

"Little things would also help market my services to the local public," she explains. She wore her chef coat when grocery shopping. "People would stop me and ask me what I was doing. (*Note:* This is a perfect time for an elevator speech. See chapter 5.) I was generous with my time and became their on-the-spot expert on food. This certainly helped demonstrate the services my personal chef business could provide."

With her knowledge of computers and the Internet, she also started an e-newsletter featuring recipes and food tips. This newsletter provided a web link back to her business's website, which helped raise her rating on the Google search engine; she was always in the top three search hits for personal chefs in her area.

She also learned what *didn't* work for her. She says, "The normal advertising resources, such as newspapers, were too expensive and their distributions too wide for my target market, so I didn't use them." Some personal chefs donate services at charity events, hoping the exposure will create new business, but Chef Betsy never found this type of marketing successful. "Don't donate your service to a charity unless it is one you would actually write a check for," she says. "There are a lot of good causes out there, but small businesses must by selective about how they spend their advertising dollars."

She offers this advice to fellow personal chefs: "Know what your niche is. I did a good gift certificate business with new moms and such. Know what your area needs and how you can serve that need—and not just by doing what you feel like doing. People get into cooking because of their love and passion for food and cooking, but remember, it is still a business, and your personal chef service needs to be run like a business. It's hard because we want to be generous with our food, but remember to treat it like a business."

Discussion Questions

1. Chef Betsy used a variety of promotional methods and low-cost advertising to her advantage. How is cooking at the farmers' market a promotional event rather than an advertisement? What types of marketing materials would you make available to the people who sampled the foods? Is there a nonintrusive method of following up with possible clients from the farmers' market?

2. Explain how Chef Betsy capitalized on her competitive advantage (chapter 5) in marketing her business.

3. Create a one-page e-newsletter using your school as the subject. Include a recipe and a food tip. Have other students review and critique it.

THE SALES AND SERVICE PROCESS

chapter 9

Your most unhappy customers are your greatest source of learning.
—Bill Gates, *Business @ the Speed of Thought*

Introduction

The preceding chapters dealt with starting and organizing your business. From writing your business plan to establishing financial goals, these steps provide your business with a foundation. In this chapter we explore the sales and service process, personal contact with potential customers, the process of conducting client assessments, how to write client specific menus, and how to close the deal by completing a transaction and having the customer sign the agreement.

Generating sales revenue requires constant thought and action on your part as the business owner. Few clients will come to you with the sale already completed, as a relationship has not yet been established. It is important to keep in mind that what works for one person may not work for another. This means that in order to make sales, you should have several strategies in place. Having these sales strategies in mind at all times is part of the sales process.

Service also plays a large role in the sales process, particularly for the personal chef. Good food is and always will be good food, whether it is served in a fine white tablecloth restaurant, cooked at home on the barbecue, or prepared by a personal chef. The service provided within each of these scenarios is what differentiates the experience for the customer.

This chapter is about sales and service and how the two intertwine to help create a successful personal chef business.

Learning Outcomes

After reading this chapter, you will be able to

✎ Explain the sales service cycle as it relates to the personal chef service industry.

✎ Describe the relationship between establishing a sale and servicing the sale.

✎ Identify various sales strategies based on customers' requests for information.

✎ Understand the function of a telephone sales presentation.

✎ Conduct a potential client assessment meeting.

✎ Explain the process of transforming a potential client into a paying client.

✎ List the pricing structures available to the personal chef.

✎ Classify menu styles.

✎ Identify the importance of the service agreement.

✎ Explain the importance of client follow-up.

Key Terms

Sales and Service Cycle

Response

Telephone Sales Presentation

Cost per Entrée

Closing the Deal

Sales and Service Plan

Potential Client

Potential Client Assessment Process

Customized Program

Flat Fee

Service Agreement

Private Chef

Personal Chef

Initial Contact

Assessment Meeting

Professional Service Plus Cost of Food

Entrée Suggestion List

Matrix Format

Customization

The Sales and Service Cycle

The **sales and service cycle** for the personal chef includes a series of tasks that should be part of a plan to ensure customer satisfaction and repeat business. This process provides a feedback loop that ensures service improvement and reaction to clients' demands. Your business plan, mission statement, and vision statement provide the foundation for a personal chef's sales and service cycle. Each task within this cycle is related and helps form the **sales and service plan** to ensure proper service. The steps listed below may be modified or eliminated to meet different circumstances. You should use these as a guide and incorporate your own style to suit your needs. The steps in the sales and service cycle for a personal chef include:

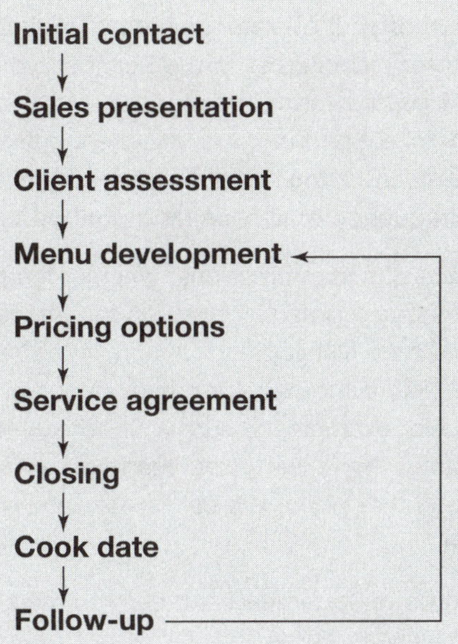

Exhibit 9.1
Sales and Service Cycle for a Personal Chef

Initial contact
↓
Sales presentation
↓
Client assessment
↓
Menu development
↓
Pricing options
↓
Service agreement
↓
Closing
↓
Cook date
↓
Follow-up

- Initiate contact with the potential client.

- Provide sales presentation.

- Perform client assessment.

- Develop menu.

- Establish pricing options.

- Create service agreement.

- Close the deal.

- Describe the process of the cooking session.

- Follow up with client.

The balance of this chapter goes into detail about each of these tasks.

Initial Contact and First Impressions

Depending on the methods you decide to use to market your business, the **initial contact** with potential clients may be in the form of an e-mail, phone call, written response, or even face to face. No matter which method you choose, your timely, professional response is critical and will help you make a good first impression on your potential clients. Your **response** usually consists of a combination of sales-manship, providing information about your services, and guiding the client through the process of hiring a personal chef.

Learning to respond to different forms of client requests takes practice and critical review. As you put together your response to a request, draw on snippets from your

> You can never recover from a bad first impression.
>
> —Folk saying

Hello, you've reached Candy's Personal Chef Company. We're the folks who custom design your home dining program. My name is Chef Candy Wallace, and I'll be happy to call you back as soon as possible. Please leave your name, telephone number, and the best time to return your call. Thanks again for calling Candy's Personal Chef Company. I look forward to speaking with you personally. Bon Appétit!"

business plan, mission statement, and vision statement and blend them into a natural-sounding extension of your elevator speech. Remember, in this situation, the **potential client** has expressed interest in the services you provide as a personal chef and has approached you for further information. Your responses must fulfill the informational needs of the client and be persuasive enough to get the client to commit to a live **assessment meeting** to define the client's likes, dislikes, dietary requirements, preferred frequency of service, and method of payment.

We all know the importance of first impressions, whether it's meeting your boyfriend's or girlfriend's family or talking to a potential client on the phone for the very first time. It is difficult to recover from a poor first impression, and, in the business world, a bad first impression can kill a deal before the negotiations even begin. Minor details can make or break first impressions. For example, be sure your contact number for your personal chef business is a dedicated phone line rather than your everyday phone line, with a specific voice mail message that plays, if a call is not answered. The message in the margin is a good example.

Written responses should be on letterhead and easy to read, with no grammatical or spelling errors. Include business cards that list your contact information when responding to a written request. If responding via e-mail, attach an electronic business card and brochure. Be careful when responding to potential clients with form letters. A request from a client usually asks for some specific information, and many canned responses do not address the client's questions. It is best to personalize your responses as much as possible.

If responding to a phone call, be prepared to turn the call into a **telephone sales presentation** that sounds like a natural, free-flowing conversation yet informs guides and sells your services to potential clients. Do not force the sales presentation on the client, but learn to manipulate the conversation in your favor.

An informal yet informative telephone sales presentation has great potential to lead to new clients. Remember, it is a two-way conversation led by you. During your presentation, ask questions such as:

1. What is the size of the family?
2. Does the family have dinner together each evening?
3. If you have small children, do they eat what you eat or are they in the pasta-and-tomato-sauce only phase?

Be sure to present potential clients with information about your personal chef service during the telephone sales presentation. Make sure the client understands the scope of your service by including key points such as these:

1. You do the shopping.
2. You cook the meals requested in the client's kitchen.
3. Your service is customized to the requirements of the client.
4. Your cooking session process is as follows:
   a. You buy the groceries and bring cooking equipment to the client's home.
   b. You cook all meals in the client's kitchen and then package, label, date, and store them in the client's refrigerator or freezer, as necessary.
   c. You provide handling and heating instructions for all meals.
5. You use only the best and freshest ingredients available, and you do not skimp on portions.

As the conversation continues, it is important to arrange for a face-to-face meeting where you can assess the dietary needs of your client and evaluate the kitchen where you will be cooking. Some clients will be sold on the idea of your service after your telephone sales presentation and may be ready to arrange a cooking date for your services. Be flexible and adjust your conversation accordingly.

Potential Client Assessment Meeting

The **potential client assessment process** is one of the most important aspects of your personal chef business. It is the backbone of the service you are promising to provide to your client. This is where you begin to form the partnership with your client that is necessary for you to succeed as a personal chef and as a business owner. Dress professionally and arrive at the agreed time with all the written materials you will need.

The assessment meeting is your opportunity to assess your potential client and determine exactly what he wants to accomplish by using a personal chef. You will also learn what he likes to eat, how he likes to eat, and whether or not he has allergies, sensitivities, and medical parameters that must be addressed, or certain tastes and textures he does not enjoy. This process also helps you and the client determine how little or how much he intends to participate in the client/personal chef relationship. Does the client want the chef to simply assemble a portobello mushroom lasagna and store it appropriately so the client may bake it at a later date, or does he want the lasagna baked, portioned, and stored for him?

The more specific the information you are able to obtain, the better the **customized program** you will design to fit the needs of your client. The more satisfied the potential client, the better chance you have to gain a long-term client for your service. You will even want to find out which appliances your client wants to use to heat her meals and whether she wants disposable or reusable containers. All of this information is important to you as you strive to provide the top-notch service you claim to offer. It is also at this meeting that you tell your potential client three important things about you and your business:

1. You are a certified safe food handler.
2. You carry $2 million in general liability insurance coverage.
3. You have a valid municipal business license.

This provides the peace of mind your potential client needs in order to be able to invite you into his home for an initial cook date—and make no mistake, on that first cook date you are an invited guest in his home. Once he has had the opportunity to taste your delicious meals and experience the top-notch service you provide, you may well be invited back as a regular personal chef. Remember, you only have one chance to make a first impression, and this meeting is when you do it.

Client Assessment Sales Presentation

It is important to remember that you are offering your potential client a personalized service, and you want to establish a long-term relationship with him. So you must look like and behave like a professional. Take the time to get to know this potential client and express your interest in his needs. This is the personal part of your personal chef business, and it will contribute greatly to your overall success.

Practice makes perfect. Before your first sales presentation, practice in front of classmates, family members, or friends. Have them play the role of a client with a list of questions and concerns. Break the presentation into the components listed below. Each component flows naturally into the next.

A. Introduction or Warm-Up:

"Hello, Mr. Smith, I'm Candy from Candy's Personal Chef Company. You have a lovely home. Thanks so much for taking time from your busy schedule to allow me to tell you more about the personal chef service I have to offer you." (Chat for a few minutes, but don't become so mired in small talk that the client thinks you are wasting his time.)

B. Sales Presentation:

"As I mentioned to you on the phone, I am a personal chef, and after we have completed this interview, I will be able to custom design a meal program for your approval. When you and I have reserved your cooking date, I will do the grocery shopping for your meals and come to your home with my own equipment to prepare the meals you have selected. I will be preparing the number of entrées you have selected (each of which serves four), and I will package these entrées as you've requested (either single servings, servings for two, or family style). I will label the containers and leave heating instructions so there is no question about how to handle them. It couldn't be simpler, and your job is just to enjoy your meals."

C. Client Assessment Form

"Let's complete the food portion of the interview now—all I have to do is ask a few questions." (Fill in client's responses on the client assessment form.)

D. Suggested Entrée List

"Why don't we select a list of entrées for your first cook date while we're here together? (Give client a copy of your suggested entrée list. For the sake of variety, suggest that he select entrées from each of the categories, unless he is a vegetarian; that way he can enjoy an entrée from the soup category as well as beef, chicken, turkey, lamb, or pork as well as a delicious meatless entrée.)

E. Reserve the Cook Date

"Since we have your first entrée selections, let's reserve your cooking date now."

F. Service Agreement Form

"The date is set, and now all we need to do is fill out your service agreement and for you to issue payment for the scheduled services." (Explain the service one more time while you fill out the service agreement which is a nonbinding agreement that outlines the services to be provided, the method of payment, and the responsibilities of both the personal chef and the client).

G. Close the Deal

"Thank you, Mr. Smith, for choosing Candy's Personal Chef Company. I'm looking forward to seeing you on Wednesday at about 9 A.M. Good-bye, Mr. Smith."

As you can see, this is a simple process, but it does require practice and honest self-evaluation. If possible, record your practice sessions for review. You'll be amazed at how much listening or watching yourself can improve a presentation. Do a full dress rehearsal before your first assessment meeting, and remember to keep the conversation as smooth and natural as possible. Anticipate questions from the client, and prepare your responses. Prospective clients often ask the following questions:

1. **What is the difference between a personal chef and a private chef?**

   A **private chef** is an employee, employed by one individual or a family on a full-time basis, who often lives in with the family and prepares up to 3 meals per day. A **personal chef** is a small business owner who serves several clients, usually one per day, and provides multiple meals that are customized for each client's requests and requirements. These meals are packaged and stored so the clients may enjoy them at their leisure.

2. **Do you cook in my kitchen?**

   "Yes, I will prepare your meals in the safety of your own kitchen. On our agreed-upon cooking date, I will bring the fresh ingredients for your meals along with my own pots, pans, and utensils, and prepare your entrées on site. At the end of the day, I will leave your kitchen clean and filled with the aroma of good home cooking!"

3. **How long will you be here?**

   "I'll be cooking several entrées and side dishes from scratch, so it will take several hours. I cannot say exactly how many hours; however, I am willing to work around your schedule or situation, and we can make arrangements, in advance, so my scheduled cooking date is compatible with your schedule."

4. **I'll be home that day. Is it okay if I watch—or help?**

   This can be a delicate situation. You don't want to seem rude, but you want to convey that this is your business, that you are a professional hired to do a job, and being under someone's watchful eye or being distracted by conversation or inquiries will not only slow the process but can also distract you and cause burns, cuts, and forgotten ingredients. Tell the client he is welcome to come in and visit for, say, fifteen minutes, but after that you need to be in command of the kitchen in order to complete the job you've been hired to do.

5. **Do I heat the food?**

   "Yes. Any entrées that have been stored for you in your freezer should be defrosted overnight in your refrigerator and then heated so you can enjoy them at the peak of their flavor. I will be leaving you easy-to-follow heating instructions for each entrée."

6. **How much freezer space do you need?**

   "It depends on the number of meals you request and the size of the containers, but my entrées do generally require a considerable amount of freezer space. Why don't we take a look at your freezer to see just how much room you have available?"

   Efficient storage is one of the reasons we recommend that you select the appropriate uniform-sized storage containers for your clients.

8. **What types of side dishes do you prepare?**

   "I prepare side dishes that complete the entrées you have selected. For instance, if you have ordered a beautiful savory stew entrée, I will prepare a rice or polenta side dish to be enjoyed with the stew.

9. **What if I want you to prepare additional side dishes as well?**

   "I'd be happy to provide that service to you; however, it will entail an additional fee."

10. **The cost seems to be about what I would pay for an entrée in a restaurant. Why is that? There doesn't seem to be a difference between dining out in a restaurant and hiring you to prepare my entrées.**

    "I'm glad you asked that. It's a really good question. The difference is really in the personalized service and convenience in using a personal chef.

    "Although my fees are per entrée or per serving, they actually represent all of the components that make up a professional personal chef service. For example, the assessment process we complete to determine what you like to eat, how you like to eat, and whether or not you have allergies, sensitivities, or medically specific requirements is included in the fee. One of the features of a personal chef service is that the factors uncovered during the assessment process are taken into account when I prepare your entrées. Other features of this service include customizing my recipes to reflect your wants and requests, submitting meal selections for your approval, doing the grocery shopping, and coming to your home to prepare your entrées in the safety of your own kitchen, in addition to packaging, labeling, and storing your entrées for your future consumption.

    "If you compare a personal chef service to a restaurant service, you will see that to eat at a restaurant, you must drive to get there. Once you arrive, you may wait for a table, and you take the chance that your server is having a bad day. Also, if you have allergies or special requests, you don't always have the guarantee they will be honored by the line chefs, as most entrées are prepared by an assembly line in the kitchen. Finally, after eating your meal, you must pay for it, tip the server, and get back in your vehicle to drive home.

    "On the other hand, if you have hired a personal chef service, you can heat a beautiful entrée that has been prepared specifically for your palate and requirements, and you can eat it in the comfort of your own home. You can even enjoy it curled up on the couch in your jammies if you want."

11. **Do I pay you in advance of each cooking date?**

    "Yes, it is customary to pay for the service in advance of your cooking date. If you like, you may leave me a check for the upcoming cooking date on the day I am cooking."

12. **How long will the food last us?**

    "Depending on how many entrées you order and how many evenings you eat at home, I can determine approximately how long your meals will last. If you travel for business, entertain in restaurants during the week, or just enjoy eating out on occasion, the meals will take you further than if you eat them each night. The beauty of a service like this is that we can adjust it to your needs at any time."

13. **How often will we need your service?**

    "I would be happy to help you determine just how often you will want to schedule my personal chef service to best serve your needs. I will make sure it supports your busy lifestyle without putting any pressure on you."

Pricing Structures

In addition to the traditional **flat fee** many personal chefs start out charging their clients, which includes the cost of food and service, you may also consider other pricing structures that accommodate the needs of a broad base of potential clients. Consider these options:

1. Flat Fee.　One advantage of a flat fee service is that it is straightforward. This pricing method includes all costs except for the food storage containers. Your client pays you in advance so you can buy groceries with the client's money and have no receivables to collect after you have performed your service. The flat fee includes the cost of food, so the clients who use this system leave the shopping and menu planning decisions up to you. These are clients who do not have special needs or requirements—they place the decisions in your hands and have only to sit back and enjoy life, now that you are providing home-cooked fine foods for them. The fee is always the same for this basic service model, so it is easy for these clients to remember to write you a check and leave it for you each time you come to their home on a cook date. The check they leave for you each time is for the upcoming cook date. It doesn't get much simpler.

How the Flat Fee Pricing System Works:

Your client selects five entrées and you schedule a cook date. Unless you are in a rural and remote area, the recommended fee structure tends to be in the range of:

- **$15 per serving, or $60 per entree (4 servings) and a side dish (4 servings)**

- **5 entrées × 4 servings = 20 servings**

- **$300 per cooking date, including the cost of food**

Food usually costs slightly less than $75 at the supermarket, so the personal chef earns approximately $225 for the day.

2. Fee for Professional Service Plus Cost of Food.　If your client has special needs, special requests, or consistently requests premium entrées, this pricing structure is a great way for them to have their food their way. A fee is set for services to which the cost of food is added.

If your client requests that all ingredients be organic, wants you to use his personal butcher or fishmonger, wants you to shop only at suppliers and purveyors of his choice, or requests foie gras, Maine lobster, and black truffles frequently, the fee for professional service and cost of food model is the way to go.

Current fees for professional services provided for the day can range from $225 to $300, plus the cost of food to a much higher amount in many markets. Of course, each market is unique; it is acceptable to charge more in an urban area than in a rural area. Many personal chefs who are just starting out in the business are tempted to UNDERCHARGE clients for their services. This can lead to frustration on their part when they discover just how much service they are providing their clients for their established fee. We strongly suggest you charge a minimum of $200–$225 per day for your services if you are using the fee for **professional service plus cost of food** pricing structure we just described.

In order to ensure that you are shopping for ingredients with your client's money, arrange for the client to pay you a monthly food deposit that can be reconciled at the end of each month. The fee for your professional services is paid in advance of any scheduled cooking date, as in the flat fee system.

At the end of each month, you must prepare an invoice for the client. If you do not, you should provide one at each cook date. This end-of-month (EOM) invoice should indicate the cost of ingredients for any individual cook dates and a total for the month. Your company's EOM invoice should also indicate whether or not there is a balance left in the food deposit fund that can be applied toward the upcoming month's food costs, or the amount of money the client needs to contribute to replenish the fund. This system requires more administration, but it allows the client to have exactly what she wants without jeopardizing your profitability.

Some personal chefs arrange for their clients to add them as signors on the client's monthly accounts with their purveyors so the client is billed by the butcher or fishmonger of their choice on a regular basis and the chef is not handling money for these necessary transactions.

Other personal chefs have arranged for the client to supply them with a credit card with a specific limit for the chef's to use when shopping for the client's food. The client pays the credit card monthly so once again, the chef is not handling money nor does the chef have to prepare an EOM accounting of monies spent for the client's food.

3. Cost per entrée.   This pricing option is for clients who do not choose the classic five-entrée configuration and works well if your clients tend to order a different numbers of entrées for each service date. Similar to an à la carte menu, the price of the entrée includes charges for professional services. This pricing method combines the cost of entrées cooked during a session and the charge for your professional services.

Once you have determined which pricing option is appropriate for the service you are offering a particular client, you must also consider several other factors prior to setting your final fee.

LOCATION

Are you in a large metropolitan area or a less urban setting? This will have a direct impact on your pricing structure, as personal chefs in New York City must charge more than personal chefs in Des Moines in order to account for the higher cost of living.

RESUMÉ

Are you a culinary school alumnus or a restaurant professional with extensive experience? If so, you may wish to pursue a client base with a more experienced palate and those who are interested in more complex fare. If you go this route when determining your target market, adjust your pricing structure accordingly.

If you are cooking for clients who live in large gated estates and prefer fine dining or clients who are your neighbors and live just down the street and prefer less complex fare, you may also want to take the level of requested service into consideration when developing your pricing structure. It takes more time and experience to build a vegetable tower than it does to prepare a meatloaf, although both are wonderful, and there are clients out there who prefer one or the other—and, on occasion, both. Once you have considered location and the complexity of the fare you anticipate your clients will want, select the appropriate pricing option for each potential client.

ADDITIONAL CHARGES

You will, on occasion, be asked to supply additional courses, entrées, or servings. We suggest adding $50 per additional portion requested over four servings on each cook date. This will cover the cost of food for the additional portions. You may also wish to charge separately for additions such as:

- Salads

- Breads (if requested for each entrée)

- Desserts

- Cookies (by the dozen), baked, or cookie dough, frozen for later use

- Any other request(s)

Food Storage Containers

As we've mentioned previously, no two clients are alike. In order to achieve our goal of personalized service for each client, we, as personal chefs, must cater to our clients' preferences for serving size, and provide containers appropriate for the appliances they will use to heat their entrées.

DISPOSABLE CONTAINERS

If your client chooses to dispose of her containers rather than use them again, supply her with appropriate disposable containers or vacuum-sealed meals at each cook date. Add a fee of $12–$15 per cook date depending on the type and number of containers used. This means your client can use and toss all of her containers with abandon because she owns them!

Many younger clients have only learned to warm meals in the microwave, and they love this option. The fact that most microwave ovens ruin good food is of no consequence to them because they have been consuming commercial frozen foods since childhood. What they care about is convenience, and you should be happy to give it to them.

There are quite a few disposable container options, including Gladware®, Ziploc® freezer containers, Ivex®, and Tenneco®, as well as the packaging used with a Food-Saver® vacuum sealer and other brands of sealers. Ziploc® freezer bags are excellent for pastas and vegetable side dishes, and disposable aluminum containers are great for entrées heated in conventional ovens. If a client has brand preference for containers, obviously you should try to satisfy her request.

REUSABLE CONTAINERS

Clients who are willing to take the extra fifteen minutes to heat their beautiful entrées in their conventional oven are going to enjoy better results and more pleasing presentation by using containers such as Corningware®, Pyrex®, or Anchor Hocking®.

All of these brands manufacture appropriately sized containers with tight-fitting plastic lids for single (individual), dual, and family-size servings.

If the client selects this option, you should supply him with an appropriate configuration of reusable containers and charge a $20 shopping fee in addition to the cost of the containers. This way, the client owns a collection of useful containers, and you need not replenish the stock at each cook date.

Part of the client assessment process which you use to determine the scope of services and your customer's desires, is to also identify which appliance your client will use to heat your entrées and what container type he prefers so you can give it to him. Remember, people eat with their eyes, and if disposable containers offend them, they will not enjoy the process or the entrée.

Clients who learn to use a personal chef service efficiently and easily are clients who stay with you. It's your job to help your client learn how to best use your service for optimum results.

CONTAINER CONFIGURATIONS (EXAMPLES)

1. 20 Single Servings

It is a good idea to start out with a few extra containers. This example includes eight extra containers, in case some items haven't been eaten by your next cook date.

24   15-ounce Corning oval containers with plastic lids for entrées

<u>24</u>   15-ounce Corning oval containers or 1 7/8-cup Pyrex containers with vented blue lids for sides

<u>48</u>   Total containers

2. 10 Dual Servings

Following is an example of packaging for two servings per container. In this case, you will need only twelve of each type of container.

12   5-cup Pyrex containers for entrées

<u>12</u>   3-cup Pyrex containers for sides

<u>24</u>   Total containers

3. Family-size Servings

Family-size packaging is possible, of course. However, sticking with two servings per container is usually better because the family-size containers take longer to defrost

Menu Selection

Even though the personal chef business is about customizing foods to meet the taste and health demands of each client, you should also offer a menu of food choices. The menu serves several purposes. First, it creates a starting point for the food types and styles from which your client can choose. Second, it allows you to feature foods or cuisines you are particularly proud of and consider your signature dishes. Third, the menu allows you to control cost, especially if you are using the fixed-price or flat fee pricing strategy. Menus can be presented in numerous ways. The **matrix format** creates a checklist for the client to use as he chooses entrées from different columns.

> You don't have to cook fancy or complicated masterpieces, just good food from fresh ingredients.
>
> —Julia Child, America's first celebrity chef (1912-2004)

Exhibit 9.2   Example of a Matrix Format Menu

Menu Selection

Please check your selections for the month.

Entrées

Beef		Chicken		Pork		Pasta		Soups	
Stew	____	Oven-Fried	____	Tenderloin	____	Spaghetti		Minestrone	____
Meatloaf	____	Parmesan	____	Ham	____	Lasagna		Bean	____
Stroganoff	____	Poached Lemon	____	Chops	____	Baked Ziti		Barley Mushroom	____
Stir-Fry	____	Stir-Fry	____	Stir-Fry		Alfredo		Chicken Noodle	
Chef's Choice	____	Chef's Choice	____	Chef's Choice	____	Chef's Choice	____	Chef's Choice	

Side Dishes

Cooked Vegetables		**Potatoes**		**Rice**		**Pasta**	
Glazed Carrots	____	Mashed	____	Pilaf	____	Rotini	____
Green Beans	____	Baked	____	Fried	____	Penne	____
English Peas	____	Oven-Roasted	____	Steamed	____	Fettuccine	____
Stir-Fry	____	Au Gratin	____	Brown	____	Egg Noodles	____
Chef's Choice	____	Chef's Choice	____	Chef's Choice	____	Chef's Choice	____

Categorized menus allow more space for item descriptions and look more like restaurant menus. Remember, the purpose of this menu is to give your client the opportunity to choose the foods he wants to enjoy and the foods you will cook during your cooking session. The time you spend on this aspect of your business is critical—preparing the menu is at the heart of the service aspect of your personal chef business. The information you gathered during the client assessment comes into play here as you personalize each client's program and present it for approval. Always have the client's file with you so you can refer to the client assessment.

Exhibit 9.3
Example of a
Categorized Menu

Soups, Fresh or Frozen

Lentil Soup

French yellow lentils simmered with onions, celery, carrots, and tomatoes.
Served with French bread.

Chinese Winter Soup

Sliced mushrooms, spinach, and tofu in an Asian chicken broth.
Finished with cilantro and green onions. Served with brown rice.

Vegetable Soup

A garden selection of fresh vegetables cooked in a vegetable broth.
Served with Italian bread.

Poultry, Fresh or Frozen

Breast of Chicken Piccata

Sautéed boneless chicken breast with lemon butter–caper sauce.
Served with orzo pilaf.

Chicken Cacciatore

Sautéed boneless chicken breast with garlic, fresh
tomatoes, mushrooms, and wine.
Served with fettuccine.

Szechwan Chicken

Stir-fried chicken in a spicy sauce, finished with raw peanuts.
Served over steamed jasmine rice.

Roasted Mushroom-Stuffed Chicken Legs

Boneless chicken legs stuffed with wild mushrooms.
Served with dried fruit couscous.

There are two ways to complete the menu selection process. If you have presented your client with a list of entrée suggestions, she may phone or fax in her choices one week prior to her scheduled cooking day. Alternatively, you may present suggestions to your client, if that is what she prefers, via phone or fax approximately ten days before her scheduled cooking day.

If a client communicated his dislike for mushrooms during the client assessment meeting, any recipe you submit for approval must either contain no mushrooms or be unaffected by the omission of mushrooms. You should also pay close attention to client requests for low-fat and low-salt recipes and any specific medical requirements.

It is also important that you provide a variety of tastes and textures. If you present a number of similar dishes for any one cooking date, your client may easily become bored. For example, you may wish to submit recipes from several food groups, such as Soup as an Entrée, Chicken, Beef or Veal, Turkey, and Meatless. If the meatless entrée is a tomato-based sauce with pasta, make sure the other recipes on your menu are not similar in taste or texture.

Cost of food is another area you should consider as you prepare your menus. Because you are developing the menus, make certain to balance expensive entrées like swordfish and lamb chops with less expensive items such as eggplant parmigiana and turkey Tettrazzini unless you are offering your clients the Fee Plus Cost of Food pricing option. You must keep your menus interesting and enjoyable without cooking up all of your profits. That's why you are in business for yourself—you like the challenge, but you also want to make a profit.

You should also include a plan for stove time in your menu selection process, as you will be working on residential equipment, for the most part. You may want to plan an entrée to roast in the oven and another that can marinate while you sauté a third on the stovetop and grill a fourth. Make a plan that uses the equipment and your time efficiently, or you will have a very long day.

If you store and catalog your recipes in Mastercook or another recipe software program, you can customize them for your clients' preferences, do a Save As of the adapted recipe, and store it under your client's name in an individual client cookbook. This way, you can keep a record of each recipe you prepare for that client and offer him the same meal on request. You can keep your recipes in three-ring binders, on 4 × 7 recipe cards, or in some other organized manner. When you have received your client's approval of a menu, pull the recipes from your binder or file and slip them into plastic sleeves. This way, if you spill or splash on a recipe while cooking, you haven't ruined it—just wipe off the plastic cover.

Ask your clients to keep notes of their impressions of each entrée they eat. Remember, you will not be present when your clients enjoy your food, and feedback is critical to your continued success. Some personal chefs ask their clients to write their impressions on the handling instructions. Other personal chefs use simple check-off forms with space for additional comments. The client should tell you if she loved the entrée, hated it, how she would alter it, if she would alter it at all, and whether or not she would like to have it again. This information is invaluable because it allows the personal chef to fine-tune his service. This **customization** demonstrates one significant difference between dining in a fine restaurant and enjoying the services of a personal chef. How many restaurants do you know that can keep a record of each customer's likes and dislikes and adjust the menu accordingly? Keep good records of your clients' food preferences and refer to them each time you plan an **entrée suggestion list** for a client.

The format below may be useful if you wish to supply your customers with a list of the recipes you've chosen to offer for their selection. You may also want to prepare seasonal lists. Simply list your recipes under each appropriate heading.

Soups/Salads	_____
Seafood	_____
Poultry	_____
Meats	_____
Vegetarian	_____
Children's Food	_____

Service Agreement and Closing the Deal

You may wish to have your clients sign a **service agreement**. This agreement is not a legally binding contract, and you or the client may choose to discontinue service at any time with no penalty. The agreement confirms the decisions you and your client made at the assessment meeting. It reiterates the services you agreed to provide to the client and the specific information the client provided that relates to your services.

Keep the agreement in your client's information folder and use it to compile your client database system. The service agreement should include the following customer data:

- Name(s)

- Address

- ZIP

- Home phone

- Work phone

- Cell phone

- First cooking day

- Entry/Alarm/Pet instructions

- How did you hear about my service?

- Fuse or breaker box location

- Do you have any friends or family you would like to refer?

- Do you have anyone for whom you would like to purchase a gift certificate?

The service agreement should also contain a statement outlining your responsibilities as well as your client's with respect to your business relationship. The following is a good example of such a statement:

We have conducted a Client Assessment to determine what and how you like to eat, whether or not you have any allergies or sensitivities, or any dietary or medical parameters that must be addressed. I will use this information to design a custom program for you and/or your family. Together, we have selected your first set of entrées and reserved your first cook date on ____. On that day, I will bring all of the ingredients to prepare your meals and prepare all of your meals in the safety of your own kitchen. At the end of the day, I will package your meals for you per your instructions, label them, and leave complete heating instructions for your convenience. I will leave your kitchen clean and orderly, taking all of my equipment with me.

Of course, the service agreement includes pricing information formatted for the pricing structure you and your client have determined:

FEE: Number of Entrées   _____

    FLAT FEE (Service and Food) $_____

FEE plus FOOD

    1. Fee for Professional Services $_____

    2. Food Deposit $_____

Container Options

    1. Disposable Container Fee $ 15/Cook Date

    2. Reusable Container Shopping Fee $ 125–150

Total Amount Due $_____

Instructions for heating the foods may be included in the service agreement, attached to each food item, or listed on a separate sheet. The service agreement also includes the client's responsibilities. The following example points out some of those responsibilities:

CLIENT AGREEMENTS

Payment for the initial cook date should be made today. All payments for upcoming service should be left for me on the cook date preceding the next service. As I mentioned in our meeting, on a cook date, I consider your kitchen to be my office. In order to avoid any mishaps in the way of forgotten ingredients or, worse yet, an accident caused by distracted attention, I request that you allow me to perform my professional service without interruption. If you would like me to arrive and spend a brief time visiting or answering questions, I will be happy to make arrangements to do so, and will also be happy to spend a short visit at the end of my cook day.

CANCELLATION POLICY

Because cook dates for regular clients are scheduled on a quarterly basis, it is necessary for any cancellations to be requested at least 10 days in advance of your regular cook date. There can be no guarantee of a rescheduled date before the end of the quarter.

PLEASE NOTE EACH OF THE ITEMS BELOW:

✓ Have the kitchen area clean and ready for use on the scheduled cook dates.

✓ Make arrangements for children and pets to be away from the kitchen area on scheduled cook dates.

✓ Leave containers ready for use in the agreed-upon area.

✓ Client signature:____ Date____

✓ Chef Signature:____Date____

Client Follow-Up

As mentioned earlier in this chapter, follow-up is a critical part of the service cycle. It enables you to deliver superior customer service and differentiates the personal chef business from many other foodservice businesses. Wait only a couple of days after you've cooked for a client and then call to follow up on how your client enjoyed

> Quality is never an accident; it is always the result of intelligent effort.
>
> —John Ruskin (1819-1900), poet and author

the food. You may even want to pick a day of the week to make all your follow-up calls to all the clients you've served most recently. You can tell clients in advance, "I'll be calling you Sunday evening."

QUESTIONS TO ASK

- Did you enjoy the service?

- What did you like best?

- Did you have any problem reheating the dinners?

- How many dinners have you had? (Have the client's file in front of you for reference).

- Do you want to continue the service on a regular basis?

- It is best to schedule a regular cooking day every two, three, four, or six weeks. What would you like to try?

- Whom do you know who would enjoy the service? (Describe your referral program—for example, "I offer 10 percent off a regular service for every referral.")

Follow-up is essential to establish repeat clients. Do it, and you will reap the benefits. If you are nervous about calling (due to fear of rejection), find a call buddy—someone you call *before* you make the follow-up calls for encouragement and *after* to report your success. Accountability and support are amazing and wonderful!

Conclusion

The personal chef business is a service business offering clients the ability to enjoy healthy and wonderful foods in their own home. What differentiates the personal chef from a restaurant is not only the service setting but also the level of service and customization offered by the personal chef. As stated in the chapter, "good food will always be good food." Good food offered with outstanding service and follow-up makes for a great experience for your clients. It is this type of experience that creates repeat customers.

Just as good cooking requires a plan (mise en place), so does good service. The successful personal chef has a sales and service plan that reflects her business plan, vision statement, and mission statement. This plan should be under constant review and adjusted as needed.

Key Terms

Sales and Service Cycle
A feedback loop that ensures service improvement and reaction to clients' demands.

Sales and Service Plan
A method to ensure proper service as part of the sales cycle.

Initial Contact
A potential client's first contact with your business.

Response
Your follow-up generated by a potential client.

Potential Client
A person who expresses interest in the services of a personal chef.

Assessment Meeting
An interview between a personal chef and a client to define the client's likes, dislikes, dietary re-

quirements, preferred frequency of service, and method of payment.

Telephone Sales Presentation

A sales tool used in which the goal is to inform, guide, and sell the services of a personal chef to an initial contact.

Closing the Deal

Ending the conversation or meeting with the desired result: making a sale.

Potential Client Assessment Process

The interview a personal chef conducts with a potential client to discover the scope of services desired.

Customized Program

The personal chef's complete menu cycle that fits the needs of a particular client.

Service Agreement

A nonbinding agreement that outlines the services to be provided, the method of payment, and the responsibilities of both the personal chef and the client.

Private Chef

An employee employed by one individual or a family on a full-time basis who often lives in with one family and prepares up to 3 meals per day.

Personal Chef

A small business owner who serves several clients, usually one per day, and provides multiple meals that are customized for each client.

Flat Fee

A method of pricing that includes all costs except for the food storage containers.

Professional Service Plus Cost of Food

A method of pricing that sets a fee for services to which the cost of food is added.

Cost per Entrée

A method of pricing similar to an à la carte menu.

Matrix Format

A check-off menu where a client chooses entrées from different columns.

Customization

The ability of the personal chef to create menus and foods that meet the individual tastes and dietary requirements of each client.

Entrée Suggestion List

The personal chef's list of entrées that fit the profile for a particular client.

Review Questions

True / False

1. A sales cycle and a service cycle are the same thing.

2. The sales cycle and the service cycle are a loop in that there is an evaluation process that regenerates the cycle continuously.

3. You are providing a response as a personal chef when you contact a potential client who has contacted you.

4. First impressions mean little for the personal chef.

5. It is a good idea when responding by e-mail or mail to include a business card.

6. Most of the time, a telephone sales presentation is all you need to book a client.

7. The purpose of a telephone sales presentation is to arrange for a potential client assessment meeting.

8. A potential client is one who is interested in the services of a personal chef but has not yet committed to employing those services.

9. One of the unique components of the personal chef business is the ability to customize a menu to match the requirements of the client.

10. A client assessment plays a critical part in identifying the needs, likes, and dislikes of a client.

11. A flat fee is the only method of pricing personal chefs use.

12. A flat fee ensures the same level of profit from each client no matter what he chooses to include on his menu.

13. Your locale has little to do with the pricing structure a personal chef provides you.

14. Because a personal chef customizes the client's entrées and sides so well, there is no need for a menu to present to potential clients.

15. The service agreement is a legal and binding contract between you and the client.

1. Which is not part of the sales/service cycle?

    a. Client assessment

    b. Service agreement

    c. Closing

    d. Projected profit

2. A response to a potential client's request involves

    a. Salesmanship, guidance, and profit projections

    b. Salesmanship, information, and a discussion of food safety

    c. Information, guidance, and profit projections

    d. Salesmanship, guidance, and information

3. A potential client is one who has

    a. Responded in some way to your marketing.

    b. Indicated an interest in the services provided.

    c. Is the same as a current client, except no cook date has been established.

    d. A and B are correct.

4. When responding to a phone call, you should try to

    a. Sell the client, sight unseen.

    b. Work the conversation into a telephone sales presentation.

    c. Tell the client how wonderful your food is.

    d. Respond by mail only.

5. During the potential client assessment meeting, you will

    a. Assess your client's needs, likes, and dislikes.

    b. Meet the client's children and pets.

    c. Point out repairs needed in the client's kitchen.

    d. Bring samples of entrées and sides for the client to try.

6. A customized cooking program for each client starts with

    a. Looking through her cooler and freezer.

    b. Gathering general information from her.

    c. Gathering specific information from her.

    d. Having her meet with health professionals to determine her dietary needs.

7. A flat fee includes

    a. All costs associated with a cooking session, such as containers, food, and professional services.

    b. All costs associated with a cooking session, such as food, professional services, planning, and shopping.

    c. Only the cost of food; professional services are added separately.

    d. The cost of all the entrées cooked during a cooking session.

8. A fee for professional service plus cost of food tends to

    a. Stay the same week to week.

    b. Change as the menu changes.

    c. Provide the personal chef with a changing level of profit depending on the cost of food.

    d. A and C are correct.

9. During the client assessment process, you should determine
   a. What type of food storage containers to use
   b. What type of wines will be served with the meal
   c. How much food you are going to buy
   d. The time of day for the clients to have dinner

10. A matrix style menu allows the client
    a. To see the full range of styles and types of entrées you offer.
    b. To check off entrées and side dishes he would enjoy.
    c. To write in his own choices.
    d. To know the price ahead of time using the professional service plus cost of food pricing strategy.

11. A good service agreement outlines
    a. The personal chef's responsibilities
    b. Method of payment
    c. The client's responsibilities
    d. All of the above

12. Client follow-up should
    a. Be done a week or two after the cook date.
    b. Only point out the foods the clients really enjoyed.
    c. Be done two or three days after the cook date.
    d. Be done only when re-booking a client.

Discussion Questions & Activities

1. Within a group, create several scenarios for a call to a potential client. Scenarios may include clients who are concerned with price only, clients who want specific food types, and clients with health concerns. Respond to each client and record the responses for evaluation.

2. Evaluate your home kitchen from the viewpoint of a personal chef. Does it have adequate counter space? Is the stove and all its burners working? Does the cooler or freezer have enough storage space? Do the same at a friend's or family member's house and compare the differences between the kitchens.

3. Create a menu for a client focusing on a five-day cycle with a wide variety of flavors, colors, and textures. Have others evaluate the menu for variety.

4. Go to www.personalchef.com. Select an area with enough personal chef businesses to compare the methods of pricing used. Prices are usually shown on the personal chef's home page. Are there trends in the pricing structures? If so, please explain.

From the Field

Chef Javier Fuertes, *TheDinnerMaker*, and Chef Meredith Erickson, *Whisk for Hire*

DESIGNING YOUR MENU

In 2000, Chef Javier graduated with honors from Johnson and Wales University with a degree in culinary arts. Before attending culinary school he was a software engineer for a small firm in Cambridge, Massachusetts, where an inner calling drove him to explore his passion for cooking. Upon graduating from Johnson and Wales, he cooked in the Boston area for some of the finer restaurants. Several years ago, however, he realized that the restaurant life style was too hard on his fam-

From the Field...continued

ily life, and so he decided to become a personal chef. He developed a menu featuring global fusion cuisine, with items such as Thai-inspired pork tenderloin, beef satay, Jamaican jerk chicken, curries, pastas, and upscale traditional entrées such as maple thyme glazed salmon.

His customers can choose anything from his menu, which he then customizes based on the individual food profile. "If I am using squash in a recipe and they don't care for squash, I will substitute something for it," he says. "If a customer is watching his fat intake and my recipe calls for heavy cream, again I would substitute for the cream to meet the customer's needs.

"I customize my menu per customer. I have a different approach; I know that some personal chefs build a menu per client, with each client having separate recipes. I just found that too time-consuming, so I customize my own menu for each client."

Prices are adjusted for special diets or menus that require special attention or increases research. He is currently working with a family of vegetarians who have restrictive dietary food profiles, which is taking extra time and research. Their prices will reflect the extra time he spends researching their food choices.

"I had a client who wanted to follow the Pritikin diet. After doing the research on the diet I discovered the client was already buying the foods from the Pritikin Longevity Center and getting the real deal from them. I told him it was going to cost him a lot more for me to cook it and that is was in his best interest to keep buying from Pritikin. I may have talked myself out of a job, but at the same time his wife was interested in home-cooked meals, and now I have them as clients."

Chef Javier's most enjoyable clients are those who ask him to choose their menu for them. "Those are the fun ones. I get to play with their menu items, and they love it. The more open-minded the client is the more fun I have." On follow-ups Chef Javier adjusts menus to meet clients' individual tastes. "I always tell them it takes a few cook dates to nail down their palate; I am always looking for feedback."

Chef Javier has enjoyed a successful career as a personal chef. He cooks four days a week and has time to enjoy his family. At the time of this interview he was considering methods of expanding his business and how to get to the next level.

In contrast to Chef Javier's approach is Chef Meredith Erickson of Whisk for Hire. Chef Meredith believes her business is "mostly about service, not just food—but it's got to be good food," she adds. "I work at understanding what the clients want and cooking what they want. Some chefs cannot bring themselves to make normal foods; some would rather die than to serve a porcupine stew." She adds, "Find your target; your ability to listen and communicate is just as important as your cooking and business skills."

Here are examples of two personal chefs, both successful, with two different approaches toward menu development. Chef Javier uses a more upscale restaurant menu-style approach, while Chef Meredith customizes each of her clients' menus. Both methods work.

Discussion Questions

1. Chef Javier presents a menu to a client and makes minor adjustments to the recipes to fit the taste profile of the customer. Chef Meredith takes a more customized approach by cooking what the client wants, "from porcupine stew to beef tenderloin." Both chefs are successful personal chefs. Contrast and compare these two approaches to menu development. Why would one or the other work for you? Which approach would you choose.

2. Chef Javier was willing to "talk himself out of a job" for the good of the customer. This is an excellent example of putting the customer first. How would this benefit a personal chef in the long run even though he may lose a client

CUSTOMER SERVICE

Great services are not canceled by one act or by one single error.
—Benjamin Disraeli, author and England's prime minister, 1837-1841

Introduction

As we emphasize throughout this text, the personal chef business is about service. Think for a moment: What is the difference between good and bad service? Is good service just something that happens if we are lucky, or is it planned? We all know bad service. The restaurant server who forgets the ketchup you asked for, the cable guy who never shows up, and the "customer service" representative who puts you on hold for hours are all delivering bad service. We also have experienced good service. The restaurant server who consistently keeps the water glass filled, the airline that gives you an enjoyable and safe flight, and the representative from a credit card company who is actually responsive to your questions and concerned about your situation are all delivering good service.

This chapter focuses on how to ensure you deliver good customer service as part of your business plan. Many cooks and chefs create wonderful foods that look beautiful and taste delicious. Successful personal chefs combine their cooking talents and good service to create an experience their clients want to revisit many times.

Learning Outcomes

After reading this chapter, you will be able to

✑ Identify the elements of good customer service.

✑ Establish the process for a customer service feedback loop.

✑ Determine the difference between being reactive and proactive with respect to customer service.

✑ Define the hospitality attitude.

✑ Identify how quality of customer service affects a business's profitable sales volume.

✎ Identify the key elements of an assessment plan.

✎ Formulate an assessment plan for a personal chef business.

✎ Understand the importance of menu customization in the personal chef business.

✎ Plan an assessment meeting.

✎ Define the function of follow-up as it relates to customer service.

Key Terms

Proactive	Feedback	Hospitality Attitude
Adjustment	Action Loop	Assessment
Profitable Sales Volume	Maximizing Sales Volume	Assessment Form
Customization	Assessment Process	Evaluation
Taste Profile	Evaluation	

Customer Service

Do you walk the walk

or just talk the talk?

—Universal question in business

What is good customer service? Is it reacting to situations to please your paying clients or changing or correcting services on the fly, or is good customer service planned for and part of a system? Just as the professional personal chef does mise en place before cooking at a client's home, she also plans for good customer service. Customer service is a concept demonstrated in many ways to apply to specific situations. As the owner, it is your responsibility to establish what you feel constitutes good customer service in your personal chef business. Keep these universal truths in mind as you define what represents customer service for your business:

1. Customer service is something that a successful business does not take lightly. It plays a large role in the success of a business, and a plan must be in place to enable a business to provide good customer service. Chapter 4 of this text dealt with writing a business plan and a vision statement and mission statement for a company. As you prepare these business tools, it is important for you to consider how your business will conduct its customer service and what you plan to offer your customers to ensure good customer service. Remember, customer service is not a single act or idea; it is a concept that an organization must live up to.

**Exhibit 10.1
Creating your Customer
Service Plan**

Mission Statement ⟍
Vision Statement ⟶ Customer Service
Business Plan ⟋

2. Customer service should be proactive in nature. It is important to keep this in mind as you determine what actions will signify good customer service for your personal chef business. **Proactive** refers to your ability to anticipate a customer's unique needs and to address them even before the customer realizes them and expresses them to you. You anticipate and address clients' needs before they become problems.

3. Customer service is not about a quick fix to help deal with the complaining customer. Many times we realize good customer service has been delivered only after a problem we complained about has been rectified.

4. Customer service requires excellent communication. For the personal chef, this communication is the dialog between you and your clients as you establish your business relationship—that is from the assessment meeting to determining the menu. There should also be open communication throughout the duration of this business relationship to ensure your client's consistent satisfaction with your services.

5. Customer service requires continuous **feedback, evaluation,** and **adjustment**. In order for feedback to be meaningful, it should be timely, frank, and honest. The feedback you receive from your clients concerning one quality of your food and service is part of an **action loop** in which problems are identified, solutions are evaluated, and adjustments or modifications are made to the service or product to meet the needs of a client.

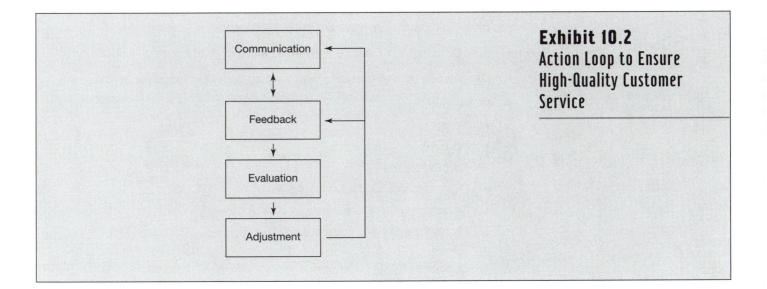

Exhibit 10.2
Action Loop to Ensure High-Quality Customer Service

6. Customer service must be timely.

7. Customer service creates customer loyalty and long-term customer retention.

As you develop your customer service plan, remember that service is based on meeting and exceeding a customer's set of wants and needs. In the foodservice business, many times this goal is referred to as the **hospitality attitude**. As you begin your career as a personal chef, you will be serving people in different settings. The act of serving is mechanical in nature. The attitude you possess as you provide this service helps differentiate you from those personal chefs still looking for customers.

Of course, even with the best planning and work to maintain the hospitality attitude, it is simply not possible to anticipate every customer's gripes and complaints before they happen. It is important that you always address customer complaints quickly and handle them effectively. Remember, clients should be treated with respect. Stay composed, communicate, listen closely, and then react. Ask your client for the same in return and work together to solve the problem. Your client must provide adequate information in order for you to evaluate and to react to the problem at hand. Two-way communication is essential to solving customer's complaints.

Firing a Client

Even with the best plans and the greatest hospitality attitude, you will encounter clients who are impossible to please. These people may complain just to hear themselves talk or to see what they can get out of a service provider, or they may require services you are unable to offer. Sometimes solving a customer problem may require so much time or cost it might not be worth it, especially if it takes away from time spent with your other customers.

Consider this client's requirements:

- Mother: On a diet and wants low-fat entrées, fresh vegetables, and low carbohydrates.

- Dad: Eats almost anything but really likes beef.

- Son: Does not eat a single vegetable; wants only Mexican or Italian foods.

- Daughter: A quasi-vegetarian who eats an occasional chicken breast.

- Other limitations:
  - No pork
  - No beef, per Mother
  - No cold salads
  - Low salt; Dad has high blood pressure
  - No soup-style entrées, such as chili or stews
  - Microwave-friendly foods only

How does a personal chef meet each family member's food preferences and still remain profitable? This may be a no-win situation. The food you prepare may please the mother, who arranges and pays for the service, but the other members of the family may be disappointed. It is extremely difficult to maintain profitability while trying to meet so many needs. Recall the discussion of **profitable sales volume** in which sales create a larger percentage of profit than the norm, versus **maximizing sales volume** by increasing sales without regard to profit from chapter 8.

If the family outlined above is not willing to pay extra for the extraordinary planning and cooking time necessary to meet all of their requirements, it might be better to focus on replacing this client with a more profitable one with fewer requirements. This is a difficult decision for a small business owner to make, and you should do so only after serious consideration. If you do decide to stop servicing a particular client, it is your responsibility to communicate the reason in a fair, honest, and respectful

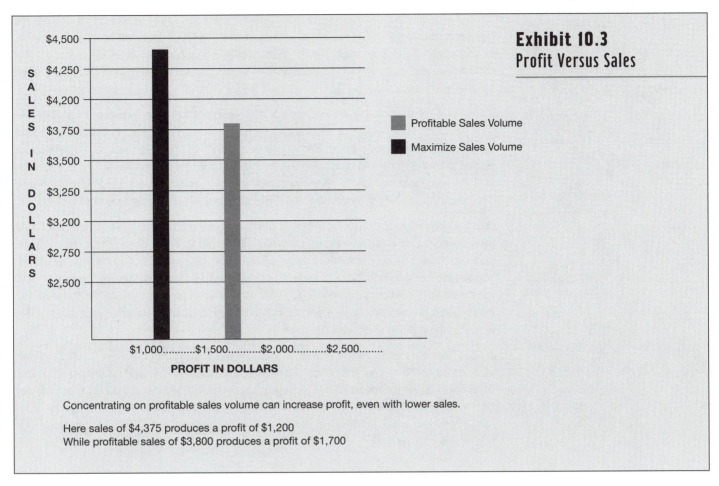

Exhibit 10.3
Profit Versus Sales

SALES IN DOLLARS

- $4,500
- $4,250
- $4,200
- $3,750
- $3,500
- $3,250
- $3,200
- $2,750
- $2,500

Profitable Sales Volume
Maximize Sales Volume

$1,000..........$1,500..........$2,000..........$2,500........

PROFIT IN DOLLARS

Concentrating on profitable sales volume can increase profit, even with lower sales.

Here sales of $4,375 produces a profit of $1,200
While profitable sales of $3,800 produces a profit of $1,700

manner. It is important that you make an effort to minimize the inconvenience and nonprofitablility that results from the family's prescriptive and diverse dining needs.

If you leave one of your clients with a negative or bad feeling, this could lead to negative word-of-mouth promotion, which could discourage potential clients. Leaving a client should be a last resort, and it must be done in a tactful way. Suggestions include explaining your decision to the client and establishing a cut off date where services will stop. This allows the client to find another personal chef if desired or make other arrangements to suit their needs. You may wish to mention that you will make an effort to locate another personal chef for them.

Assessment and Customization

After your initial contact with a potential client, the next step is the assessment of his dietary likes and dislikes. As outlined in chapter 9, the assessment process is absolutely critical to establishing a long-term relationship with a client. First impressions important when meeting a new client, and first impressions of your food can be even more important. You want that first meal to be just right. Actually, you want every meal to be just right, but the first meal should be a little special, as it is your chance to make a first impression with your food.

The **assessment process** is your chance to gather the knowledge needed to customize a menu and to select meals that meet your client's choice of palate and dietary needs. A restaurant simply cannot do this.

Putting the adventure

in front of them.

—**Chef Carol Borchardt,**
A Thought for Food

Each personal chef performs the assessment differently. Do your homework before going on your initial visit. Is the potential client the person you will be speaking with, or will other family members be there as well? Is a son arranging for service for his senior parents? Remember, what he wants for his parents may not be what they want for themselves!

Have your client complete and return your assessment form via e-mail or snail mail before your first meeting. This allows you to review food preferences and to formulate menu suggestions in advance. Some personal chefs bring a sampling of appetizers or desserts to the initial meeting with a new client, while others prefer not to do so. The professional personal chefs interviewed for this text report that providing samples to potential clients during the assessment meeting has yielded only marginal results.

Bring a presentation folder containing copies of referral letters from previous clients for whom you've cooked, copies of press clippings, several of your business cards, and brochures as well as information about your personal chef business, such as, suggested menus, prices, your policy, a description of the services you provide, and your mission or vision statements for your business. You want the client to have this information on hand to pass along to other potential customers who your client feels would benefit from your service.

In the *From the Field* section of this chapter, you will see Chef Carol Borchardt, owner of a *Thought For Food* used the detailed forms created by the American Personal Chef Institute as the base of her assessment program and personalized them for her own use. Many personal chefs personalize forms based on original material from APCI. You will want to develop a final representation of your personal assessment process forms as well.

MEETING FACE TO FACE

The initial face-to-face meeting with your client has six purposes:

1. To review the assessment form. This is the time to clarify your client's answers to the questions posed on the assessment form.

2. To review the kitchen. Some client's kitchens will feature state-of-the-art industrial gas ranges, while others' have stoves with only three working electric burners and a noncalibrated oven. Review storage areas, pantries, and cooler and freezer space with the client.

3. To present menu options to the client based on the information provided on the assessment form. Even if the client wants to customize every choice, this step provides you with valuable feedback. Eventually the client will become accustomed to using your service, and you will be able to improve your degree of **customization**.

4. To explain your fees to the client. Many potential clients express surprise when hearing the fees for a personal chef service for the first time. Generally they are comparing your fees to what they would spend in a restaurant, and they think (mistakenly) that your fees involve the cost of food only. Of course, when you are highlighting the features and benefits of using your personal chef service, you should gently enlighten your clients about just what you provide:

    -   Conduct an **assessment process** interview to determine what and how your client likes to eat, whether or not he has allergies or sensitivities or just doesn't like some foods, and whether or not medical parameters call for special attention.

- Customize an appropriate program based on the information the client provides on his **assessment form**.
- Conduct whatever research is necessary to accommodate each client's wants and needs.
- Plan menus of interest that feature a wide range of tastes and textures using only the freshest ingredients selected at the peak of season or quality.
- Shop for all ingredients at the sources you deem appropriate to provide top quality and freshness.
- Transport your mobile kitchen containing cookware, utensils, containers, etc., along with the client's groceries, to the client's home.
- Prepare the client's meals in the safety of his own kitchen while practicing food safety techniques and standards.
- Package each meal as requested by the client, then clearly label each container.
- Supply simple, understandable heating instructions for each meal.
- Leave the client's kitchen in a clean and orderly state at the end of your cook day.

5. To establish a cooking date and review and sign the service agreement. As discussed in chapter 9 the service agreement is a nonbinding agreement that outlines the responsibilities of both the personal chef and the client.

6. To collect the appropriate fees for your first cooking date, as stated in the service agreement.

THE FOLLOW-UP PROCESS

As discussed earlier in this chapter, providing customer service is a proactive process rather than a reactive one. The follow-up process (chapter 9) that occurs shortly after a cooking session is part of the proactive planning to ensure you are providing good customer service to your clients. This is your opportunity to gather additional information leading to even greater ability to customize future menus for the client.

The follow-up process can be a rewarding experience for the personal chef. We all like to hear compliments about the wonderful food we prepared, but we should be more interested in the foods the client did not enjoy. While it is sometimes hard to hear a client say the pot roast did not meet her expectations, even though other clients have raved about it, it is important for the personal chef to be aware of a client's dissatisfaction with a particular meal or service in order to prevent it from happening again. Remember, you are dealing with individual tastes. Your clients have the right to dislike something you have prepared or a service you have provided even though others love it.

Hearing what the client liked and did not like is the most important feedback you will receive. It will help you ensure your clients are completely satisfied with the services you provide going from this point forward in your partnership with them. The **feedback** clients provide during the follow-up process helps you thoughtfully evaluate the options you offer in an effort to make the adjustments that will keep your clients happy and satisfied with your services. This follow-up process completes the customer service loop which then repeats itself continuously.

> You have to have confidence in your ability, and then be tough enough to follow through.
>
> —Rosalynn Carter, First Lady of the United States, 1977-1981

Conclusion

Good customer service does not just happen. It is planned, anticipated, evaluated, and adjusted continuously. Customer service is the backbone of the personal chef industry, and maintaining good customer service is one of the keys to the success of your business. A personal chef's ability to customize a menu that appeals to a specific **taste profile** and meets dietary requirements makes the industry uniquely service-oriented.

To ensure good customer service, you must recognize your own abilities and limitations. Do not promise the moon unless you can deliver. Delivering service starts when you contact potential clients to explore exactly what they are looking for. You are then able to develop a customized menu program during the assessment process and to fine-tune the program during the follow-up phase to ensure your client's satisfaction with your services. The customer service loop repeats as you complete each cooking date with your client. The goal of outstanding customer service is to create loyal customers who not only become long-term clients but also refer their friends and family members to you, expanding your pool of clients.

Key Terms

Proactive
Anticipating and addressing a need before it becomes a problem.

Feedback
Information provided by a client about the results and quality of a service or product.

Evaluation
The act of judging the results or value of a service, product, or person.

Adjustment
A modification or change made to a service or product to meet the needs of a client.

Action Loop
The ongoing process of receiving feedback, evaluating it, and ad-justing the services provided in order to improve a product or service.

Hospitality Attitude
A state of mind or feeling about serving the needs and requirements of customers in the hospitality industry.

Profitable Sales Volume
Sales that create a larger percentage of profit than the norm.

Maximizing Sales Volume
The act of increasing sales without regard to profit, which will generally be lower than the norm.

Assessment
The gathering of information in order to customize a menu plan and ensure a smooth business transaction.

Customization
The act of changing or creating new menu items to meet the flavor profile and dietary requirements of a particular client.

Assessment Process
Gathering information from a potential client before a cooking date in order to prepare a specific meal plan.

Assessment Form
A form used during the assessment process that poses key questions to the client regarding his dietary needs, and preferred food styles. A kitchen assessment is also included.

Taste Profile
The grouping of flavors and textures of food that a particular client enjoys or dislikes.

Review Questions

True / False

1. Because each customer requires a unique service, customer service cannot be planned but rather is an ever-evolving process.

2. The actions and practices you feel embody customer service come from your vision statement, mission statement, and business plan.

3. Customer service relates only to your ability to react to a customer's complaint.

4. Customer service should be constantly evaluated and changed as needed.

5. In certain cases, "firing a customer" may be best for both the service provider and the customer.

6. The assessment process begins the personal chef's customization service.

7. The ability to customize food for a client is a major selling point for the personal chef.

8. The assessment process deals only with the client's likes and dislikes regarding food.

9. As a personal chef, it is wise to review the client's kitchen during your first assessment meeting.

10. Follow-up includes listening to your client's comments about your food and service.

Multiple Choice

1. In the personal chef industry, the concept of customer service may be defined as:
   a. Reacting to the needs and desire of the customers to solve unforeseen problems.
   b. Evaluating services and products and adjusting them as needed to meet the needs of future and current clients.
   c. Serving good food that clients really enjoy.
   d. Picking up a few extra items at the store per the client's request.

2. Which is not true about good customer service?
   a. It is planned for.
   b. It is proactive.
   c. It is reactive.
   d. It requires excellent communication.

3. An action loop is made of
   a. Feedback, adjustment, and change
   b. Adjustment and communication
   c. Feedback, change, and communication
   d. Feedback, evaluation, and adjustment

4. The concept of profitable sales volume suggests it may be acceptable in specific cases to
   a. Fire a customer.
   b. Raise prices across the board.
   c. Take any business with no concern for profit.
   d. Leave any customer who does not meet your profit profile.

5. The assessment process involves
   a. The exchange of information between the client and the personal chef.
   b. Creating a record of the client's likes and dislikes.
   c. Performing a review of the client's kitchen.
   d. All of the above.

6. Customizing a menu for a client

   a. Requires buying the most inexpensive foods for them to enjoy.
   b. Requires changing and researching menus and recipes to meet the flavor profile of a client.
   c. Requires changing the flavor profile of the client to meet your cooking style over time.
   d. Has little effect on the success of the personal chef with a particular client.

7. A taste profile includes

   a. The cost of foods the client enjoys
   b. The flavor of foods the client enjoys
   c. A listing of foods the client does not enjoy
   d. The flavor and texture of foods the client enjoys

8. Which of these tasks is not necessary before an initial assessment meeting takes place with a potential client?

   a. Review the potential client's completed assessment form.
   b. Prepare samples of entrées the client might enjoy.
   c. Prepare a presentation folder.
   d. Determine who will be present this initial meeting.

9. Included within the price of a personal chef's service are such items as

   a. Research, shopping, planning, and food preparation
   b. Cost of storage containers
   c. Separate cost of reusable items
   d. Cost of food only

10. During the follow-up process, the personal chef

   a. Learns how much the clients enjoyed the food prepared by the personal chef.
   b. Determines if he should charge the client more for the next cook date.
   c. Creates an action plan to improve or adjust any service or product on which the client has commented negatively.
   d. Allows the client to vent his complaints about the services provided with no adjustment to that service or products.

Discussion Questions & Activities

1. Have a group discussion with other students about what customer service means to you. Compare your thoughts with those of others and point out the differences and similarities. Use examples to define good customer service. Define poor customer service using examples.

2. Write a customer service plan for your personal chef business. Outline what you feel is important to address in terms of the services you provide based on your business plan, mission statement, and vision statement.

3. You have a client who always complains. No matter how hard you try, nothing is right for this client. She continues to use your service but always wants something free as compensation for her complaints. Due to the style of foods she enjoys, she has been a profitable client, but you are getting tried of the complaints. Role play with fellow students to try to work through this situation and identify solutions so you can maintain the business relationship.

From the Field

Chef Carol Borchardt, _A Thought for Food_

CLIENT ASSESSMENT

At A Thought for Food, Chef Carol Borchardt's personal chef service, she begins her assessment process by setting up a non-obligation meeting of a potential client. She sends the client the forms in advance, allowing him time to work through the questions and reduces the amount of time Chef Carol spends at the home during the assessment meeting. Before the meeting, she directs the client to her company's website, where he can review the services, costs, and menu selections she provides, which again saves time for both the client and Chef Carol.

Most of the important questions on Chef Carol's assessment form focus on the food styles that appeal to her clients. She offers four food styles for her clients to choose from:

1. Simple foods and comfort foods
2. Gourmet, upscale foods
3. Spicy, adventurous foods
4. Health-conscious foods

When a potential client selects one of these styles, Chef Carol is able to focus on the food suggestions she makes at the assessment meeting. She likes first-time clients to make selections from her website menu. This helps her define their taste profile. "There is nothing worse than having someone say "Make whatever you want" for the first cook date, and then they come back and say, "No, that's not what I am looking for." You make what you think is the right food and then you feel terrible if the meal does not meet the client's expectations," she states.

Some people ask Chef Carol to make all the selections for the menu. When this occurs, she relies on the information provided by her assessment of the client. Others have her select a menu and then approve via e-mail. At times, Chef Carol presents an expanded list of possible menu items from which the client can choose. She may even present some clients with an index of entrées—over four hundred possible choices. She has had clients e-mail her recipes, which she includes in their menu plan, even if the request is a little bit off the wall. She recently was asked by a client to make a root beer cake as a special surprise for her husband. Of course, as a service provider who prides herself on good customer service, she made her first root beer cake after some recipe research.

Some clients are not as adventurous as others. They want the same thing time after time. For these clients, Chef Carol makes a few suggestions based on their taste profile, and occasionally they agree to try a different meal. Her goal is to keep the menu interesting by continually offering new options to her clients. "This will keep them interested and keep their taste buds happy," she states.

Chef Carol sees her assessment form as the key to her success. Her clients' completed assessment forms enable her to customize foods to suit their palate. She has earned the loyalty of customers by catering to their individual needs and desires as she prepares their entrées—one of the keys to the success of any business.

Chef Carol also has potential clients complete an allergy and taste preference form. This yields specific information about foods to avoid when cooking for particular clients. Clients are able to identify foods they simply do not care for or foods that may cause an allergic reaction.

The following is Chef Carol's assessment form. As mentioned above, she sends this form to the client and evaluates it before the face-to-face assessment meeting in order to save time for both parties. As you read through the form, notice the non-food-related questions as well as the more obvious food issues.

Some personal chefs come prepared for a day in their client's kitchen only to find themselves wandering around with a flashlight when a circuit breaker blows. Imagine if you have a client in a high-rise apartment building and the elevator requires a key code to access a particular floor. The best-prepared cooking plans may come to a complete stop because you cannot gain access to the client's kitchen. The client's assessment form should provide the sort of information you need for each cook date to progress without obstacles.

A Thought for Food

Personal Chef Service

Dear Client: So I can better serve your needs, would you kindly provide me with the following information?

Name

_____

Address

_____

Phone – Daytime _____ *Evening* _____
Mobile _____

E-mail Address

_____

Children's Names and Ages (if living with you)

_____

_____

Other relatives living with you (such as a parent): _____

Service Requested   _____   *Weekly Super-Fresh Service*
                            _____   *Standard Freezer-Friendly Service*
                            _____   *Entrée Only*
                            _____   *Other* _____

Number of Entrées _____   *Number of Servings:* _____

Overall Diet by Choice   _____   *Includes Red Meat (Beef, Pork, etc.)*
                            _____   *Excludes Red Meat (Chicken, Fish, Vegetarian)*
                            _____   *Mostly Vegetarian (Includes Fish)*
                            _____   *Ovo-Lacto Vegetarian (Includes Dairy and Eggs)*
                            _____   *Vegan (No Dairy or Eggs Whatsoever)*
                            _____   *High Protein, Low Carbohydrate*
                            _____   *Weight Loss*
                            _____   *Other* _____

Dr.-Recommended Diet   _____   *Low/No Cholesterol, Low/No Fat*
                            _____   *Low/No Salt / Sodium*
                            _____   *Weight Loss (Specific Plan?* _____ *)*
                            _____   *Other* _____

If you do eat meat, poultry, etc., would you like an occasional vegetarian meal?

_____

Please specify any medical conditions you or a member of your family have where diet is a serious factor (for example, diabetes, heart disease or other heart condition, high blood pressure):

_____

_____

On a scale of 0 to 10, with 0 being absolutely none to 10 being no limit, please indicate where you or family members are on the scale for:

<u>Heat/Spiciness</u> – 0 to 3 is mild, 4 through 6 is a fair amount of heat, 7 through 10 is quite hot.

Name of Family Member

_____	0	1	2	3	4	5	6	7	8	9	10
_____	0	1	2	3	4	5	6	7	8	9	10
_____	0	1	2	3	4	5	6	7	8	9	10
_____	0	1	2	3	4	5	6	7	8	9	10

<u>Salt Level</u>

Name of Family Member

_____	0	1	2	3	4	5	6	7	8	9	10
_____	0	1	2	3	4	5	6	7	8	9	10
_____	0	1	2	3	4	5	6	7	8	9	10
_____	0	1	2	3	4	5	6	7	8	9	10

<u>Garlic Level</u>

Name of Family Member

_____	0	1	2	3	4	5	6	7	8	9	10
_____	0	1	2	3	4	5	6	7	8	9	10
_____	0	1	2	3	4	5	6	7	8	9	10
_____	0	1	2	3	4	5	6	7	8	9	10

Favorite Global Cuisines

_____   American / Regional (Southern, New Orleans, etc.)
_____   Caribbean / South American
_____   Indian
_____   Asian / Thai
_____   Mediterranean / European (Includes Italian, French
Greek, Spanish, German, etc.)
_____   Middle Eastern
_____   Moroccan / North African
_____   Southwestern / Mexican
_____   Other _____

Which of the following closest describes your food style? (Choose all that apply.)

Meat and Potatoes / Comfort Food (simple, classic)   _____

Gourmet (upscale)   _____

Spicy / Adventurous (no limits)   _____

Health Conscious (no special diet, but conscious of eating right)   _____

What are your favorite dishes and favorite comfort foods?

_____

What is your favorite fish / seafood?

_____

How do you prefer chicken?   _____ Dark Meat   _____ Off the Bone

_____ White Meat   _____ No Preference

How do you prefer potatoes?   _____ *Peeled*   _____ *No Preference*

                                        _____ *With Peel On*

Type of rice you prefer?   _____ *Brown*   _____ *White*

How well cooked do you like vegetables? _____

Beef? _____

What is your favorite cut of beef?

_____

May I use wine or other alcoholic beverages in cooking your selections? _____

Is there anything else I should know about your food preferences?

_____

Do you have any favorite recipes you no longer choose to prepare yourself that I can prepare or that I can modify for your health reasons?

_____

Would you like meals prepared for you to cook on your outdoor grill?

_____

Do you have a working meat thermometer?

_____

Menu selection process: _____ *Chef Chooses for Me – Surprise Me*

                                        _____ *Chef Chooses for Me – I Will Approve (Via E-Mail)*

                                        _____ *Chef Chooses for Me from Select List*

                                        _____ *I Want to Make All Selections*

How do you want your meals packaged?   _____ *Individually*

                                        _____ *For Two*

                                        _____ *Family Style*

How do you prefer to heat the food?   _____ *Microwave*

                                        _____ *Conventional Oven*

Cooking and Storage   _____ *Gas Cooktop* ____ *# of Burners*

                                        _____ *Electric Cooktop* ____ *# of Burners*

                                        _____ *Cooktop with Grill*

                                        _____ *Microwave Oven*

                                        _____ *Single Conventional Oven*

                                        _____ *Double Conventional Oven*

                                        _____ *Convection Oven*

                                        _____ *# of Freezers*

Does all cooking and storage equipment work properly?

_____

Please list any indoor pets, their names, and where they will be contained:

_____

Entry and security system instructions:

_____

Fuse or breaker box location:

_____

Location of heat and air conditioning controls:

_____

May I adjust these controls?

_____

How did you hear about my service?

_____

Thank you. I look forward to serving your culinary needs!

Allergy and Taste Preferences

Please circle any items you or a family member are allergic to, sensitive to, or do not care for the taste or texture of:

Vegetables

Artichoke	Asparagus	Bamboo Shoots	Beets	Belgian Endive
Bok Choy	Broccoli	Broccoli Rabe	Brussels Sprouts	Cabbage
Carrot	Cauliflower	Celery	Chayote	Corn
Cucumber	Daikon	Eggplant	Fennel	Garlic
Ginger	Green Beans (String)	Horseradish	Jerusalem Artichoke	Jícama
Kohlrabi	Leek	Mushroom	Okra	Onion
Parsnip	Peas	Pea Pods	Peppers (Hot)	Peppers (Sweet)
Potato	Pumpkin	Radish	Rhubarb	Rutabaga
Shallot	Squash (Spaghetti)	Squash (Winter)	Squash (Summer)	Sweet Potato
Tomatillo	Tomato	Turnip	Water Chestnut	Zucchini

Greens and Lettuces

Arugula	Collard	Endive	Kale	Lettuce
Mustard	Radicchio	Spinach	Swiss Chard	Watercress

Fruit

Avocado	Apple	Apricot	Banana	Blackberry
Blueberry	Cantaloupe	Cherry	Cranberry	Currants
Dates	Figs	Grapefruit	Grapes	Kiwi
Lemon	Lime	Mango	Orange	Papaya
Peach	Pear	Pineapple	Plum	Prunes
Raisins	Raspberry	Strawberry	Tangerine	Watermelon

(Continued)

Herbs and Seasonings				
Allspice	Anise	Basil	Cardamom	Caraway
Cilantro	Cinnamon	Cloves	Coriander	Cumin
Curry	Dill	Fennel	Fenugreek	Ginger
Marjoram	Mint	MSG	Mustard	Oregano
Paprika	Parsley	Pepper (Black)	Pepper (Cayenne)	Pepper (White)
Rosemary	Saffron	Sage	Savory	Sesame
Tarragon	Thyme	Vanilla		

Nuts and Seeds

Almond	Brazil	Cashew	Chestnut	Coconut
Hazel	Macadamia	Peanut	Pecan	Pine (Pignoli)
Pistachio	Pumpkin	Sesame	Sunflower	

Grains and Legumes

Barley	Beans (Dried)	Black-eyed Peas	Bulgur	Couscous
Lentils	Peas (Dried)	Quinoa	Soybeans	Wheatberries

Cheeses

Aged	Blue	Cottage	Feta	Goat

Miscellaneous

Buckwheat	Chocolate	Dairy / Lactose	Food Coloring	Iodine
Mayonnaise	Mustard	Olives / Pickles	Seafood / Shellfish	Wheat / Gluten
Dried Fruits (Raisins, etc.)	Alcohol			

Please list any others you can think of: _____

Discussion Questions

1. Using the above assessment form, interview a fellow student as a potential customer and complete the form. What changes would you make to the form? What, if any, important information is missing?

2. Using the completed assessment form, offer menu suggestions that fit the taste profile identified by your mock assessment.

A DAY IN THE LIFE
OF A PERSONAL CHEF

chapter
11

The kitchen can be a place of magic or a place of terror.
—Chef's saying

Introduction

As a personal chef, you control your own work schedule, cook for clients, and do the paperwork necessary for your business to continue functioning. The most enjoyable part of the personal chef business is probably going to the stove to cook for a client. The services you provide, the food you prepare, and the paperwork and planning you do are all part of your business. This chapter looks at a day in the life of a personal chef, focusing primarily on a cook session.

Learning Outcomes

After reading this chapter, you will be able to

✎ Identify the value of recipe testing when planning menus for your clients.

✎ Understand the importance of buying high-quality ingredients.

✎ Identify the purpose of the shopping form.

✎ Identify ways to set up mise en place in a client's kitchen most efficiently depending on the menu planned and the kitchen configuration.

✎ Apply the principle of mise en place to your cooking session to maximize your time in the kitchen.

✎ Explain proper cooking and freezing methods to your clients.

✎ Understand methods of handling and warming food items and provide clearly written instructions to your clients.

✎ Identify the cooking equipment needed for a specific cook session.

Key Terms

Grocery Shopping
 Form

Mirepoix

Condensation

Drip Loss

Freezer Burn

Handling Instructions

Mise en Place

Recipe Testing

It is important to do some recipe testing while you are setting up your personal chef business. Written recipes are important tools since they provide a way of applying basic techniques to specific ingredients, and help to provide consistency in the product you supply your clients.

Start cataloging your personal recipes for your personal chef clients. Offer your personal chef clients menus including recipes where your confidence is highest—you know, the dishes you prepare that your family, colleagues, and loved ones rave about. As you build your repertoire of recipes you should test them in several areas such as was it easy to find all of the required ingredients?, was the cooking time accurate?, did it store well?, and most important, did you like it/will your clients like it?

Remember, while you are in the recipe testing phase of your business, save your grocery receipts and write them off as a legitimate business expense in the area of Research and Development.

Grocery Shopping Tips

An herb is the friend of physicians and the praise of cooks.

—Charlemagne, A.D. **742-814**

Shopping wisely will help you succeed as a personal chef. Introduce yourself to the produce, meat, and seafood managers in the stores you will be using regularly and let them know you are a personal chef. Be prepared to explain your business to them and to emphasize the importance of the quality of the foods you are buying. Often, the fish and meat managers will order what you need if you tell them about forty-eight hours in advance.

You should also use a good local butcher shop for those cuts your grocery meat market does not provide. If you call ahead and tell them what you need, they will usually have it waiting for you. The quality of your meat, fish, and seafood dishes speaks volumes about your personal chef service, so you should not accept anything but the best.

Exhibit 11.1
Top 3 USDA Grade
Levels of Beef

USDA PRIME   USDA CHOICE   USDA SELECT

Doing research on your local specialty markets and making your own decisions should be fun. You may even receive referrals from some of your friends at the markets. Once you have decided where to shop for the best quality at the most reasonable prices, you can get started with your day.

An investment in canvas shopping bags will reduce the volume of plastic and paper bags you amass. Keep a supply of ingredients such as bulk seasonings, herbs, oils, vinegars, flour, beans, and canned goods like tomatoes, tomato paste, and defatted chicken broth on hand at all times. This will save you time and enable you to focus on fresh foods for your planned menus.

Use your clients' approved recipes when planning the menu for a particular cook session and complete a **grocery shopping form** or grocery list for a particular cook session, before you go to the market. The first page of the shopping form lists exactly what you need to buy that particular day. The second page indicates the ingredients you already have at your disposal.

When you begin your day, pack your vehicle with the kitchen equipment and the on-hand ingredients and seasonings needed. Once the packing is done, you are ready to leave for your shopping trip. If you are charging fee plus food (chapter 9), you will be stocking your client's pantry and working with the items you've purchased for your client. Usually, when you use a fee-plus-food client's kitchen for the first time, you will need to stock the pantry with the food staples you will be using.

Shop only for the ingredients called for on your shopping form at the grocery store, butcher shop, or seafood market. Always pack these perishables in a cold case.

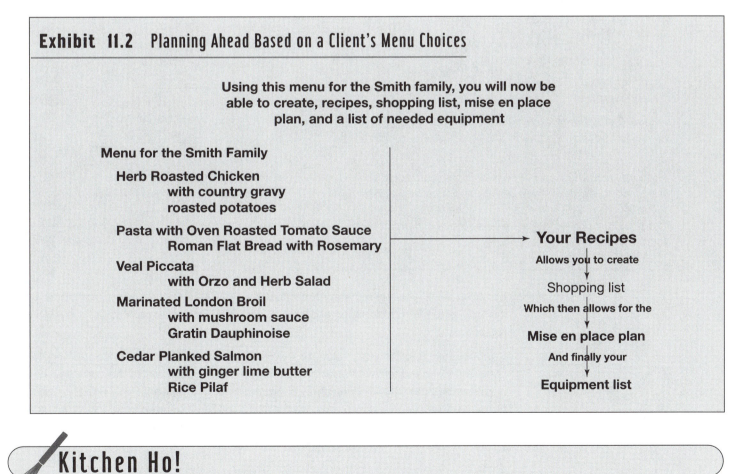

Exhibit 11.2 Planning Ahead Based on a Client's Menu Choices

Using this menu for the Smith family, you will now be able to create, recipes, shopping list, mise en place plan, and a list of needed equipment

Menu for the Smith Family

Herb Roasted Chicken
    with country gravy
    roasted potatoes

Pasta with Oven Roasted Tomato Sauce
    Roman Flat Bread with Rosemary

Veal Piccata
    with Orzo and Herb Salad

Marinated London Broil
    with mushroom sauce
    Gratin Dauphinoise

Cedar Planked Salmon
    with ginger lime butter
    Rice Pilaf

Your Recipes

Allows you to create

Shopping list

Which then allows for the

Mise en place plan

And finally your

Equipment list

Kitchen Ho!

Now that you have completed the shopping portion of your day, it is time for you to head to your client's kitchen, where the fun begins! Keep in mind that each kitchen,

Chef = any cook who

swears in French

—Henry Beard, founder, *National Lampoon*, and Roy McKie, illustrator

like each client, is different. That is why it is helpful to have your own familiar kitchen equipment with you so you can control your environment as much as possible.

When you reach the client's home, either ring the bell or use the key the client supplied. Once again, each client is different, and arrangements for entry on the day of the scheduled cook session must be made in advance and on a client-by-client basis. Once you have unloaded your equipment, take a moment to mentally organize how you will proceed. Put the perishable items in the refrigerator and begin to set up in the kitchen by placing all needed equipment on the counter. Place all of your on-hand pantry supplies in a box on the floor near you so they are readily accessible as you work. Put the container holding your pots and pans near the stove and the dry and fresh ingredients for the recipes elsewhere within your reach.

Based on the principle of **mise en place**, you should prioritize your recipes so you start with the entrées that take the most cooking time to prepare.

Exhibit 11.3 Preparing mise en place for a Cooking Session

Sautéed Veal Piccata
4 Servings

Veal scallops, 2 to 3 oz each	8 each
Seasoned flour	4 oz
Clarified butter	2 oz
Shallots, chopped	2 Tbsp
White wine, dry	4 oz
Lemon juice	2 oz
Brown stock	4 oz
Unsalted butter	1 oz
Lemon wedges	8 each

Pound the veal into uniform thin scallops. Dredge in seasoned flour and sauté in clarified butter until lightly brown.

Remove from the pan, add the shallots, and cook until translucent. Deglaze the pan with the wine and lemon juice. Add the stock and reduce by half. Mount with the unsalted butter. Adjust seasoning, and garnish with lemon wedges.

Mise en place would dictate

Food

Earlier in the cooking session

    you clarified butter
    you made brown stock
    you chopped shallots
    you pounded the veal

As you start to cook

    you have seasoned flour
    you have wine and lemon juice
    you have unsalted butter

Equipment

    A sauté pan
    A holding plate for the cooked veal
    A small bowl for the seasoned flour

For example, if you have a stew that must be simmered for two hours, start preparing this recipe first. Marinades and sauces also take priority over less time-intensive recipes.

You may also wish to chop, dice, or mince all of the **mirepoix**, or chopped vegetables, you will need for all of your day's recipes at the beginning of the cook session. If you write down the amount and configuration of the mirepoix you need for each recipe and prepare it accordingly, then all you will have to do is reach for it when it is needed. You may have three plates—one with 2 cups minced, another with 1 cup chopped, and the third with 2 cups diced mirepoix.

If you are preparing pasta or rice as side dishes, put them all on the stove first. This way, you can prepare other recipes while these dishes are boiling and you do not have to fight for room on the stove to prepare these side dishes later.

You will become experienced at multitasking as you cook in the kitchen over time. Initially, it is important not to panic about the number of food items being prepared at the same time and to pay attention to the recipe you are currently making. Learning to multitask requires a little practice; remember, you may have to adjust your cooking plan according to the client's kitchen. Use common cooking sense as you work, and finish dishes such as stews and braised items in the oven to free up stovetop space. Just a reminder: Taste each dish you are preparing so you can avert disaster by making adjustments, if necessary, as you prepare your entire planned menu.

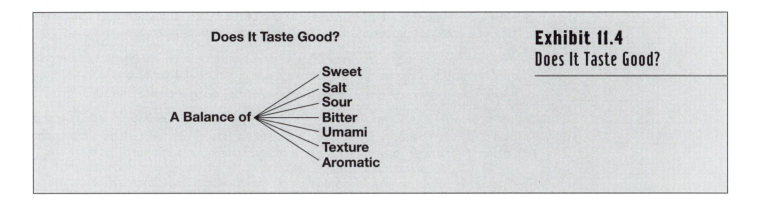

Does It Taste Good?

A Balance of
- Sweet
- Salt
- Sour
- Bitter
- Umami
- Texture
- Aromatic

Exhibit 11.4
Does It Taste Good?

In a perfect world, all recipes come out perfectly every time. However, in the real world, this is not always the case. If you realize a specific recipe has failed and cannot be redone that day, leave the client a note of apology with an I.O.U. for that recipe on another day. When you deliver the make-good recipe, leave a small gift (perhaps a bottle of wine or a dessert) and some fresh flowers. This is your way of saying "Thank you for being so understanding." It is crucial that this does not happen often with any one client. If it does occur repeatedly, your client will grow less and less understanding.

In order to have enough utensils and pans to prepare everything on your menu, you will have to wash dishes periodically. As you wash, review where you are in your day's plan. Doing dishes is a way to step back and take a deep breath. Do not forget to eat your lunch and drink fluids to maintain your strength. You do not want the client to come home to find you on the kitchen floor, limp from exhaustion!

When all of your entrées and side dishes are cooked and cooling (a small fan is helpful for this phase of the cooking process), it is time to package and label your day's work. You should consider using Rubbermaid and Tupperware containers, IVEX®, aluminum baking/broiler pans, and Ziploc® freezer bags for packaging the food. Make your own decision about which containers to use, but remember to choose containers that freeze well and are microwaveable. *Note*: IVEX® can go from freezer to microwave or oven.

You can use either commercial freezing labels or masking tape and an indelible felt-tipped marker to identify the food items in each container. Once again, it is your decision to make. Label each food container clearly so your client can see what it is, how many servings it provides, and the date it was prepared.

Leave a list of entrées you prepared during a particular cook session, along with handling and warming instructions for your client (see example). Attach this sheet to the freezer door with a magnetized business card for your personal chef service. This way, if your clients have questions while heating the food, your telephone number is right there on the card. It makes them feel secure and keeps your name in their mind.

Freezer Facts

As a personal chef, your primary concern is to find fresh, high-quality ingredients and to capture that freshness in the delicious meals you prepare for your clients. Because you are preparing entrées prior to their consumption, you must find a way to freeze them without compromising their quality.

When your client sits down to eat, she expects an excellent meal. Scallops should taste the same whether they just came out of the ocean or the freezer. The freezer is unbeatable for preserving food in a way that retains its original fresh flavor.

You will find that using the freezer as a basic kitchen tool, like a blender or a stockpot, can both preserve the perfect freshness of your ingredients and work to make meal preparation easier and less-time consuming for your clients.

Of course, if your client has a microwave oven, cooking foods from the freezer is even more convenient. Defrosting and heating frozen entrées is fast, simple, and clean. The freezer-to-microwave process is tailor-made for personal chefs.

Freezing 101

The freezer is only as good as the food you put into it. The first rule in freezing food is to buy fresh, high-quality food items. Using mediocre food items yields mediocre results.

Freezing food is not difficult, but some ways of freezing produce superior results. Here are general rules:

- **Chill first**. Make sure the food is cool before you freeze it. This allows it to freeze faster and reduces condensation and drip loss during defrosting. You may wish to carry and use a small fan to help cool cooked food. Cooling the foods first reduces the burden on the freezer, allowing for better freezing. Spread out the food as much as possible (half-sheet pans work well for this), as exposing surface area makes it cool quicker.

- **Condensation** is the moisture that collects on the surface of the food. If food is warm when you put it in the freezer, condensation occurs, and when you eventually defrost it, the excess water resulting from the condensation will make the food soggy and tasteless.

- **Drip loss** is the leakage of natural moisture that occurs when you defrost food. Water expands as it turns into ice, causing the food fibers to splinter. This is what causes a limp or soggy texture in defrosted food. However, if the food is chilled before freezing, the ice crystals that form will be smaller, causing less damage to fibers and therefore less drip loss. The result is better texture and flavor. Chill cooked foods uncovered, then cover and seal them before freezing to prevent another source of condensation.

- **Cool it**! Before you freeze cooked food, it is important to cool it quickly so bacteria do not grow. A slick way to cool large amounts of cooked food quickly is to place the containers of warm food in an ice bath. Simply fill your sink with ice, and then wedge the containers into the ice and stir the food occasionally. Stirring ensures the center of the food cools also.

- **Wrap well**. The goal is to isolate the food from the atmosphere of the freezer by sealing the wrapping tightly to keep as much air as possible from the container. Ordinary plastic wrap is too thin and can crack in the freezer. Use heavy-duty microwave plastic wrap and heavy-duty plastic freezer bags rather than the everyday kind. Freezer-safe plastic containers that can also be used safely in the microwave are another good choice. Seal the packages well, squeezing out as much air as possible, and label clearly.

- **For liquids and semi-liquid foods**: Use freezer jars or plastic containers. Remember, liquid expands by over 10 percent when it freezes, so leave up to 1 full inch of headroom when you are freezing soups, stews, or purees in containers. After the food is cooled, place a layer of plastic wrap directly on the surface and then put the top on the container. Food that has not been properly wrapped will suffer **freezer burn**, which means it may be dry, stringy, and have an off taste due to dehydration resulting from moisture loss when food is stored below freezing. Needless to say, your client will not be pleased if the entrées you've prepared have freezer burn.

A freezer enables you to preserve the freshness of the marketplace, prepare your own frozen "convenience" foods for your clients, and control the quality (the amount of fat, salt, and sugar) of your meals. Remember, it is best to defrost foods in the refrigerator or in the microwave oven. Most foods should be left in their freezer packaging while defrosting.

Handling and Warming Instructions

Your clients are adopting a lifestyle change and establishing new habits by employing you as their personal chef. They need to plan ahead and decide what they want for dinner each night after you leave them the prepared menu items. They can easily do this by referring to the **handling instructions** consisting of specific guidelines for storage, defrosting, and heating specific food items you supply for each entrée. Post the handling instructions on each client's freezer with your business card magnet. Your instructions should recommend defrosting overnight in the refrigerator, although it is acceptable to defrost in the microwave.

Handling instructions cover reheating as well as defrosting. List each entrée, describe it, and note whether it warms better in the microwave or the oven. Note that ovens and microwaves vary in power, and your clients may have to adjust warming times as a result. They will most likely have to experiment a bit before mastering the heating process for each entrée, but they tend to catch on quickly.

What garlic is to salad,

insanity is to art.

> —Augustus Saint-Gaudens,
> American sculptor, 1848-1907

SAMPLE HANDLING INSTRUCTIONS FOR A CLIENT

Personal Chef's Business Name

Handling Instructions for the Smiths

Date

For best results, all frozen entrées should be defrosted OVERNIGHT, in the refrigerator, before being heated and consumed.

BLACK BEAN SOUP: Heat in a saucepan on the stovetop at medium to low heat. Remember to stir. Serve with lime and salad with chopped egg and rolls.

CHICKEN ROTOLO: Place the frozen cheesecloth-wrapped rotolo in boiling water. Boil for 30 minutes and remove from the water. Unwrap the cheesecloth and let rest for several minutes before slicing. Pour the sauce over the slices and serve with tossed salad and rolls.

SCHEHERAZADE CASSEROLE: Bake, covered, at 375°F for about 20 minutes, then uncover and bake 25 minutes more with the oven turned down to 350°. Serve with rolls.

TURKEY BASIL MEATLOAF: Remove from the container, slice, place on microwave-safe plate, and heat 2 minutes, or place in a 325°F oven, covered, and bake 15 minutes. Serve with sauce, steamed or baked potatoes, and the green vegetable of your choice.

Shopping and Packing Tips

To avoid lugging cases and coolers that are heavier than necessary, pack only what you need rather than a whole bottle or container of each required ingredient. If your recipe calls for 1 cup red wine, pack only 1 cup in an appropriate-sized jar or container with a screw lid. For instance, you should use the small 6–8 (Styrofoam®) egg cartons rather than packing a whole dozen-sized container if you need eggs. Ziploc® type bags are great for transporting flour, rice, beans, and other dry ingredients. The bags take up very little room in your case.

Buy oils and vinegars in large sizes, but transfer measured amounts to smaller bottles and jars for transport in your dry pantry container. There is no need to carry your entire supply of staple ingredients with you each day. You are going to get plenty of exercise without lifting unnecessarily heavy containers.

Use your day's recipes to guide you in packing each day. Always pack based on your recipes! Pack only the pots, pans, roasting racks, and appliances called for in your day's recipes. This way, you will have everything you need.

EQUIPMENT LIST

Below is a guideline list of equipment. You know what you use and do not use, so you should add or delete items according to your cooking needs. Also, you may have many of these in your kitchen now, or you can check out the thrift stores for great deals on items you need to complete your collection.

- Set of pots and pans (the lighter, the easier to carry)
  - Sauce pots, assorted sizes
  - Medium-size fry pan
- Two flexible cutting boards
- Two or three plastic bowls in different sizes
- Salad spinner, food processor, and blender, if needed
- Splatter screen
- Pot holders, towels, rubber gloves

- Sponges, scrubbers, aprons, and dish soap
- First-aid items
- Heavy-duty foil and plastic wrap
- Ziploc® freezer bags and containers in assorted sizes
- Grater and strainer
- Measuring cups, 2 wet sets and 1 dry set
- Wire whisk
- Chef's knife plus medium and small knife, steel
- Spatulas and wooden spoons
- Large slotted spoons and serving spoons
- Ladle and potato masher
- Tongs and kitchen shears
- Mushroom and vegetable brush
- Hand juicer
- Manual can opener
- Garlic press and pastry brush
- Instant thermometer
- Vegetable peeler / zester
- Measuring spoons
- Graduated aluminum bowls
- Black felt Sharpie® pen
- Freezer labels or masking tape
- Matches and timer
- Baster
- Funnel
- Scale
- Wine corkscrew
- Shrimp deveiner
- Pastry bag with assorted tips
- Half-sheets for cooling food
- Small electric fan to cool food prior to freezing

ON-HAND PANTRY ITEMS

Your on-hand pantry supply of staple ingredients will grow as your client base grows. Remember to pack based on your recipes so you carry only what you need each day!

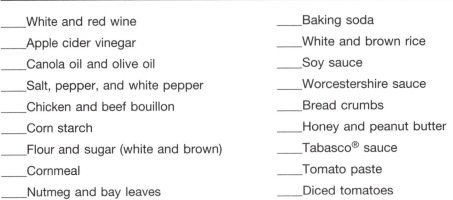

Suggestions

____White and red wine	____Baking soda
____Apple cider vinegar	____White and brown rice
____Canola oil and olive oil	____Soy sauce
____Salt, pepper, and white pepper	____Worcestershire sauce
____Chicken and beef bouillon	____Bread crumbs
____Corn starch	____Honey and peanut butter
____Flour and sugar (white and brown)	____Tabasco® sauce
____Cornmeal	____Tomato paste
____Nutmeg and bay leaves	____Diced tomatoes

To track the cost of your on-hand pantry items, write the cost on each package as you purchase it. For example, on a gallon of extra-virgin olive oil you might write $16.00 or 12.5 cents per fluid ounce at 128 fl oz (12.5¢/oz × 128 fl. oz = $16.00)

Conclusion

No two personal chefs are alike. From their cooking style to service methods, each is different, but certain tasks are universal regardless of work style. All personal chefs need to plan for their shopping, choose the equipment needed for each cooking session, and plan a mise en place list. Different clients require different resources for storing foods and use different equipment to heat their foods. You must be sure to customize the handling and heating instructions for each client.

Key Terms

Grocery Shopping Form
Your grocery list for a particular cooking session.

Mirepoix
A traditional French cooking term used for a mixture of chopped vegetables. In this text, it refers to any chopped vegetables used in mise en place.

Condensation
Formation of water droplets caused by cooling foods.

Drip Loss
Loss of natural moisture in frozen food when it is defrosted.

Freezer Burn
Dehydration of foods resulting from moisture loss when food is stored at temperatures below freezing.

Handling Instructions
Specific guidelines for the storage, defrosting, and heating of a spe-

cific food item written for a specific client.

Mise en Place
A traditional French cooking term used for all the preparation work necessary before the assembly of the final dish. May include both the food items and equipment necessary to produce the final dish.

Review Questions

True / False

1. For the personal chef, is it wise to buy the lowest cost and quality of protein items.

2. Client approved recipes are used to complete your grocery shopping form.

3. It is better to pack all of the equipment you might need during a particular day than to plan for equipment you will need for a scheduled cooking session.

4. The way you set up a client's kitchen determines your efficiency in it.

5. If a cooking session calls for a stewed item, it might be wise to cook it last because it takes too much room on the stovetop.

6. Any vegetables used in recipes should be cut separately for that recipe.

7. If you have a recipe that fails, it is best to try and recook it before the client sees it.

8. The best way to freeze an item is to wrap it and place it in the freezer while it is still hot.

9. Drip loss is the leakage of natural moisture from a food item as it defrosts.

10. Handling and warming instructions will be the same for all the foods your clients order.

Multiple Choice

1. The proper order for the top three grades of beef are
   a. Prime, select, choice
   b. Prime, good, choice
   c. Prime, choice, select
   d. Prime, choice, good

2. The grocery shopping form is generated from
   a. What is on sale that day
   b. Recipes to used in the cooking session
   c. What is fresh that day
   d. Your personal choice of foods you enjoy

3. When packing your cooking equipment
   a. Take extra equipment, as you never know what you will need.
   b. Take only equipment needed for the cooking session.
   c. Use the client's equipment as much as possible.
   d. Take equipment that is heavy and conducts heat well, such as cast iron.

4. Which sequence of tasks best reflects the principle of mise en place?
   a. Cut all mirepoix items, cook sauté items, marinade items, cook stews.
   b. Cook stews, cut all mirepiox items, cook sauté items, marinade items.
   c. Marinade items, cook stews, cut all mirepiox items, cook sauté items.
   d. Cut all mirepoix items, marinade items, cook stews, cook sauté items.

5. If a recipe fails, it is best to
   a. Leave a note explaining what happened and return with the entrée at a later date.
   b. Give credit on the client's invoice.
   c. Substitute the failed item with another.
   d. Try to fix the failed item as best as you can.

6. Because you are freezing foods for heating later, it is best to use
   a. The highest-quality food items
   b. Only foods that freeze well
   c. Food bought from the store in a frozen state
   d. None of the above

7. When freezing cooked foods, it is important to

   a. Wrap the food, cool it, and then place it in the freezer.
   b. Wrap the food and place it in the freezer.
   c. Cool the food, wrap it, and then place it in the freezer.
   d. Freeze food unwrapped until frozen, and then wrap it.

8. Well-written handling and warming instructions are

   a. Specifically written for the food and the client.
   b. Written specifically for the food item.
   c. The same for every client.
   d. Not important because each client and their food is different.

9. When doing a price-plus-fee style of service, you will

   a. Bring all foods items with you for each cooking session.
   b. Stock the client's pantry with items you will need to prepare your menu of recipes.
   c. Buy only protein and vegetables; it is the client's responsibility to have pantry items.
   d. Follow the same procedure as for an all-inclusive style of service.

10. To develop your equipment list for a client's cooking session, you should

   a. Evaluate the method of heating the client will use.
   b. Review the recipes you will use to match the equipment.
   c. Choose equipment that is disposable.
   d. Evaluate the cost of the food being used.

Discussion Questions & Activities

1. In a group, equally divide the menu items listed in Exhibit 11.2. Develop a recipe for each item listed. Develop a shopping list and combine with other recipes from the group. As a group, develop the mise en place plan for preparing this particular menu.

2. Using the menu in Exhihit 11.2, prepare a mise en place plan that gives you the most efficient use of your time as if you were preparing the menu in your own kitchen.

3. Cook and freeze two or three of the same proteins. Write warming instructions for the items using different methods to reheat the foods. Try each method and evaluate each.

From the Field

A DAY IN THE LIFE

Here we examine a day in the life of three very different professional personal chefs: Chef Dale Pyle, CEC, a career culinarian who specializes in romantic dinner parties; Chef Heather Mader, who describes herself as a passionate home cook who offers a traditional personal chef service; and Chef Pete McCracken, a world traveler and entrepreneur turned personal chef.

Chef Dale Pyle, CEC, *At-Your-Service Chef*

Chef Dale Pyle, CEC started his personal chef business in central Florida several years ago. He was a chef for thirty years, trained through the ranks, and eventually burned out on the rigor of a high-volume commercial kitchen. "I just wanted to cook and not deal with the administrative end of the business," he says. After considering his career options, he decided to open a personal chef business.

Chef Dale found he enjoyed preparing the dinner parties more than providing the more conventional service of a personal chef and chose to design his business around that preference. He recalls that for his first dinner party, "The kitchen was a matchbox, two burners working and no counter space, which was a big challenge. But I did it, and the client loved the food. I fell in love with the job right then." He adds, "If I could make a meal like this in that kitchen and have the clients love it, what I could do in a bigger kitchen would be great!"

Chef Dale's wife is a massage therapist, and his service offers a spa package that includes a dinner party along with a half-hour massage session for each customer while the chef cooks dinner. "People love it, and working with my wife is great," he says. With a well-rounded culinary background, Chef Dale does not need to do much research as he prepares customized menus and chooses recipes. "The business has been a natural progression for my culinary career.

"After clients contact me and describes the type of the dinner party they want, I offer five or six menu choices. They pick a selection for each course, and then we talk a little about what they like and don't like so I can customize the selection to their liking. I try to gear the menu to exactly what they want.

"On the cook date, I pack my cooking equipment specifically for what I am cooking, go shopping, and then show up at the client's home and start cooking. The clients supply all the tableware, and I ask them about their kitchen. I like to know in advance if any of the kitchen appliances are not working properly. I cook the meal, serve it, and leave the kitchen cleaner than I found it," he says. Feedback on his entrées is immediate, as Chef Dale interacts his clients as each meal is served.

The hardest part of the business for Chef Dale is lugging all the stuff from his car to the client's kitchen. He also says getting the business going was a challenge, as he had to plan his time efficiently and prioritize his to-do list carefully. He advises new personal chefs "to do this on the side until you get established. For me, it is so amazing how easy it was to start up and how rewarding it has been. It's a great lifestyle—better than working the line."

Chef Heather Mader, *Black Radish Personal Chef Service*

Chef Heather, who recently started her business in Portland, Oregon, describes herself as a passionate home cook. After working in a bakery, a gourmet take-home shop, and as a private chef, she learned about the personal chef business from her mother. "I always wanted to cook for people but never wanted to run a restaurant, and this was right for me."

Most of her clients are fresh-service clients, which she says is more fun than cooking for clients who prefer freezer-style service. Her day starts early with "office stuff," such as responding to e-mails, researching recipes, and writing menus and heating instructions. "As I write the menu, I also create my shopping list," she says. As she writes the menus she reviews the client's likes and dislikes, ensuring she is cooking food that will appeal. "I do a ton of stuff for customer feedback because it's really important that I become a better chef for them," she adds. "I supply a list of all the items I have cooked for them during the last month, and I have them star the ones they want again, circle the ones they liked, and cross off the ones they don't want again."

Packing her kitchen kit takes about fifteen minutes, and she has learned to pack light. "I do not carry my best cookware; I carry my lightest. I love stainless-steel bowls but take plastic ones because they are lighter," she says. She also has a pantry staple kit containing spices, oils, vinegars, and other cooking essentials, which stays in her car.

Shopping usually takes about ninety minutes, resulting in five or six bags of groceries and a cooler on wheels for proteins. As she drives to the client's home, she thinks through her menu and the timing of the foods. "Foods that need to cook for a long time go on the stove and in the oven first," she says.

The cooking session takes about four hours. "I have become a master at multitasking," she states. Due to the size of her cooking kit, she cleans the kitchen as she works. "I bring only three pans, so I have to constantly clean them. My cooking sessions take about four hours, and I guess I spend about a quarter of my time cleaning."

Because most of her clients are not at home while she cooks, they leave her a blank check to pay for the service; she leaves them an invoice and copies of the food receipts. She sweeps the floor and leaves the menu and handling instructions for each food item.

When she returns to her home, she checks her e-mail and responds to potential clients. She also makes notes about the food she just cooked for her future reference. Although she has been in business only six months as she interviewed here,

From the Field...continued

Chef Heather has a full list of clients and is cooking five days a week. In fact, she currently has a waiting list of customers wanting her service. She uses her time off to work on the business side of her service.

Her customers' favorite foods tend to be comfort foods. "They love simple dishes. I was expecting to cook more upscale foods, but they love stews, curries, and roasts."

The part she dislikes the most about the business is hauling all the stuff, which is a common feeling among personal chefs. She also has found she has less time to cook for her family. "We eat out more than we used to," she says. "The part I love the most is being able to share my food with so many people in a direct and personal way. Nothing is better than having clients come home to a refrigerator full of all this wonderful food I've prepared specifically for them," she says with passion.

Chef Pete McCracken, *Personal Chef Services*

Chef Pete McCracken started his personal chef business about six years ago in Porterville, California. He had always enjoyed cooking and in his previous profession had traveled the world. When he returned to California, he wanted to recreate the foods he discovered during his travels. He had been an entrepreneur most of his life, and the idea of becoming a personal chef seemed to fit his needs.

As discussed earlier in this chapter, most personal chefs prefer to pack as light as they can. Chef Pete has a different point of view. He drives a minivan that "carries everything I need or could possibly need," he says. "Moving into a kitchen takes about half an hour. I have a rack where I set up for all my equipment. It speeds things up. If I need a spoon, I can wash it and hang it up and it's ready to go again. During my first few cook dates, I cooked for a while and then cleaned for a while. I felt that all the time I was spending cleaning equipment was not worthwhile, and that's when I came up with this rack idea."

He brings a mise en place list with him and does all his prep work first, placing food into containers for later use. Upon completion of his mise en place, he goes to the stove and multitasks by using all the burners and ovens available to him at once so he can prepare several food items simultaneously. He also stores a few portable butane burners in his van, so that "even if the client's range does not work I can cook." He also carries two collapsible worktables in his van in case he needs more counter space. The van is also home to countertop equipment such as a food processor, vacuum sealer, and blenders. "I know a lot of chefs worry about how much they are packing. I am fortunate out here; most everything is ground level, and I don't have to carry anything I've packed for a cook session up stairways or anything like that," he adds. "In a sense, I set up a small commercial kitchen in the client's home. I ask my clients to clear their countertops before I arrive, and if I need more space I always have the tables in the van."

His client's favorite foods are those he calls "Americanized Mediterranean with a lot of Italian influence." Chef Pete says, "There are two types of people in this world—those who are entrepreneurs and those who are not. There's a big difference between running your own business and working for somebody else. A lot of people are used to working for somebody else and picking up a paycheck and making so much per hour. "One of my biggest frustrations with new personal chefs is that they keep talking in terms of dollars per hour. They have not yet learned that the issue is dollars per cook date. With the dollar-per-hour mentality, the more hours you work the more money you make, but with the entrepreneur's mentality, it's not the hours you put in, it's the end product." As a personal chef, if you provide high-quality service and customized entrées to your clients' liking, you will have repeat business, and your clients will help market your business via word-of-mouth advertising.

Discussion Questions

1. All three personal chefs are highly successful, yet they offer different types of services. Chef Dale targets a niche market—those who like romantic dinners—while Chef Heather and Chef Peter provide more traditional services. Which style would you prefer? Why? What would be the advantages and disadvantages of each? Refer to the discussion of niche markets in chapter 7.

2. A common dislike of personal chefs is hauling all their cooking equipment along with the groceries for a particular cook session. Plan a romantic three-course dinner for two. Make a list of the equipment you will need to bring to your client's house and how you plan to use each piece when preparing the meal. Review the list and eliminate items the client may have in his kitchen.

3. Chef Heather makes it a point to follow up with her customers to "become the best chef for them," while Chef Dale receives feedback as he serves his clients their meal. Are there advantages or disadvantages of written feedback compared to immediate feedback from clients? Which method do you think would be more useful to a personal chef?

4. As Chef Peter describes his personal chef business, he explains that he brings a much larger kitchen kit than most personal chefs do to his client's house. Aside from the obvious issue of weight, what are the advantages and disadvantages of his method? Would you prefer Chef Peter's approach over keeping it light and simple? Why or why not?

REVENUE STREAMS

Because the personal aspect of the personal chef service works both ways, no two clients and no two personal chef services are alike. The only thing that limits your potential range of services as a personal chef is the limit of your own imagination.
—Candy Wallace, founder and executive director, APPCA

Introduction

As your personal chef business expands, new opportunities may present themselves. Being able to take advantage of these opportunities will allow your business to grow and diversify. It is important for you to plan carefully for the growth and expansion of your personal chef business, just as you planned for its start-up.

Not every personal chef wants to expand his business. While some who are satisfied with the income and lifestyle their business provides may not choose to take advantage of additional business opportunities, others want to explore them.

This chapter discusses additional **revenue streams** for the personal chef. These allow you to diversify your services as a personal chef and spread out your sources of revenue. Diversification is beneficial for a business because if one revenue source decreases, the others may be able to make up for the loss. Being receptive to the possibilities of alternate revenue streams can enhance your business.

Learning Outcomes

After reading this chapter, you will be able to:

✎ Identify a wide range of revenue steams for the personal chef business.

✎ Explain the advantages of using a commercial kitchen.

✎ Identify common equipment found in a commercial kitchen.

✎ Describe the difference between a storefront kitchen and a production kitchen.

✎ Define a dinner club and describe how it operates.

✎ Explain off-premise catering.

✎ Describe a home meal replacement business.

✎ List types and styles of dinner parties.

Key Terms

Revenue Stream
Production Kitchen
On-premise Catering
Commercial Kitchen

Dinner Club
Home Meal
  Replacement
Storefront Kitchen

Off-premise Catering
Dinner Parties

Commercial Kitchen

Although it can be expensive, using a commercial kitchen expands the business opportunities for a personal chef tremendously. A **commercial kitchen** is one that meets the fire, health, and business codes of your particular area. In most areas, this means obtaining licenses to operate the kitchen from one or more governmental agencies. The size of your commercial kitchen and the amount and type of equipment included will depend on your growth plan, but most share similar equipment:

- **Exhaust hoods**: These can be the most expensive part of the commercial kitchen. Hoods are designed to exchange the air in the kitchen with fresh air. This exchange creates a more comfortable working environment and reduces fire risk. Exhaust hoods often require expensive ductwork and fire suppression equipment.

- **Cooler and freezer**: The size of these units depends on your plans for the commercial kitchen. Large operations may require walk-in coolers with shelving, while smaller businesses might use roll-in or reach-in coolers. Most chefs say they can never have too much cooler space.

- **Three-compartment sinks** (for pot washing): These sinks have drainboards on both sides and come in different sizes to fit different space requirements. It is a good idea to picture your largest pot or pan to determine what size sink you need. The right sink makes it easier to wash dirty pots and pans. There is nothing worse than wrestling large pots and pans into dishwater.

- **Two-compartment sinks** (for food washing): Again, these come in different sizes. Some kitchens use a three-compartment sink both to clean dirty equipment and to clean vegetables and fruits. Some health departments do not allow this configuration.

- **Work surfaces**: These can be stainless-steel worktables, tables with a wooden surface, or possibly even counter space. The amount of work surface needed depends on the purpose of the commercial kitchen.

- **Floor surface**: The flooring is often overlooked in a commercial kitchen. Flooring is important; it must be easy to clean, comfortable to stand on, and resistant to chemicals. Some of the new floors are seamless and offer some degree of slip protection even when wet.

- **Lighting**: Many health departments have requirements for commercial kitchen lighting. Measurement of the amount of lighting is typically taken at work level and must meet local requirements. A commercial kitchen is easier to work in and clean with proper lighting.

- **Heating equipment**: Cooking foods requires a wide range of steamers, ranges, ovens, broilers, fryers, and other such equipment. Most, if not all, of this equipment comes powered by either gas or electricity and in many sizes and configurations.

- **Pots and pans**: A good-quality sauté pan or roasting pan can be expensive. Pots and pans come in all sizes and are made in many materials. Whether you choose pricy copper pans or cheap aluminum pans, the cost for stocking a commercial kitchen can easily be in the thousands.

- **Small wares**: From spoons to rolling pins, pastry bags to whisks, the list is endless.

- **Other equipment**: Mixers, blenders, slicers, food processors—the list goes on and on. Some chefs like to have every new gadget that slices or dices. But remember: Every piece of equipment not only costs money but also takes up space and may require costly repairs.

Equipment choices must be driven by your intended use for the kitchen. Many professional planners design kitchens based on menu and volume. Equipment might change to fit a particular space requirement or use. Try to plan for equipment that has multiple uses. This could save you the cost of buying a single-use piece of equipment.

In certain markets, you might be able to find high-quality used equipment. Used restaurant equipment can save you considerable money if you know the difference between good and bad. For example, a single-tank dish machine may cost upwards of $8,000 new but between $800 and $1,200 used—a substantial savings. However, if the pumps do not work or the fill tanks do not heat, the saving is reduced. Worse yet, if the used dish machine breaks down and requires major repairs, the business may have to close while the repairs are made. The cost of the repairs plus the cost of lost sales due to closing might be much more than the price of a new machine. With most used equipment, shipping and installation is extra. If you are thinking of buying used equipment, spend the extra time or money to have the equipment evaluated by a professional.

Another consideration when setting up a commercial kitchen is whether you need a storefront kitchen or a production kitchen. As the name implies, a **storefront kitchen** is one where customers interact with you or your employees. For this type of kitchen, location is more important than for a production kitchen. Typically, a storefront kitchen should have excellent exposure from the road, walkway, or parking area.

The storefront kitchen itself is likely to be more upscale than a production kitchen, possibly using a mix of commercial and home-style cooking equipment. Often, this style of kitchen is broken into workstations or teaching areas, depending on the planned use for the facility. This style of kitchen is most suited for dinner clubs which offer customers the ability to prepare entrées on site that are later cooked at home or teaching customers on site.

The **production kitchen**, in contrast, is simply a kitchen designed to produce food. Aside from it being convenient for your and your staff to get to, location and visibility aren't important. The production kitchen lacks some of the touches found in the storefront kitchen and usually costs less to build and equip. This kitchen is typically used by those in off-premise catering who prepare the food at one location and serve it at another, or those who serve home replacement meals customized for their clients' tastes and nutritional needs, which clients heat at a later time.

Dinner Clubs

The **dinner club** concept is based around a storefront commercial kitchen where customers assemble a predetermined number of pre-prepared components into entrées, salads, side dishes, and desserts which they cook at home. Some personal chef businesses expand their services by offering this dinner club concept to their clients. It not only provides clients with an additional service but also gives the business an additional revenue stream.

Some dinner clubs use fully equipped commercial kitchens, while others have limited, if any, cooking equipment. Some franchise models are built around price and convenience, offering meal service for as low as $3.00 per serving. In this case, the food offered is no better than the canned or frozen entrées found in most grocery stores, but the clients enjoy the socializing and being able to put meals together for their families. Customers choose ahead of time from a menu that usually changes monthly. Each station is supplied with recipe cards and heating instructions for the meals being prepared. Some of these operations offer a salad bar of common ingredients that customers bag to take home along with their main course. Customers supply their own storage containers and coolers.

A more upscale variation is the dinner club where the client prepares some of the food items used. In this style of operation, a client may have a chef prepare the sauce, chopped shallots, butter, and herbs for a snapper en papillote at her workstation. After following the supplied recipe, the client places the fish in its parchment bag to cook at home later. Of course, this variation is focused more on upscale foods and a more mature taste profile. Upscale clubs charge more than the other dinner club variation.

The important point here is to know your market. In most markets there is room for both styles of business.

Catering

Using a commercial kitchen, also allows the personal chef to become an off-premise caterer as well. **Off-premise catering** is the ability to prepare food in your commercial kitchen and serve it at a different location. Catering can be profitable, but the start-up costs can be high. Along with the commercial kitchen, a caterer needs:

- A vehicle to deliver the food while keeping it hot or cold. This involves insulated hot or cold food storage boxes, or possibly even heated hot or refrigerated cold cabinets.

- Plate and tableware for the customer. For an informal party this can be paper or plastic, but china, flatware, and glassware are required for a more upscale event.

- Chafing dishes, serving trays, and other service utensils. An inexpensive chafing dish might cost about $75, while a more elegant one can cost approximately $600. If your party requires eight chafing dishes, six serving trays, and other serviceware, it is easy to invest $5,000 in serving equipment.

- Some caterers supply tables, chairs, tents, bars, and other such services for their clients.

- Specialty equipment ranges from carving stations to chocolate fountains. This equipment can be a major expense, but, if fully utilized it will bring in increased revenue resulting in increased profits.

- For the personal chef who caters to larger parties, renting the service equipment occasionally may be an option. Many rental stores and large commercial catering operations can supply wide choices of table top ware and service ware, some even allow you to return the used items dirty! Of course, this can add as much as $2.00 per person to the cost of the function, which makes this choice very costly.

An off-premise caterer must hire employees to cook and help with delivery, set-up, breakdown, and clean-up. For more on off-premise catering, refer to books that provide a more detailed account of this profession, such as *Off-premise Catering Management, 2nd ed.,* by Bill Hansen and Chris Thomas (John Wiley & Sons).

Home Meal Replacement

A commercial kitchen also allows for the personal chef to expand her business into the **home meal replacement** market. This concept is a variation of the typical personal chef method of cooking in a client's home, but the chef uses a commercial kitchen instead. Clients order this service from a website or by phone. The food is cooked and packaged in the commercial kitchen and then either delivered to the client's home or picked up by the client.

In an effort to distinguish this style of service from a restaurant offering take-out, it is important for the personal chef to retain the services provided when she cooks in the client's home kitchen. Customized menus that meet the client's taste and nutritional concerns still remain key elements. Menu offerings that change monthly, personalized service, and small-batch cooking also help differentiate the home meal replacement concept from restaurant take-out service.

Teaching in a Commercial Kitchen

A commercial kitchen can also help you expand your personal chef service so it includes culinary teaching. However, teaching can be more difficult than it looks. Not every chef has the personality to be a good teacher. Teaching people to cook at any level takes planning, research, patience, and a sense of humor. If you are considering this revenue stream, start by working with small groups of three to six students. Keep to a common theme and stay focused. You will be amazed at how much preparation time you need to teach a simple class—typically, about

In teaching, you both learn.

—Jim Davis, personal chef and culinary educator, RGF Culinary Services

three hours of planning and research per one-hour class. This rule has not changed much over the years.

Subjects could include soups, stews, appetizers, desserts, or international cooking.

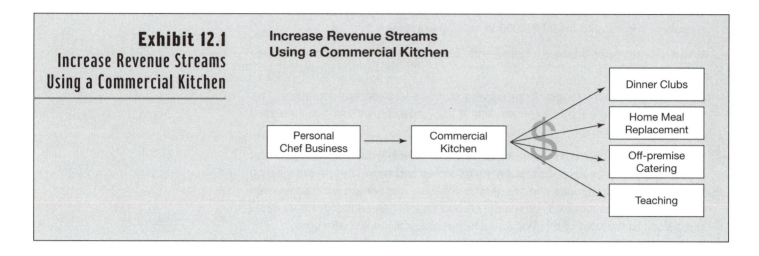

Exhibit 12.1
Increase Revenue Streams Using a Commercial Kitchen

Dinner Parties

You have to sell service.

You cannot make a

living selling food.

—Jim Davis, personal chef
and culinary educator,
RGF Culinary Services

Dinner parties are a natural extension of a personal chef's business. In fact, some chefs prefer to do only dinner parties and shy away from weekly client service. Dinner parties come in all styles, with a wide variety of services and menus. Personal chefs we interviewed for this text have done the following dinner parties:

- **Wine pairing dinners** where each course is matched to a different wine. This may require you working with a wine expert to match the right wine to each food on the menu. In some states, the client may need to purchase the wine separately to avoid legal conflicts.

- **Intimate dinners**—small, special dinners that are romantic and possibly theme based. Creating a mood with food, table decorations, and even background music such as Chef Shari Aupke described in chapter 7 can be rewarding.

- **Special event parties**—any holiday from Thanksgiving to Easter. Special events such as birthdays, engagements, retirements, birth of a child, or summer solstice can become a party. A good party creates a theme and a memorable experience for the clients and their guests. It takes planning and research along with good organizational skills as well as cooking skills to make a party a success.

- **Tea and dessert service**—The classic English tea service has enjoyed an increase in popularity in the past few years. Personal chefs create and serve tea, traditional sandwiches, and petit fours to small groups. Proper equipment, service, and uniforms can help this event develop into excellent revenue stream.

- **On-premise catering**—With this form of catering, all the food is prepared and served at the client's location. The difference between a dinner party and a catering party can be in the minor details. Both involve planning, cooking, and service. A catering party might involve buffet service, while a dinner party calls for plate service.

- **Cooking class dinner parties**—Depending on the size of the kitchen and number of guests, this class can be either hands-on or demonstration. This is becoming a popular way to entertain. Guests can learn a skill or technique and enjoy a meal at the same time.

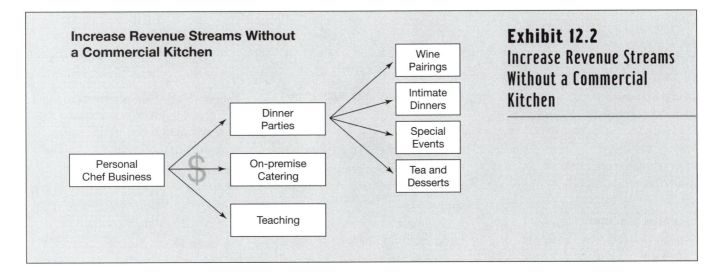

Increase Revenue Streams Without a Commercial Kitchen

Exhibit 12.2
Increase Revenue Streams Without a Commercial Kitchen

Teaching in a Client's Home

Even without a commercial kitchen, you can teach small groups in a client's home. As with teaching in a commercial kitchen, the fundamental rules are: Stay within your knowledge base, be prepared and organized, and have a sense of humor while entertaining your students. Your teaching should be based on a particular theme or idea. The final test of your effectiveness is often your students' enjoyment of the food prepared during the teaching session.

Teaching specific groups with common interests and goals has been a successful avenue and additional revenue stream for some personal chefs. People in retirement communities, where small portions and nutritional concerns are important, make for an excellent student base. Athletic groups with specific nutritional needs also make a good market. Some personal chefs specialize in teaching children to cook simple meals safely.

– Sushi	– Desserts
– Hot or cold appetizers	– Tasting menus
– International cooking	– Outdoor grilling
– Healthy cooking	– Bread making

Exhibit 12.3
Teaching Possibilities

Conclusion

Using your personal chef business to springboard into other revenue streams can provide countless opportunities for the growth of your business. Some personal chefs become food writers for local papers or regional publications, while others venture into teaching, catering, sales, and specializing in some undiscovered branch of the personal chef business. It is important to remember, however, that you must plan and research potential avenues for the expansion of your business just as you did when you started out.

Key Terms

Revenue Stream

A business activity that earns money for the business. The more revenue streams a business establishes, the more potential for greater revenue and resulting profits.

Commercial Kitchen

A kitchen licensed by the appropriate local governmental agencies for a specific use.

Storefront Kitchen

A kitchen that provides good exposure to potential customers, usually set up to accommodate

customer interaction within the facility.

Production Kitchen

A kitchen designed for food production with little concern for customer interaction within the facility.

Dinner Club

A storefront kitchen that offers customers the ability to prepare entrées on site that are later cooked at home.

Off-premise Catering

The act of preparing food at one location and serving it at another location.

Home Meal Replacement

Preparing foods, customized to a client's taste and nutritional needs, that the client heats later.

Dinner Parties

A broad range of food events prepared by a personal chef to meet a predetermined standard.

On-premise Catering

The act of preparing and serving the food at the same location.

Review Questions

True / False

1. A revenue stream is a source of sales for a business.
2. A commercial kitchen is one that has obtained all the necessary licenses to operate legally.
3. The floor surface in a commercial kitchen is not an important issue.
4. Used equipment always saves you money as compared to buying new.
5. A storefront refers to exposure of the business to potential customers.
6. Potential customer visibility is a key factor when planning a production kitchen.
7. Off-premise catering refers to food prepared at one location and served at another.
8. An off-premise caterer needs a wide range of food holding and serving equipment.
9. Home meal replacement is the same as take-out food from a typical restaurant.
10. Dinner parties include a broad range of events that encompass many styles of foods and services.

Multiple Choice

1. Which of these would not be considered a new revenue stream for a personal chef business?
   a. Catering, either off- or on-premise
   b. Dinner parties
   c. Writing non-paid food articles for a local paper
   d. Starting a dinner club

2. Exhaust hoods

    a. Provide for the exchange of fresh air within a kitchen.

    b. Are inexpensive.

    c. Are not needed in most commercial kitchens.

    d. Are easy to install.

3. A good flooring material should be

    a. Easy to clean

    b. Slip resistant

    c. Comfortable to stand on for long periods

    d. All of the above

4. When buying used kitchen equipment, it is wise to

    a. Inspect the equipment for excess dirt and grease.

    b. Trust the seller's word that it works.

    c. Offer the seller a price just to take it off their hands.

    d. Hire a professional to evaluate the equipment.

5. A production kitchen is one that

    a. Supports large-scale food production.

    b. Has excellent visibility to potential customers.

    c. Is highly decorative and offers customers a homey atmosphere.

    d. Uses only the newest and best equipment.

6. In off-premise catering, the caterer

    a. Cooks and serves the food at the same location.

    b. Cooks the food at a location where the customer picks it up.

    c. Cooks the food at one location and serves it at another.

    d. Delivers the food to the client, allowing the client to cook and serve the food.

7. A dinner club is

    a. A group of people who enjoy dining out

    b. A storefront operation where customers prepare foods they then cook at home

    c. A delivery-style foodservice operation

    d. A private restaurant open to members only

8. A home meal replacement business is

    a. The same as take-out from a restaurant

    b. A meal that is ordered by the customer and customized to meet her needs

    c. The same as an in-house cooking session

    d. Similar to a catered dinner party

9. Which is not an example of a dinner party?

    a. English high tea service

    b. A birthday party

    c. Intimate dinners

    d. A boxed lunch delivered to a customer

10. Teaching how to prepare the food items on a menu in a client's home involves

    a. Greater preparation than just cooking the meal.

    b. Less preparation than cooking the meal, because the students will do all the work.

    c. Getting a licenses to teach from the state you are in.

    d. Bringing an assistant to help in the teaching.

Discussion Questions & Activities

1. Using ¹/₄-inch graph paper, make a floor plan for a commercial kitchen that is designed for production. Place the equipment to allow for the proper flow of food through the kitchen. Write a list of needed equipment and use the Internet to price the pieces.

2. Visit a storefront kitchen by visiting a dinner club or an upscale home kitchen equipment retailer. Study the design of the kitchen to look for ease of workflow. What would you change? If there are no such businesses in your area, take an online kitchen tour by visiting such sites as www.chefdanes.com, www.evanssupperclub.com, or www.dreamdinners.com.

3. Design a teaching station. Consider what the station should include based on both the instructor and student perspectives. What equipment do you need? How will the students see and interact with the instructor?

4. Design a one-hour teaching course using a subject you are both knowledgeable about and enjoy. Teach your fellow students and ask for constructive criticism about the strengths and weaknesses of your lesson. How much time did you put into designing the class? What would you change? How was the lesson received by the students? Did you enjoy it?

From the Field

Chef Jim Davis, *RGF Culinary Services*

EXPANDING REVENUE STREAMS

Chef Jim Davis and his son Bryan opened their personal chef business, RGF Culinary Services, seven years ago as a result of a discussion Jim had with a real estate agent at a luncheon. Jim described the new concept of a personal chef to the real estate agent, and a few days later, the agent became Jim and Bryan's first client; they still cook for him today. At the time, Jim was a mortgage broker and enjoyed cooking as a passionate hobby. Bryan had been professionally trained at l'Academie de Cuisine and was cooking in the Washington, D.C., area. Their first cooking date was a much longer day than they had planned for. It took sixteen man-hours, numerous trips to the store, and most of the pots and pans from their personal kitchens to prepare their planned menu. After they left the client's home that day, Bryan said to his father, "Dad, are you sure we want to do this?"

From this rough beginning, RGF Culinary Services grew into a full-time business. In a short time, Jim and Bryan were cooking for clients five days a week. As they evaluated their business, they concluded that Bryan could cook for only four or five clients a week and that Jim should handle the paperwork and other business activities. Even though the income was good, they wanted to expand their business opportunities, so they decided to find a commercial kitchen from which to operate.

About three years ago, they shifted their business from cooking in the client's home to cooking in catering kitchens where they rented space. Even with the use of the commercial kitchen, they found they could still do only two full clients a day. One of their biggest problems was the travel time needed to deliver their food to their clients. Another problem was working around the schedule of the caterers who owned the kitchen. "Most days they were done in the later morning, but at times they would use the kitchen until late afternoon. This created problems for us," Jim explains. He and Bryan realized they needed their own space and kitchen, not a shared space, to ensure they continued to service their clients efficiently.

Eventually they found a cooking school for sale. The building offered a 1,200-square-foot kitchen, where they started a home meal replacement service. Using their background and experience as personal chefs, they built the business around small-batch cooking customized to fit the needs and taste of their clients. Established clients order meals off their business's website, while new clients go through the same assessment process Jim and Bryan used when they cooked in their clients' homes. The menu features a wide range of entrées, salads, and side dishes. All menu items are sold à la carte, so the client just orders the amount he wants, and the next day the meals are delivered for an additional fee. To allow Bryan the time he needs for cooking, they enlisted a delivery service with a limited delivery service area. Clients can also opt for curbside pickup, where food is brought to the client's car at no additional charge.

They have also expanded their dinner party offerings. Jim enjoys cooking for a party once a week, and they hire additional help for service during these parties. They customize each menu to the client's liking and handle the cooking, service, and clean-up. Jim says there is enough business for dinner parties to cook every night, but he prefers to pick and choose which events they cook for.

Earlier this year, RGF opened a dinner club business, using their kitchen facility in the cooking school. Their version features high-quality foods. The customer participates assembles the meal and then cooks it at home. The club provides everything a client needs, from recipes to containers. Key elements such as sauces, meats, seafood, and poultry, are prepared by Chef Bryan, which enhances the experience for the customers. The club has been open a short time, but it enjoys a full house and rave reviews.

Jim and Bryan Davis's RGF Services is an excellent example of a traditional personal chef business that successfully extended its revenue streams by expanding its services to include catering, dinner parties, home meal replacement, and dinner clubs. With each expansion, the core concepts stay the same, and the team continues to provide outstanding customer service and support. The new revenue streams have enabled the original personal chef business to become a multifaceted enterprise enjoying great success.

Discussion Questions

1. Visit the *RGF* website at http://www.rgwdgroup.com/reallygoodfoodonline/ and review their home meal replacement offerings. What other services or food choices could they offer? Speculate on how increasing their offerings might affect their business. Consider the potential increase in revenue as well as the added pressures on the staff and facility.

2. Does the website navigation clearly indicate the services provided by their business? If not, what would you improve or change?

3. Do you think *RGF Services'* growth is typical of the personal chef business? What changes in the business occurred as the business grew? Are these positive or negative changes, in your opinion?

APPENDIX

Within this section you will find assorted forms, a few selected recipes, and suggested heating instructions for different types of foods. Some of the forms are the same as those found in the text, while others are alternate versions. Choose the resources that work for you and make changes as necessary.

A. General Food Heating Tips

B. Sample Recipes

C. Heating Tables

D. A Personal Chef Business Description

E. Checklist—Starting Your Personal Chef Service

F. Client Assessment Form

G. Allergy Assessment Form

H. Service Agreement

I. Monthly Accounting Journal Categories

J. Equipment List

K. Sample Press Release

GENERAL FOOD HEATING TIPS

AMERICAN PERSONAL & PRIVATE CHEF ASSOCIATION

★ PARTNERS IN ★
LIFESTYLE SOLUTIONS

These instructions provide you with guidelines to relay to your clients. We have designed them based on cooking the regular service for two people. All of the times are approximate and depend on the operation of your clients' equipment, whether it be a conventional, convection, toaster, or microwave oven. Some people may choose to heat on the cooktop, transferring the food to a saucepan or sauté pan. Once you have done your client interview, you will know that client's preferences for heating their entrées.

As we all know, microwave ovens vary in heating power. What is high power for one is not high power to another. All times given for microwave heating are approximate within 1–2 minutes based on our experience using many brands and models of microwaves. Times given for conventional ovens, assuming proper calibration, should not differ.

When heating foods in a microwave oven, we recommend, for two reasons, that either a commercial microwave cover or plastic wrap be used. The cover locks moisture in the container and helps prevent food from drying out, and it keeps the splattering of inside microwave walls to a minimum. If your client is heating food in a Rubbermaid® container, have her remove the lid and cover with plastic wrap as the Rubbermaid lids tend to warp.

When heating in a conventional oven, you may want to suggest that Ivex® containers or foil pans be covered loosely with foil. This is to protect the top of the entrée from becoming dried out, and it also aids in heating.

The average temperature setting for heating foods ranges between 325 to 400 degrees F. Of course, this will vary depending on the size and type of food item being reheated. Always refer tothe heating instructions you provide to your client.

Toaster ovens may be used for smaller portions or single servings. This is particularly convenient for senior citizens. If using a toaster oven, decrease the oven temperature by 25°. Because they are smaller than conventional ovens, they distribute heat faster and with greater intensity.

Tips for Microwave Cooking

NOTE: Timing depends on the wattage and size of the oven.

Most microwave cookbooks are written for 700-watt ovens. To convert the cooking time for a 650-watt oven, add 10 seconds (or less) for each minute stated in the recipe. For a 600-watt oven, add 20 seconds for each minute stated in the recipe. For a 500-watt oven, add 40 seconds for each minute stated in the recipe.

Foods that are low in moisture or high in fat or sugar cook faster.

As a rule of thumb, cover any food that would be covered when heating by conventional methods.

Plastic wrap makes a great dish cover, but there's some concern that at higher temperatures the plastic in some brands could come into contact with the food.

When an airtight plastic-wrapped container is removed from the microwave oven, the wrap often collapses onto the food. This problem can be avoided simply by poking a tiny hole in the center of the plastic wrap after it's stretched tight over the container. Alternatively, the dish can be vented by turning back a corner of the plastic to allow steam to escape while the food is cooking.

Room-temperature food cooks faster than refrigerated or frozen foods.

Source: Sharon Tyler Herbst, *The Food Lovers Tiptionary.*

Convection Oven Cooking

Convection ovens have a fan that provides continuous circulation of hot air, which cooks food more evenly and up to a third faster than conventional ovens, even when the oven is crowded. The hot-air circulation makes convection ovens particularly suited for baked goods and roasted and broiled meats and fish.

When converting conventional heating instructions to convection oven instructions, reduce the temperature by 25° to 75° or follow the manufacturer's manual.

Convection ovens usually require little or no time for preheating. Unlike microwave ovens, convection ovens require no special cookware or major adjustment in cooking time or technique.

For meats and fish, the convection oven temperature can be lowered by 25° and roasting time decreased by 25–30 percent.

Convection ovens can easily over-brown baked goods, so be on the safe side and lower the oven temperature by 50° to 75°, but keep the baking time about the same.

Source: Sharon Tyler Herbst, *The Food Lovers Tiptionary.*

Sample Recipes

Salmon Gone Wild Chef Jody Peppler, *Reservations at Home Personal Chef Service*
Award-winning recipe from the American Personal Chef Association Annual Recipe Contest

Serves 4

4 Chinook salmon fillets, about 6 ounces each

Salt

Pepper

2–4 tablespoons olive oil

1 pound assorted wild mushrooms

$1/_2$ cup chicken stock

7 ounces Italian-style canned diced tomatoes

2 tablespoons finely diced shallots

2 cloves garlic, minced

$1/_2$ tablespoon capers, drained

$1/_4$ cup chopped kalamata olives

2 cups arugula

2 tablespoons butter

3 tablespoons chopped parsley

3 tablespoons pine nuts, toasted

1 cup raw orzo, cooked in salted water

Method

1. Season the salmon with salt and pepper. In a skillet over medium heat, pan-sear the salmon in the olive oil on both sides. Remove the fillets and hold warm.

2. Add a touch more olive oil to the pan and sauté the mushrooms until lightly browned. Add the stock and tomatoes and simmer until almost all the liquid evaporates.

3. Add the shallots, garlic, capers, and olives to the mushroom mixture. Season to taste. Let cook for 3 to 5 minutes, allowing only a bit of moisture to remain.

4. Toss in the arugula and allow to wilt.

5. Remove the pan from the heat and add the butter. Toss until the mixture is fully incorporated.

6. Toss the cooked orzo in olive oil; season with salt and pepper.

7. Serve on orzo and garnish with the chopped parsley and pine nuts

Note: Mushrooms can include any full-flavored mushroom such as oyster, shiitake, porcini, lobster, or black trumpet. If using portobello, remove the gills before cooking.

Asian Beef and Green Beans   Chef Karen Tursi, *CHOP Personal Chef Services*

Serves 2

$^1/_2$ pound green beans, washed and trimmed

1 tablespoon cornstarch

$^1/_4$ teaspoon ground ginger

1 tablespoon soy sauce

3 cloves garlic, minced

8 ounces flank steak, sliced into thin strips

$1^1/_2$ tablespoons canola oil

1 tablespoon peanut butter, smooth style

$^1/_2$ tablespoon lime juice

1 tablespoon chopped cilantro

Method

1. Blanch the beans in salted water until tender, shock, and hold.

2. Mix the cornstarch, ginger, 1 teaspoon of the soy sauce, and half the garlic. Add the sliced beef and marinate for 20 minutes.

3. Heat half of the oil in a wok or skillet over medium heat. Add the beans and stir-fry for about 3 minutes or until the beans develop a few brown spots.

4. Add the remaining garlic and fry an additional 30 seconds. Remove from the pan and keep warm.

5. In a small bowl, mix the peanut butter with 4 ounces hot water and mix until smooth. Add the remaining soy sauce.

6. To the same skillet add the remaining oil and heat. Add the beef and stir-fry for about 3 minutes or until the beef is brown.

8. Stir in the beans and peanut sauce, cook for an additional 1 minute, and thicken slightly. Add the lime juice; adjust seasoning.

9. Serve over rice and garnish with cilantro.

Note: Many personal chefs prefer not to recommend heating stir-fries in a microwave. It tends to toughen the protein and overcook the vegetables.

Salmon with Parmesan Crust and Pesto Cream
Chef Peggy Waller, *Culinary Cottage Cuisine*

Serves 8

8 salmon fillets, skinless, pinbones removed

Salt

Pepper

1 cup fresh bread crumbs

$\frac{1}{4}$ cup grated parmesan

2 tablespoons olive oil

1 cup whipping cream

1–2 tablespoons pesto

Method

1. Place the salmon on a baking pan. Season with salt and pepper.

2. Mix the bread crumbs, parmesan, and olive oil in bowl. Press on top of salmon.

3. Bake at 350° until the salmon is flaky and topping is browned.

4. Mix the cream with pesto to taste.

5. To serve, plate the salmon and finish with the pesto cream.

Note: The recipe will work well with other firm fish. Adjust the flavoring of the pesto cream to the client's preference.

Green Beans with Lemon and Fried Prosciutto Chef Kristin Lyon, *The Chefmeister*

Serves 4 to 6

$^1/_2$ cup olive oil

4–6 ounces prosciutto, thinly sliced and julienned

6 tablespoons extra-virgin olive oil

$^1/_4$ cup fresh lemon juice

1 pound green beans, trimmed and washed

Lemon wedges

Salt

Pepper

Method

1. Heat the $^1/_2$ cup olive oil in a sauté pan. Add the prosciutto and fry until crisp. Drain and set aside.

2. In a large mixing bowl, combine the extra-virgin olive oil with the lemon juice. Mix well and set aside.

3. Blanch the beans in a large pot of boiling salted water. Cook until just tender, then drain. While the beans are still hot, add to the olive oil–lemon mixture. Top with the fried prosciutto and garnish with lemon wedges.

4. Adjust the seasoning with salt and pepper.

Note: This recipe works very well with broccoli and other green firm vegetables.

Au Poivre Sauce   Chef Donna Douglass, *What's Cooking*

4 portions

1$\frac{1}{2}$ tablespoons unsalted butter

2 shallots, minced

3 tablespoons cognac

1 cup beef stock

1 cup whipping cream

2 teaspoons Dijon mustard

Kosher salt

Cracked black pepper

Butter, cubed

Method

1.   Melt the 1$\frac{1}{2}$ tablespoons butter over medium heat. Add the shallots and cook until translucent.

2.   Add the cognac and increase heat to high. Let simmer until only 1 tablespoon liquid remains.

3.   Add the stock and bring to a simmer. Reduce by two-thirds.

4.   Add the cream and reduce to $\frac{3}{4}$ cup.

5.   Whisk in the mustard and season with salt and pepper.

6.   To finish, mount with the cubed butter.

Note: This sauce should be finished by the client; have him add the cubed butter after reheating. This is an excellent sauce for use with tender red meat dishes.

Pumpkin Hummus   Chef Tom Herndon, *Full Fridge*

Serves 10

4 pitas, cut into 8 wedges each

Spray oil

2 tablespoons tahini

2 tablespoons fresh lemon juice

1 teaspoon cumin, ground

1 teaspoon olive oil

$3/_4$ teaspoon salt

1/8 teaspoon ground red pepper flakes

One (15-ounce) can pumpkin

1 clove garlic, chopped

2 tablespoons chopped flat-leaf parsley

1 tablespoon pumpkin seeds, toasted

Method

1. Place the pita wedges on a sheet pan, spray with oil, and bake at 425° for about 6 minutes or until toasted. Remove from the oven and set aside.

2. Place the tahini, lemon juice, cumin, olive oil, salt, red pepper, pumpkin, and garlic in a food processor and blend until smooth. Add the parsley and blend again.

3. To serve, place the hummus in a bowl, top with pumpkin seeds, and serve with toasted pita wedges.

Note: This makes a great alternative appetizer. Leave it for the client at room temperature.

Beef Stew with Mushrooms, Onions, and Dark Beer
Chef Meredith Eriksen, *Whisk for Hire*

Serves 6

2 pounds beef chuck, cut in 2–3-inch cubes

1 cup flour, seasoned with salt and pepper

2 tablespoons olive oil

2 pounds onion, halved, thinly sliced

$^1/_4$ pound smoked ham, diced

4 cloves garlic, chopped

$1^1/_2$ pounds mushrooms, quartered

12 ounces dark beer, such as porter or stout

$1^1/_2$ cups beef or chicken stock

1 teaspoon fresh thyme

2 bay leaves

1 teaspoon Worcestershire sauce

4 carrots, cut in 2-inch cubes

Salt

Pepper

Method

1. Dredge the meat in the seasoned flour. Brown in the hot oil; remove from the pan and set aside.
2. Sauté the onions in the same pan, cover, reduce heat, and allow to cook for about 10 minutes.
3. Add the ham and garlic, allow to cook for 5 minutes
4. Add mushrooms and cook for an additional 2 minutes
5. Return the meat to the pot along with the beer, stock, thyme, bay leaves, and Worcestershire sauce.
6. Bring to a simmer and allow to cook for about $1^1/_2$ hours.
7. Add the carrots 15 minutes before finishing.
8. Adjust seasoning

Note: Before service, discard the bay leaves. The thickness of the sauce may be adjusted by adding more stock to sauce that is thin or by adding cornstarch slurry to thicken. Diced potatoes may also be added to this recipe 20–25 minutes before finishing.

Beef Barley Soup Chef Carol Borchardt, *A Thought for Food*

Serves 6 to 8

1 pound beef chuck, diced medium

Salt

Pepper

1 tablespoon canola oil

1 large onion, diced medium

3 stalks celery, diced medium

3 carrots, diced medium

3 cloves garlic, minced

2 tablespoons tomato paste

1 cup medium-diced mushrooms

16 ounces beef stock

16 ounces chicken stock

2 teaspoons dried thyme

$1/2$ cup pearl barley

1 tablespoon balsamic vinegar

$1/4$ cup chopped parsley

Method

1. Season with beef with salt and pepper.
2. Heat the oil in a soup pot. Add the onions, celery, and carrots. Allow to cook over medium heat until the vegetables are soft. Remove from the pot and set aside.
3. Add the seasoned beef and allow to brown on all sides. Add the garlic, cook for 30 seconds, add the tomato paste, lower the heat, and cook for an additional minute. Return the cooked vegetables along with the mushrooms to the pot. Use the moisture in the pot to deglaze the bottom.
4. When the mushrooms are tender, add both stocks along with the thyme. Bring to a simmer and add the barley. Allow to simmer until the barley is tender.
5. To finish the soup adjust seasoning with salt, papper, and thyme, top with balsamic vinegar and garnish with chopped parsley.

Note: This is a thick barley soup. For a different style of the same soup, cook the barley in boiling salted water until tender. Drain and rinse under cold running water. Add the cooked barley to the finished broth when it is done.

Thai Fish Cakes   Chef Heather Mader, *Black Radish Personal Chef Service*

Makes 12 to 16 cakes

2 pounds fresh fish fillets (see Note)

1 pound shrimp, peeled and deveined

4 green onions, chopped

3 cloves garlic, peeled

2 teaspoons fresh grated ginger

$1/2$ red bell pepper, chopped

$1/4$ cup chopped cilantro

5 leaves basil

1 tablespoon fresh mint

zest of $1/2$ lime

1 tablespoon fresh lime juice

1 teaspoon sugar

1 egg

1 tablespoon Thai curry paste

1 tablespoon Thai fish sauce

Method

1. Place all ingredients in a food processor and pulse into a chunky paste. Chill until firm.

2. Form the fish cakes and fry in hot oil until brown on both sides.

3. Remove the pan from the heat, cover it with a lid, and allow the steam within the pan to cook the cakes.

4. Serve with jasmine rice and sweet chili stir-fried green beans.

Note: These cakes can be made with any fresh saltwater white fish. Fish such as tilapia, cod, haddock, or even grouper form a nice fish paste when ground in the food processor. Halibut and other firm white fish should not be used for this dish.

If time allows, freeze the bowl and blade of the food processor before using. This helps ensure a better cake by keeping the protein in the fish firmer.

Orzo and Black Bean Salad with Spinach and Roasted Yellow Squash
Chef Carol Borchardt, *A Thought for Food*

This recipe was a category winner in the America Personal Chef Association annual recipe contest.

Serves 8 to 10

1$\frac{1}{2}$ cups orzo

2 tablespoons extra-virgin olive oil to coat vegetables

2 yellow squash, quartered lengthwise and sliced into $\frac{1}{2}$-inch slices

Salt

Pepper

1 tablespoon Dijon mustard

1 tablespoon honey

1 clove garlic, minced

$\frac{1}{2}$ cup extra-virgin olive oil for the dressing

$\frac{1}{4}$ cup white balsamic vinegar

One 15-ounce can black beans, drained and rinsed

5 ounces baby spinach, cleaned and chopped

$\frac{1}{2}$ cup finely diced red onion

1 carrot, finely dice or coarsely grated

Method

1. Cook the orzo in boiling salted water. Drain, rinse, and toss in 2 tablespoons of olive oil.

2. Toss the squash in some of the olive oil, season with salt and pepper, and roast at 400°F until tender. Remove from the oven and allow to cool.

3. Make the vinaigrette by placing the mustard, honey, and garlic in a bowl. Whisk in the $\frac{1}{2}$ cup olive oil and finish with the balsamic vinegar.

4. Combine the cooked orzo with the black beans, spinach, onion, and carrot. Toss with the vinaigrette and adjust seasonings.

Note: This salad can be made with any style of cooked legume. If fresh arugula is available, try substituting it for the spinach and then adding a squeeze of fresh lemon to finish the salad.

Stuffed Rolled Flank Steak with Spinach and Prosciutto
Chef Lisa Waldschmidt, *Have Whisk, Will Travel*

This recipe was a category winner in the America Personal Chef Association annual recipe contest.

Serves 6

2 tablespoons olive oil

2 tablespoons balsamic vinegar

2 cloves garlic, crushed

$1^1/_2$ pounds trimmed flank steak, butterflied

$1^1/_2$ cup fresh spinach leaves, cleaned and stemmed

8 thin slices mozzarella

6 slices prosciutto

$1/_2$ red bell pepper, roasted and julienned

Kosher salt

Pepper to taste

Method

1. Whisk together the oil, vinegar, and garlic. Pour into a Ziploc bag with the flank steak. Allow to marinate at least 20 minutes.

2. Remove the steak from marinade and open it.

3. Leaving a 2-inch border free of all fillings, lay a thin layer of spinach leaves, overlapping slightly, on the steak. Place the prosciutto slices overlapping slightly on the spinach. Cover with the cheese slices, and then finish with three evenly spaced rows of roasted red pepper. Season with salt and pepper.

4. Starting from the side closest to you, roll up the steak jelly roll fashion. Tie with kitchen twine. Season with salt and pepper.

5. Roast at 350°F on a rack until desired degree of doneness is reached. Let cool a bit before slicing.

Note: If your flank steak is thick, pound it with a meat mallet. This recipe can be modified in numerous ways. For example, stuff the steak with a mushroom duxelles or a puree of dried sweet fruits instead.

Pesto Peppers   Chef Christina Phipps, *Culinary Comforts by Christina*

This recipe was a category winner in the America Personal Chef Association annual recipe contest.

Serves 4

3 red bell peppers (or other colors)

1 cup orzo

1 tablespoon olive oil

1 clove garlic, pressed

1 tablespoon oregano, fresh

4–6 cups fresh baby spinach, cleaned

$1/2$ cup chopped oil-packed sun-dried tomatoes

$1/2$ cup large-diced fresh mozzarella

$1/4$ cup pesto

$1/4$ cup toasted pine nuts

Salt

Pepper

Method

1. Cut the bell peppers in half lengthwise so each pepper provides two stuffing containers that lie fairly flat. Remove all stems, seeds, and ribs. Blanch the peppers in simmering salted water 3–4 minutes. Remove from heat and drain. Place a paper towel on each pepper to blot excess water.

2. Cook the orzo in boiling salted water until al dente, drain, and rinse. Place in a mixing bowl.

3. In a large skillet, heat the olive oil over medium heat. Add the garlic and cook for 20 seconds. Add the oregano and cook for about 1 minute. Add the chopped spinach, a handful at a time, and stir with tongs until wilted. Add the sun-dried tomatoes and toss. Remove from heat and add to the orzo.

4. Stir in the mozzarella along with the toasted pine nuts. Season to taste.

5. Oil a Pyrex pan and fill the pepper halves with the mixture. The amount depends on the size of the peppers.

6. Bake at 375°F for about 15 minutes or until the cheese starts to melt. Remove from the oven and cool for storage.

Note: If offering for a fresh service, place a little of the filling on the bottom of the container to steady the peppers.

Tuna and Scallop Ceviche Chef Wendy Po, *Lean and Mean Cuisine*

Serves 6 to 8

1 pound tuna steak, sliced into 1-inch squares

Cajun seasoning

Spray oil

1 pound bay scallops

2 ounces fresh lime juice

1 tomato, concassé

2 ounces red onion, finely diced

1 tablespoon chopped cilantro

Method

1. Season the tuna with Cajun seasoning mix and spray with the oil. Using a nonstick pan, sear the tuna on all sides, leaving the inside raw.

2. Wrap the tuna tightly in plastic wrap and chill for at least 1 hour.

3. Leaving the plastic wrap in place to hold the shape of the fish, slice the tuna into thin slices.

4. Mix the tuna, scallops, lime juice, tomato, and red onion in a stainless-steel bowl. Allow to marinate at least 4 hours.

5. Portion into chilled martini glasses and garnish with the chopped cilantro. Serve with crackers.

Note: Ceviche is a marinated seafood "cooked" (the protein denatures) by the acid in the lime juice. You must use freshly squeezed lime juice. In this recipe, the heat of the Cajun seasoning is balanced by the acid of the lime juice and the sweetness of the bay scallops. Bay scallops are small, very sweet scallops. You can use capes or sea scallops if bays are unavailable, but they should be cut into the size of a small marble.

Heating Tables

SOUPS				
Food Type	**Container Type**	**Conventional Oven**	**Microwave Oven**	**Stovetop Transfer to Saucepan**
	Reynolds® – pts/qts		2–5 minutes	Simmer 6–8 minutes
	Rubbermaid®, Glad®, or Ziploc® (plastics)		4–6 minutes	
	Individual cup or bowl		2–3 minutes	
			Stir halfway through heating	
Notes: Creamed soups are not freezable. Heat to a slow simmer. Do not boil creamed soup (or any other creamed products) as they tend to separate. Stir often.				

POULTRY (DELICATE)				
Food Type	**Container Type**	**Conventional Oven**	**Microwave Oven**	**Stovetop Transfer to Saucepan**
Piccata, turkey cutlets, croquettes, turkey steaks				
	Rubbermaid®, Glad®, or Ziploc® (plastics)		3–4 minutes	
	Ivex®	15–20 minutes @ 325°F	3–4 minutes	
	Disposal aluminum	15–20 minutes @ 325°F		
	Corningware®	15–20 minutes @ 325°F	3–4 minutes	
Notes: When cooking any chicken entrée, cook just to point of doneness, without overcooking. This will allow for heating without drying out.				

POULTRY (DENSE)

Food Type	Container Type	Conventional Oven	Microwave Oven	Stovetop Transfer to Saucepan
Stews, casseroles, Kiev, Cacciatore				
	Rubbermaid®, Glad®, Ziploc® (plastic)		4–5 minutes	Simmer low, 10–12 minutes
	Ivex®	30–35 minutes @ 325°F	5–6 minutes	
	Disposal aluminum Loaf	35–40 minutes @ 325°F		
	8 × 8	30–40 minutess @ 325°F		
	Corningware®	30–40 minutess @ 325°F	5–6 minutes	
Notes: When cooking any chicken entrée, cook just to point of doneness, without overcooking. This will allow for heating without drying out.				

MEAT (DENSE)

Food Type	Container Type	Conventional Oven	Microwave Oven	Stovetop Transfer to Saucepan
Stews, casseroles,* cabbage rolls, short ribs, chili, osso bucco				
	Rubbermaid®, Glad®, Ziplock® (plastic)		4–6 minutes	Simmer low, 12–15 minutes
	Ivex®	30–35 minutes @ 350°F	4–6 minutes	
	Disposal aluminum Loaf	35–40 minutes @ 350°F		
	8 × 8	30–40 minutes @ 350°F		
	Corningware®	30–40 minutes @ 350°F	5–6 minutes	
Notes: *Casseroles frozen with topping to be crisped are better heated using a method other than microwave.				

MEAT (DELICATE)				
Food Type	**Container Type**	**Conventional Oven**	**Microwave Oven**	**Stovetop Transfer to Saucepan**
Veal: parmesan, piccata				
	Rubbermaid®, Glad®, Corningware®		4–6 minutes	Simmer low, 10–12 minutes.
	Ivex®	30–35 minutes @ 325°F	4–6 minutes	

	Disposal aluminum
	  Loaf
	  8 × 8
		35–40 minutes @ 325°F
		30–40 minutes @ 350°F		

	Corningware®	30–40 minutes @ 350°F		

VEGETARIAN				
Food Type	**Container Type**	**Conventional Oven**	**Microwave Oven**	**Stovetop Transfer to Saucepan**
Casseroles, lasagna, pasta, stuffed noodles	Aluminum—various sizes Ivex®	30–40 minutes @ 350°F	10–15 minutes	
Soups	Rubbermaid®, Glad®, Corningware®		4–6 minutes	Simmer low, 10–12 minutes.
Stews or similar	Ivex® Rubbermaid®, Glad®	30–35 minutes @ 325°F	4–6 minutes	Simmer low, 12–15 minutes.
Spanopokita*	Corningware® Aluminum 8 × 8 Ivex®	30–35 minutes @ 400°F		
Vegetable bundles**	Individual foil packages	15 minutes @ 400°F	2 minutes on medium setting**	
Notes: *Best cut into squares before heating for optimum crispness. **Best heated in conventional oven for optimum crispness.				

A Personal Chef Business Description

My business, a Personal Chef Company, will operate under the name of

_____

My name is _____

My background, which will contribute to the success of my personal chef company, is, (briefly) _____

_____

My personal chef company will provide individually designed cooking services of multiple entrées and appropriate side dishes, cooked on a single cooking date, in my clients' own kitchens. The markets I am targeting are two-income couples, career-oriented singles, and seniors—all of whom wish to eat healthy, delicious food but do not want to spend their time shopping and cooking.

To save time and resources, I choose to concentrate in the following county/ies:

_____

_____

My service area will include _____

I will advertise and market in this area in order to identify potential clients on a regular basis.

These targeted clients will have disposable income earnings of at least $50,000 annually and they will be health conscious. These are people who know what they want and are willing to pay a fair price to get it.

CHECKLIST—STARTING YOUR PERSONAL CHEF SERVICE

✓ Complete your business plan and vision and mission statements.

✓ Commit to starting your personal chef business.

✓ Choose a name for your new business.

✓ File a DBA for your fictitious name (if you are using one).

✓ Run your ad for your name (DBA).

✓ Procure your city/county business license.

✓ Select a bank and set up business checking and savings accounts.

✓ Select an accountant or CPA and business attorney.

✓ Set up your bookkeeping system.

✓ Sign up for and take the ServeSafe class or other CFP-approved food safety certification courses for your food handler certificate.

✓ Select stationery and design your collateral business materials.

✓ Start cooking and testing recipes on friends, family, and neighbors for feedback.

✓ Purchase and assemble your equipment and carrying cases.

✓ Schedule a cooking day with a successful personal chef.

✓ Define and implement your marketing plan.

✓ Assemble your presentation folders.

✓ Start prospecting and networking.

✓ Think positive and create success.

✓ Join a personal chef association near you.

✓ Become a successful personal chef.

Client Assessment Form

Name: _____ Date: _____

Telephone: _____ E-mail: _____

Do you enjoy soups or salads as a main dish? ____ Yes ____ No

Do you enjoy soups or salads: ____ Hot ____ Cold

Do you enjoy pastas as entrées? ____ Yes ____ No

____ Hot ____Cold

How many times per month do you enjoy the following?

____ Beef ____ Pork ____ Turkey

____ Chicken ____ Dark ____ White ____ Both

____ Fish/Seafood (List favorites so I may select the freshest catch of the day from your list of preferences.)

Do you enjoy vegetarian/vegan entrées? ____ Yes ____ No

____ Grains ____ Beans ____ Bulgur ____ Nuts

____ Cheeses ____ Real Cheese ____ Low-Fat ____ Nonfat

Are you sensitive to any of the following?

____ Garlic ____ Onions ____ Mushrooms ____ Bell Peppers

List any other sensitivity _____

Are you lactose intolerant? ____ Yes ____ No

Are you allergic to anything? ____ Yes ____ No

Are there any fruits or vegetables you dislike? ____ Yes ____ No

Like _____

Dislike _____

How do you like your portions chopped? ____ Large ____ Small

Are there any other flavors or foods you just plain dislike? ____ Yes ____ No

Foods you dislike _____

_____

May I cook with wine and/or liquors? ____ Yes ____ No

With any alcoholic substances? ____ Yes ____ No

Any medical conditions or situations? ____ Yes ____ No

____ Diabetic ____ Cardiac Condition ____ High Blood Pressure

____ High Cholesterol ____ Light Salt ____ No Salt

____ Low Fat ____ No Fat

Are you trying to lose weight?   ____ Yes   ____ No

Would you like portion control?   ____ Yes   ____ No

What global cuisines do you enjoy?   ____ Mexican   ____ Thai   ____ French

             ____ Italian   ____ Oriental   ____ Other

Spicy food scale: ____ Bland   ____ Mild   ____ Medium

        ____ Hot   ____ Laser   ____ Incredibly Painful

Do you like to eat breads or rolls with your entrées?   ____ Yes   ____ No

  If so, what are your favorites? _____

Do you like to eat tossed salads with entrées?   ____ Yes   ____ No

  Favorite greens? _____

  Do you like cherry tomatoes?   ____ Yes   ____ No

How would you prefer your entrées packaged?

  ____ Individual   ____ For Two   ____ Family Style

Would you prefer disposable or reusable containers?

  ____ Disposable Containers   ____ Reusable Containers

Which appliance are you going to use to heat your food?

  ____ Microwave   ____ Oven

Would you like meals prepared for you to cook on your barbecue grill?

  ____ Yes   ____ No

List any favorite recipes you no longer choose to prepare yourself that I can prepare
for you: _____

Do you have a microwave oven?   ____ Yes   ____ No

Stove?   ____ Gas   ____ Electric

All burners functioning?   ____ Yes   ____ No

Oven functioning and accurate?   ____ Yes   ____ No

May I see your freezer?   ____ Yes   ____ No

Do you have an additional freezer?   ____ Yes   ____ No

Where is your fuse/breaker box? _____

Do you have children?   ____ Yes   ____ No

  Name(s)/Age(s) _____

Do you have pets?   ____ Yes   ____ No

  Name(s): _____ Breed: _____

  Friendly?   ____ Yes   ____ No

  ____ Indoor   ____ Outdoor   ____ In and Out

Please note any security arrangements necessary for me to be able to enter your
home to cook for you: _____

List any other comments or concerns: _____

Emergency Numbers: Office _____

Cell Phone _____

Allergy Assessment Form

Please circle or check any items to which you are allergic or sensitive as well as tastes and textures you do not care for. (List any other known allergies on reverse side.)

Vegetables

Amaranth, Chinese	Jícama
Anise	Kale
Artichoke	Kohlrabi
Asparagus	Leek
Beans, Green	Lettuce
Beans, Chinese	Mushroom
(Yardlong, Adzuki,	Okra
Fava beans)	Okra, Chinese
Beet	(dishcloth,
Black-eyed pea	gourd, luffa)
Bok choy	Olives
Borage	Onion
Broccoli	Parsnip
Brussels sprouts	Pea
Cabbage	Pepper (red/green)
Cabbage, Chinese	Potato
Cantaloupe	Pumpkin
Carrot	Radish
Cauliflower	Radish, Chinese
Celeriac	(daikon)
Celery	Rhubarb
Chayote	Rutabaga
Chicory	Sesame
Chinese mustard	Shallots
(bok choy)	Snow peas
Collard	(edible pod,
Corn	sugar snap)
Cucumber	Soybean, edible
Dandelion	Spinach
Eggplant	Squash
Endive	Squash, spaghetti
English pea	Squash, summer
Fennel	Sweet potato
Garlic	Swiss chard
Ginger	Taro
Globe artichoke	Tomatillo
Gourds	tomato
Horseradish	Turnip
Japanese eggplant	Watercress
Jerusalem artichoke	Zucchini

Herb and Seasonings

Allspice
Anise
Basil
Borage
Carraway
Chervil
Cilantro
Cinnamon
Cloves
Coriander
Cumin
Curry
Fennel
Ginger
Marjoram
Mint
Mustard
Oregano
Paprika
Parsley
Pepper, red
Pepper, black
Pepper, white
Rosemary
Sage
Savory
Sesame
Tarragon
Thyme
Vanilla

Nuts

Almond
Brazil
Cashew
Chestnut
Coconut
Hazel
Macadamia
Peanut
Pecan
Pine Nut
Pistachio
Walnut

Seeds

Pumpkin
Sesame
Sunflower

Fruits

Apple
Apricot
Banana
Berries
Bilbery
Blackberry
Blueberry
Boysenberry
Cherry
Cucumber
Currants
Fig
Grapes
Melon
Nectarines
Gooseberry
Kiwi
Peach
Pear
Pineapple
Plum
Pluot
Plumquot
Quince
Raspberry
Strawberry
Watermelon

Chocolate

Food coloring

Iodine

Shellfish

Seafood

Service Agreement

Customer Data

- Name(s): _____
- Address _____
- ZIP: _____
- Home Phone: _____
- Work Phone: _____
- Cell Phone: _____
- First Cooking Day: _____
- Entry/Alarm/Pet Instructions _____
- How did you hear about my service? _____
- Fuse or Breaker Box Location: _____
- Do you have any friends or family you would like to refer?
  _____
- Do you have anyone for whom you would like to purchase a gift certificate?
  _____

We have conducted a client assessment to determine what and how you like to eat and whether or not you have allergies, sensitivities, or dietary or medical parameters that must be addressed. I will use this information to design a custom program for you and your family. Together, we have selected your first set of entrees and reserved your first cook date on _____.

On that day, I will bring all of the ingredients and prepare all of your meals in the safety of your own kitchen. At the end of the day, I will package your meals for you per your instructions, label them, and leave complete heating instructions for your convenience. I will leave your kitchen clean and orderly, taking all of my equipment with me.

Fee

FEE: Number of Entrées   _____

    Flat Fee (Service and Food) $_____

Fee plus Food

    1. Fee for Professional Services $_____

    2. Food Deposit $_____

Container Options

    1. Disposable Container Fee $ 15/Cook Date

    2. Reusable Container Shopping Fee $ 125–150

Total Amount Due $_____

Handling Instructions

I am a certified safe food handler and would be happy to answer any questions about food safety you might care to ask at this time.

Otherwise, please refer to the handling and heating instructions, contained in your current entrée selection list, which were prepared with your safety in mind.

Client Agreements

Payment for initial cook date should be made today. All payments for upcoming service should be left for me on the cook date preceding the next service.

As I mentioned in our meeting, on a cook date, I consider your kitchen to be my office. In order to avoid any mishaps in the way of forgotten ingredients or, worse yet, an accident caused by distracted attention, I request that you allow me to perform my professional service without interruption. If you would like me to arrive and spend a brief time visiting or answering questions, I will be happy to make arrangements to do so, and will also be happy to spend a short visit at the end of my cook day.

Cancellation Policy

Because cook dates for regular clients are scheduled on a quarterly basis, it is necessary for cancellations to be requested at least 10 days in advance of your scheduled regular cook date. I cannot guarantee a rescheduled date before the end of the quarter.

Please Note

Have the kitchen area clean and ready to be used on the scheduled cook dates.

Make arrangements for children and pets to be away from the kitchen area on scheduled cook dates.

Leave containers ready for use in the agreed-upon area.

Client signature: _____

Date: _____

Chef signature: _____

Date: _____

Suggested Monthly Accounting Journal Categories

Income

Personal Chef Services	$_____
Catering	_____
Other	_____
TOTAL INCOME$	$_____

Expenses

PERSONAL CHEF SERVICE

Cash reimbursement	_____
Recipe development/Testing	_____
Food	_____
Utensils/Small equipment	_____
Containers	_____
Uniforms/Shoes	_____
Linens/Laundry	_____
Equipment/Cookware	_____
Rentals	_____

OFFICE

Permits/Licenses	_____
Stationery/Printing/Copying	_____
Advertising/Marketing/Promotion	_____
Yellow Pages	_____
Telephone/Voice mail	_____
Cell phone and charges	_____
Postage	_____
Office supplies	_____
Computer and supplies	_____
Hardware/Software	_____
Internet service provider (ISP)	_____
Web hosting services	_____
Domain registration	_____
Liability insurance	_____
Memberships and dues	_____
Books/Magazines	_____

Vehicle or mileage	_____
Gas, oil, and maintenance	_____
Auto Insurance	_____

PROFESSIONAL SERVICES

Accounting	_____
Legal	_____
Web design	_____
Graphic design	_____
Bank fees and charges	_____
Taxes	_____

OTHER

Owner/Operator's draw (salary)	_____
Savings	_____
Container deposit escrow (savings)	_____
Assets purchased	_____
TOTAL EXPENSES	$ _____
NET PROFIT/LOSS	$ _____

EQUIPMENT LIST

This is a recommended list to be used only as a guideline. You know what you use and don't use. Add or delete items according to your cooking needs. You may have many of these as duplicate items in your kitchen currently. Check out the thrift stores in your area for great deals. (I pack each day from my recipes so I only take what I need.)

- ✓ Set of pots and pans (the lighter they are, the easier to carry)
  - ✓ Saucepots—small, medium and large saucepans
  - ✓ Medium fry pan
- ✓ Two flexible cutting boards
- ✓ Two or three plastic bowls
- ✓ Salad Spinner
- ✓ Food processor or blender (only if needed)
- ✓ Splatter screen
- ✓ Pot holders, towels, rubber gloves
- ✓ Sponges, scrubbers, aprons, dish soap
- ✓ First aid items
- ✓ Heavy-duty foil and plastic wrap
- ✓ Freezer Ziplocs®: gallon, half-gallon, quart, and pint
- ✓ Grater, strainer

✓ Measuring cups, 2 sets, wet and dry

✓ Wire whisk

✓ Knife sharpener and chef's knife, plus a medium and a small knife

✓ Spatulas and 3 wooden spoons

✓ Large slotted spoon and large serving spoon

✓ Ladle and potato masher

✓ Tongs and kitchen shears

✓ Mushroom and vegetable brush

✓ Hand juicer

✓ Manual can opener

✓ Garlic press, pastry brush

✓ Instant thermometer

✓ Vegetable peeler, zester

✓ Measuring spoons

✓ Black felt Sharpie® pen

✓ Freezer labels or masking tape

✓ Matches, timer

✓ Baster

✓ Funnel

✓ Scale

✓ Cork puller

✓ Shrimp deveiner

✓ Pastry bag

✓ Small electric fan to cool food before freezing

Sample Press Release

TOO TIRED TO COOK DINNER?

Picture this. You come home after a long day at work, dog tired. That commute really wipes you out. You want dinner, but you dread the thought of going out or fixing it yourself. SOUND FAMILIAR?

_____ (name) _____, of _____ Personal Chef Service and a resident of _____, provides time-challenged, hungry customers with beautiful, healthy dinners that can be enjoyed in the comfort of their own home any time of day or night.

Instead of opening the restaurant his/her friends and family have been encouraging him/her to open for years, _____, a longtime passionate cook, has been looking for a way to indulge that passion to cook and combine it with a way to actually touch people one on one for some time, and recently found the right recipe—becoming a Personal Chef.

"The exciting thing about being a personal chef is that I get to deal with clients individually and prepare food that is specifically designed to satisfy their needs and wants," says _____. "Each client is different."

"I conduct a personal interview with each client to determine what they like to eat and how they like to eat, and whether or not they have any special dietary needs that need to be met. I can then custom design meals for that client to satisfy those needs and desires. If that person hates Brussels sprouts, then Brussels sprouts will never cross their threshold."

After completing the client assessment interview, _____ will plan meals for his/her customer's selection, customize recipes, shop for fresh ingredients, and prepare multiple delicious, healthy dinners for clients in the client's own kitchen. The lucky client may enjoy all of these delicious, freshly prepared meals at their leisure. The personal chef not only prepares all of the mouthwatering, wonderful food; he/she also labels it and leaves specific handling instructions for each dish.

The fee for a Personal Chef Service is most affordable. Many of _____'s clients report they actually feel they are saving money because they are no longer having food delivered nightly, eating in restaurants as often, and throwing away food they had purchased with the intention of preparing it and not getting to it.

Entrée selections include choices that range from orange-ginger salmon and marinated swordfish to chicken Normandy, Cornish game hens, beautiful pastas, and mouthwatering vegetarian dishes.

You can even order meatloaf and mashed potatoes or deep-dish pot pies if you want them.

Your personal chef offers a full range of entrée selections for your review, which he/she is happy to provide on request.

When asked what kind of people become clients, _____ responded, "My clients range from busy professionals, career-focused singles, two-income couples, and busy parents who want their children to learn to eat REAL food so they don't glow in the dark to active seniors who own their own homes and want to stay there living independently but no longer want to prepare their own meals.

"I also serve people who have recently experienced a hospital stay and need culinary assistance while recuperating or learning to follow a medically specific diet. I have also been told that my personal chef service is the best gift a new mommy ever received!"

One thing _____'s clients have in common is their desire to eat beautiful, healthy, preservative-free entrées they don't want to have to shop for or prepare themselves. "Now that they have me in their lives, they don't have to shop or cook anymore," smiles _____.

"Some of my clients schedule my service every two weeks, while others find that once a month is sufficient for their needs. The one thing that all of my clients agree on is that it's a great relief for them not to have to spend their time shopping, cooking, and cleaning up, and still be able to enjoy healthy, delicious food prepared especially for them in the comfort of their own homes. I just know that some of my clients are eating my beautiful food curled up in their jammies on the couch," laughs _____. "I like that."

Index

INDEX